=

D1326402

ROBERT THORNTON AND
THE LONDON THORNTON MANUSCRIPT

MANUSCRIPT STUDIES

General Editor Jeremy Griffiths

ISSN 0267-2510

I
*Manuscripts of English Courtly Love Lyrics in
the Later Middle Ages*
Julia Boffey

ROBERT THORNTON AND THE LONDON THORNTON MANUSCRIPT

British Library MS Additional 31042

John J. Thompson

D. S. BREWER

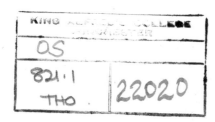
© John Thompson 1987

First published 1987 by D. S. Brewer
240 Hills Road, Cambridge
an imprint of Boydell & Brewer Ltd
PO Box 9, Woodbridge, Suffolk IP12 3DF and
Wolfeboro, New Hampshire 03894-2069, USA

ISBN 0 85991 190 X

British Library Cataloguing in Publication Data

Thompson, John J.
    Robert Thornton and the London Thornton
    manuscript: British Library MS Additional
    31042.—(Manuscript studies, ISSN
    0267-2510; 2)
    1. Thornton, Robert. *fl. 1440*
    2. Manuscripts, English
    I. Title   II. Series
    091   Z6605.E5

ISBN 0-85991-190-X

Library of Congress Cataloging-in-Publication Data

Thompson, John J., 1955–
    Robert Thornton and the London Thornton manuscript.

    (Manuscript studies, ISSN 0267-2510; 2)
    Bibliography: p.
    1. English poetry—Middle English, 1100–1500–History
and criticism.   2. English poetry—Middle English, 1100–
1500—Manuscripts.   3. Thornton, Robert, fl. 1440.
4. British Library. Manuscript. Additional 31042.
5. Manuscripts, English (Middle) 6. Transmission of
texts.   I. Thornton, Robert, fl. 1440. II. British
Library. Manuscript. Additional 31042.   III. Title.
IV. Series.
PR317.M34T48   1986   821'.1'09   86-4193
ISBN 0-85991-190-X

Printed in Great Britain by St Edmundsbury Press,
Bury St Edmunds, Suffolk

CONTENTS

LIST OF PLATES

Folio references are to the London manuscript, MS Additional 31042, unless otherwise stated.

LIST OF FIGURES

PREFACE

In recent years it has become commonplace to note that the ready availability of good-quality facsimile editions of important late medieval books
has helped to stimulate as well as sustain the interest in manuscript studies
shown by a number and range of ME scholars scattered across the globe. As
far as many of these scholars are concerned, the undoubted centrepiece in
this 'fair feeld' is the edition of the Vernon manuscript (Bodleian Library MS
Eng. poet. a.1) recently prepared for publication by Dr A. I. Doyle for
Boydell & Brewer. But there are good reasons for doubting whether British
Library MS Additional 22283 (the Simeon manuscript, sister to the Vernon)
will ever receive the same *de luxe* treatment. Spiralling costs and depleted
library budgets have conspired to produce a shrinking market for the
purchase of, as opposed to the use of, such fine modern editions. Moreover, it
is a peculiar irony that among the inevitable casualties of the present-day
recession can be counted full facsimile editions of other manuscripts that
bear witness to the phenomenal growth and health of late medieval book
production. In visual terms these books are often relatively unattractive and
they normally contain few items that have not been examined and described
over the years by a number of scholars. But the discerning textual critic can
still find some virtue in 'bad' texts which have been discarded or corrected by
earlier and perhaps less sympathetic editors. In addition, even the most
mundane manuscript collections can sometimes show traces of a fascinating
prehistory and this too is often worth retrieving. Therefore it is particularly
fortunate that, among its other ventures, a publishing house like Boydell &
Brewer can still find room for the production of illustrated studies of
manuscripts that have been forced into the second rank by their more
attractive peers. Into this category must fall the London Thornton manuscript (sister to Lincoln Cathedral MS 91) which is the subject of the present
case-study.

I have incurred many debts of gratitude during the course of this work on

Thornton's collection. Professor Frances McSparran first encouraged me to look at the London Thornton manuscript and directed my preliminary research efforts at Ann Arbor, but the role of supervisor was soon taken over by Professor Derek Pearsall at the University of York. His stimulating company and active practical support have helped to shape the present work, which itself grew out of a D.Phil. thesis. Other scholars have answered individual queries or have read early drafts of this work and their contributions are more fully acknowledged at appropriate points in the text. However they cannot be held responsible for any inaccuracies that still remain. Part of the research costs for this work have been met by grants from the Elizabeth Salter Memorial Fund at York and by the research fund administered by the Academic Council of The Queen's University of Belfast. I should also like to thank Dr Richard Barber, Mr Jeremy Griffiths, the appropriate authorities at the British Library, Miss Joan Williams and the Dean and Chapter of Lincoln Cathedral for various types of greatly appreciated practical assistance during the preparation of this volume. Finally, Dorinda deserves special mention for her help with the diagrams and for her patience.

ABBREVIATIONS

Archiv	*Archiv für das Studium der neueren Sprachen und Literaturen*
Beazeley	*Beazeley's Tracings of Watermarks at Canterbury* (British Library MS Additional 38637)
Briquet	Briquet, C. M., *Les Filigranes*, 4 vols. (Geneva, 1907, republished with supplementary material ed. Allan Stevenson, Amsterdam, 1968)
Index	Brown, Carleton and Rossell Hope Robbins, *The Index of Middle English Verse* (New York, 1943)
Manual	Severs, J. Burke and Albert E. Hartung, gen. ed., *A Manual of the Writings in Middle English 1050–1500*, vols. 1–6 (New Haven, 1967–80, in progress)
MED (Plan)	Kurath, Hans and Sherman M. Kuhn, ed., *Middle English Dictionary* (Ann Arbor, 1952– , in progress, Plan and Bibliography, 1954)
N & Q	*Notes and Queries*
NM	*Neuphilologische Mitteilungen*
SB	*Studies in Bibliography*
Supplement	Robbins, Rossell Hope and John L. Cutler, *Supplement to the Index of Middle English Verse* (Lexington, 1965)
TCBS	*Transactions of the Cambridge Bibliographical Society*
thesis	Thompson, John J., 'Robert Thornton and His Book-Producing Activities: Aspects of the Transmission of Certain Late Medieval Texts in the Light of Their Present Context in Thornton's Manuscripts' (unpublished D.Phil. thesis, University of York, 1983)
Walther	Walther, Hans, *Carmina Medii Aevi Posterioris Latina: II Proverbia Sententiaeque Latinitatis Medii Aevi*, 6 vols. (Göttingen, 1963–69)
Wells	Wells, J. E., *A Manual of the Writings in Middle English 1050–1400* (New Haven, 1916, with Supplements, 1919–51)

Introduction

British Library MS Additional 31042 (the London Thornton manuscript) is already familiar to many scholars, traditionally perhaps because it contains the only surviving copy of the important ME alliterative poem *Wynnere and Wastoure* (sometimes considered the earliest datable poem of the so-called Alliterative Revival) and two 'Charlemagne romances', *The Sege of Melayne* and *Duke Rowlande and Sir Otuell of Spayne*. This important anthology of ME verse also contains copies of two other ME romances, a fragmentary extract from *Cursor Mundi*, an incomplete copy of *The Northern Passion*, as well as an assortment of short didactic poems by John Lydgate (including Lydgate's much copied *Verses on the Kings of England* and his *Dietary*) and a cluster of other anonymous works.[1] Among the latter items, special mention should perhaps be made of an unpublished alliterating paraphrase of Vulgate Psalm 50 that is now fragmentary but which was originally written in a similar twelve-line stanza form to *Pearl*.[2] All of the other items in the manuscript have already caught the attention of modern editors.

This interesting manuscript collection has also secured its place in the history of late medieval book production by being one of two miscellanies copied in the middle years of the fifteenth century by Robert Thornton of East Newton in North Yorkshire. Although there are general thematic similarities between some of the ME material copied here and the items in the even better-known Lincoln Cathedral Library MS 91 (the Lincoln Thornton manuscript),[3] and so some obvious overlap of literary-critical interest, it is also important to notice that there is no duplication of items between the two 'Thornton' miscellanies.[4] Seen as a whole, therefore, this two-volume collection, on occasions made up of shared stocks of watermarked paper,[5] would seem to represent the sustained efforts of a fifteenth-century Yorkshire gentleman to organise a mass of the reading material available for his use into some kind of 'shape'. It is this feature, as much as the intrinsic interest of the texts Thornton copied – admittedly, some of these lie on the periphery of literature itself – that makes his collection so interesting and worthy of further detailed study.

[1] See the following chapter for a full description of the contents of the manuscript.

[2] For the curious catalogue of errors concerning recent descriptions of this fragmentary poem see 26–28. I am at present preparing an edition of the text as part of a general survey of ME treatments of Vulgate Psalm 50 (forthcoming, *Medium Aevum*).

[3] For a facsimile and description of the Lincoln manuscript and its contents see D. S. Brewer and A. E. B. Owen (revised ed., 1977). The best published description is offered by Gisela Guddat-Figge (1976), 135–42, but see too the revised account in *thesis*, Appendix 1, 427–48.

[4] The significance of the non-duplication of material in Thornton's collection is also mentioned by Dr A. I. Doyle in his brief comments on the comparison that has been made between Thornton's book-producing efforts and the activities of John Shirley. See Doyle's essay on the manuripts containing alliterative poetry in David Lawton, ed. (1982), 83–100, esp. 95, also discussion and n. 14 below.

[5] For discussion of this feature see the concluding chapter and the identification of the paper stocks in the *Appendix*.

In previous discussions of Thornton's interests and activities the Lincoln manuscript has gained most attention while, by contrast, the London manuscript has fared rather less well. Although it has attracted some critical comments the London manuscript is generally considered smaller, less varied, less well organised, and therefore less important, than its sister volume at Lincoln. One of the main objectives of this book is to gather together much of the evidence that might be used to test the validity of these assumptions. Of course, this task is made more difficult by the sheer volume of material in Thornton's collection and by the various permutations of text and physical make-up that both Thornton manuscripts represent between them. Because of these difficulties and the need to establish the terms in which we should begin to consider the relationship between Thornton's books, this short study has set itself strictly limited aims. On the one hand it offers a relatively straightforward descriptive account of the smaller London Thornton miscellany, while, on the other, it seeks to draw attention to the many bibliographical and other issues raised by the present physical state of the manuscript and the clues they provide concerning Thornton's practical compiling activities. Indeed, although there remain huge unfilled gaps in our knowledge about Thornton's scribal activities and literary associations, it is difficult to think of any other pair of related fifteenth-century manuscript collections whose histories are so interwoven and which offer quite such a wealth of material so intimately associated with the work of just one identifiable copyist. This feature alone not only seems sufficient justification for the present work but will undoubtedly ensure also a continuing scholarly interest in the reputation of Robert Thornton as an important late medieval book producer.

Identity and Life of the Scribe

In both manuscripts Thornton's name appears at the end of several items, on three occasions in the characteristic phrase, *R. Thornton dictus qui scripsit sit benedictus* (London manuscript, f. 66r; Lincoln manuscript, ff. 98v, 213r). His name also appears on f. 50r of the London manuscript and on ff. 53r, 93v, 98v, 129v (badly faded), 176r and 278v of the Lincoln manuscript. These signatures are not, of course, marks of authorship and their most likely general purpose seems to have been to draw the reader's attention to the identity of the copyist and compiler of the material. As such they are usually taken as signs of the original ownership of the two completed miscellanies, making them 'Thornton' books. But, due to the composite nature of both volumes, the evidence suggesting their gradual compilation, and the probably 'unfinished' state of the London manuscript (all these factors will be discussed further below), it is possible that some of these autographs could relate more precisely to Thornton's earliest efforts to indicate his ownership of individual portions of his work in small and originally self-contained manuscript units at some stage prior to the eventual creation of two much larger volumes.[6]

Even with this potential complication, the localisation of the Thornton manuscripts and their compiler in Yorkshire is not problematic, although it does rely heavily on evidence in the Lincoln manuscript. Due to the well-known work of J. O. Halliwell (1844), and later M. S. Ogden (1938), followed more recently by the continuing research of Professor George R. Keiser (1979, 1983), we now have an increased sense of the life and milieu

[6] This does not necessarily mean that the Thornton collection was conceived as a 'circulating library' of booklets that were originally intended to exist entirely independently of each other. The 'booklet' was also a convenience arrangement of material for the aspiring late medieval book compiler. See the recent general comments on this by N. F. Blake (1982), 71–3; A. I. Doyle in David Lawton, ed. (1982), 95, 97. In Thornton's case, parts of his work may even have been released to his readers as work in progress while the task of completing a larger collection was continuing. See my tentative comments on this and other possible uses of the booklet format in the concluding chapter.

of the Thornton scribe. Halliwell first tentatively suggested that Robert Thornton could be identified as the man who, in 1418, became lord of East Newton in the parish of Stonegrave, wapentake of Ryedale, North Riding; his findings were supported by Ogden whose work expanded on the unpublished research of Virginia Everett. These scholars based their identification of the scribe on a reference to Ryedale in a birth record on f. 49v (Lincoln manuscript), mention of Oswaldkirk, a few miles from East Newton, in Thornton's copy of the *Liber de Diversis Medicinis*, and the survival of the names of other members of the Thornton family in the Lincoln manuscript. These are William (ff. 49v, 144v), Edward (ff. 75v, 137r, 194r), Eleanor (f. 135v) and Dorothy (ff. 265r, 266r). A seventeenth-century pedigree of the East Newton Thorntons compiled by the antiquarian Thomas Comber, Dean of Durham (1644–99), supports the identification of these names as descendants of Robert Thornton of East Newton. Other names found in the margins of the Lincoln manuscript can also be associated with families who are known to have lived near East Newton in the sixteenth century. These are Louson (f. 29r), Rokeby (f. 220v) and Blande (f. 265r).

Professor Keiser's research has revealed no other candidate who seems any more suitable than the one suggested by both Halliwell and Ogden, although documentary evidence suggests that there were at least seven contemporary Yorkshiremen (including the East Newton Thornton) with the same name as the scribe.[7] Keiser has also produced impressive confirmation of the accepted view of Thornton as a member of the minor Yorkshire gentry. In particular, he highlights Thornton's work as a tax collector, his contacts with some of the leading Yorkshire families of the day, possible links with some of the religious houses in the area, and, less convincingly, his possible involvement in local disturbances caused by the rivalries of the Percies and the Nevilles. In addition, there is now some evidence from specifically Yorkshire sources to suggest the increasing availability and importance of written literature among the middle strata of fifteenth-century society.[8] Due to the nature of Thornton's known activities there remains the likely possibility that the two Thornton manuscripts were not the only documents written by him. Future examination of the remaining available sources might well produce further examples of the same hand in other local records.[9] If these do survive, they would undoubtedly provide additional valuable clues about the full range of Thornton's day-to-day life and activities.[10]

Thornton copied both manuscripts using an Anglicana hand typical of much fifteenth-century book production as well as many documents and official records of the period.[11] In 1976, Mrs Karen Stern's analysis of the functional nature of the script in the London Thornton manuscript effectively countered the earlier claims by S. J. Herrtage, followed by L. F. Casson, that the Thornton collection may have been the work of several copyists.[12] Dr M. B. Parkes has recently confirmed that, regardless of variations in the shape, size and degree of formality of the script, the Thornton scribe was solely responsible for the fifteenth-century material in the Lincoln manuscript as well.[13] Thornton's writing style was one that grew out of the need to write fluently and quickly but this feature is hardly any indication of either his 'professional' or his 'amateur' status as a book compiler. Indeed, the same fifteenth-century copyist could have been 'professional' in many aspects of his scribal activities (i.e. working for money), at the same time as he was working informally as a home-based 'amateur' collector and potential book producer. Therefore, while attempts have been made to link Thornton's

[7] See Keiser (1979), 159–60. The frequency with which the name of Thornton is mentioned in local records, often without geographical designation, means that a degree of uncertainty concerning the full range of the Thornton scribe's activities must still be allowed to stand.

[8] Here again, the identifications of some of the texts referred to in wills are notoriously problematic. But see also Keiser (1979), esp. 170–74 and Keiser (1983), esp. 115–16.

[9] A similar project, centred on a search for the Thornton scribe's hand in local records, has been suggested by A. S. G. Edwards (1980), 25.

[10] See the lead given for this type of work by Carter Revard's continuing work on the varied writing career of the main scribe in British Library MS Harley 2253 (Revard, 1979, 1982).

[11] The nomenclature used here is based on M. B. Parkes (1969), xiv–xvi.

[12] References here are to Stern (1976), 201–4; Herrtage (1880), vii–viii; Casson (1949), ix.

[13] The note recording the birth of the scribe's grandson at Ryedale and the pen trials on f. 49v of the Lincoln manuscript may well have been written by Thornton but because of the experimental nature of the script it is difficult to be sure. Thanks are due to Dr Parkes for confirming this point and also for suggesting that the material on ff. 50r–52r in the Lincoln manuscript was added in a sixteenth-century hand. It is a point of some interest that the ink in which some of this later material was added has dried to the same distinctive colour as some of the uncharacteristically crude ink sketches of knights in armour on f. 52v of the Lincoln manuscript. See too the discussion of the decorative features in Thornton's collection below and the facsimile edition of the Lincoln manuscript, introd. D. S. Brewer and A. E. B. Owen (revised ed., 1977).

[14] The fullest biographical discussion of John Shirley can be found in A. I. Doyle (1961, 1983). Dr Doyle elaborated on this published work in a lecture delivered to the second York conference on fifteenth-century manuscript studies, July 1983. For the comparison of Thornton and Shirley as 'literary speculators' see Stern (1976), 213–14 and comments by Doyle on this referred to in n. 4 above.

[15] This point is explained in more detail in the recently completed survey of fifteenth-century anthologies and miscellanies by Julia Boffey and John Thompson in *Book Production and Publishing in Britain 1375–1475*, ed. Derek Pearsall and Jeremy J. Griffiths (forthcoming, Cambridge University Press).

[16] For the processes of compilation that lie behind these collections see the forthcoming survey referred to in the preceding note. See too the accounts of the individual manuscripts in Frances McSparran and P. R. Robinson (1979), vii–xxv (facsimile edition of MS Ff.2.38); Phillipa Hardman (1978), 262–73 (MS Advocates 19.3.1); A. J. Bliss (1966), xi–xiii, M. Mills (1969), 4–6 (MS Ashmole 61).

[17] Stern (1976), 201–4, for examples see plates 25, 30 in that article.

[18] For the late additions to the London manuscript see K. Hodder/Stern (1969), 378–83; for the Lincoln manuscript see n. 13 above.

[19] See Doyle's thesis (1953), 1, 44, 199; Keiser (1983), 116–17. Both scholars comment on the inappropriateness of the feminine forms in the 'Thornton' copies of a ME version of *St Edmund's Mirror* and Walter Hilton's *Mixed Life*. Elsewhere, however, Thornton has taken some trouble to personalise a few of the Latin prayers he copied by inserting his family name at appropriate points in the text. For further details of this and the networks of manuscripts which are textually related to the 'Thornton' religious unit in the Lincoln manuscript (consideration of which begins to impose certain necessary restrictions on the assumptions that can be made about Thornton's own compiling interests) see *thesis*, 63–153.

achievements with those of the prolific metropolitan book producer John Shirley, the comparison here seems to create as many difficulties as it resolves, especially since the assumption of Shirley's 'professionalism' is itself not without problems.[14] It seems more helpful to grant Thornton's collection a place alongside other regional collections intended for family consumption.[15] Typical examples here include the anthology produced by the anonymous copyists writing in a similarly workmanlike hand to Thornton in Cambridge, University Library MS Ff.2.38; or the collection of *domestitia* mainly copied by Richard Heege (who, like Thornton, shows a tendency to name himself in several much smaller manuscript units) and now gathered together in National Library of Scotland, MS Advocates 19.3.1; or the work of the scribe calling himself Rate in Bodleian Library MS Ashmole 61.[16]

It can also be assumed that many of the variations in Thornton's script, outlined in detail by Stern,[17] and discussed alongside other physical and textual evidence in the chapter on Thornton's practical compilation procedures below, support the view that the material for both Thornton volumes was copied in different stages and compiled over a lengthy period in what was probably an extremely varied writing career. Other 'post-Thornton' hands then felt free to use some of the remaining spaces in both manuscripts, notably on f. 94v (London manuscript), and on ff. 50r–52r (Lincoln manuscript), to add extra material to the collection.[18] The identity of these later scribes remains unknown.

Several attempts have already been made to retrieve some limited impression of Thornton's scribal instincts and these too provide a useful preliminary impression of the Thornton scribe's 'personality' as a copyist. As long ago as 1844, J. O. Halliwell was warning that the texts of the 'Thornton' romances in their various extant copies, 'are not . . . to be always implicitly trusted'. In 1895. Carl Horstmann, another early editor of Thornton's texts, also recognised that many of Thornton's religious items (and especially his copies of Latin material in the Lincoln manuscript) were often 'very incorrect'. Moreover, it has been obvious to many later editors that the items in Thornton's collection have been variously contaminated in the course of their transmission. What is not so clear is the extent to which Thornton can be held personally responsible for some of that contamination, and in particular for some of the more intriguing changes that have taken place in the pre-history of his texts. For example the second-hand nature of some of the changes inherited by Thornton has already been stressed by Dr A. I. Doyle and Professor Keiser.[19] Both scholars suggest that several of the religious items in the Lincoln manuscript seem to have been prepared and intended originally for an audience of female religious. Intriguingly, these are also 'mystical' items that tend not to get copied by compilers who were interested in ME romances.[20] In a slightly different context, Mrs Stern is probably also close to the truth in her analysis of some of Thornton's more serious mechanical errors and repetitions when she states that his material is marred by a plethora of different types of scribal meddling, some of which can be laid at Thornton's door, but most of which show Thornton's general concern to reproduce his exemplar faithfully, regardless of the differing textual states in which he received his sources.[21] It will be hard to build upon this kind of conclusion until many more 'Thornton' items are made the subject of detailed textual scrutiny.[22] Even then the experience of this writer would suggest that it is unlikely that the resulting battery of textual variants will allow the emergence of any truly convincing picture of Thornton the

'editor-scribe' consistently at work. Nevertheless, David Lawton's work in progress promises to reveal more about Thornton's 'good ear' for alliterative poetry, and Mary Hamel has recently commented usefully on Thornton's general conservatism and his tendency to self-correct.[23]

In the light of this uncertainty, and with such a bewildering mass of available data, it would also be useful to know about the dialect features in some more of Thornton's items. In his study of the textual transmission of the alliterative *Morte Arthure* Professor Angus McIntosh has suggested that 'Robert Thornton was not by habit a scribe who transformed or "translated" exemplars so thoroughly as to obliterate all those characteristics in them which were alien to his own' and this information is certainly potentially useful.[24] However, it was extremely fortunate that in this work McIntosh was able to isolate the uncommon use of 'whas' (was) and 'cho' (she) in just two of the many 'Thornton' texts (the alliterative *Morte* and the pseudo-Bonaventuran *Privity of the Passion*) both now extant in the Lincoln manuscript. This exact type of particularly striking linguistic exclusivity is unlikely to occur regularly in other pairs of 'Thornton' texts. Nevertheless, an exhaustive study of common linguistic features in some of the items in this two-volume collection based on the McIntosh model has now been undertaken.[25] Eventually, it is hoped that this work may suggest possible localisations for other clusters of material now extant in one or other of the manuscripts. Such information, coupled with the types of physical and textual details used in this study, might indeed enable a much clearer picture of the nature of Thornton's sources to emerge than has hitherto proved possible.

Later Descent of the Thornton Collection

The later history of this collection, and particularly the history of the London manuscript, offers puzzles of a different nature. Paradoxically, Professor Keiser's research in this area has not only cleared up the problem of how the Lincoln manuscript probably came to Lincoln via Dean Comber's associations with both the Thornton family and Daniel Brevint, Dean of Lincoln, 1682–95, but it has also called into question the accuracy of the Comber pedigree that played such an important role in the earliest identification of the scribe.[26] Unfortunately the original Comber document is now missing but a corrected nineteenth-century transcript was published by Charles Jackson as an unnumbered page at the end of his edition of *The Autobiography of Mrs Alice Thornton* (1875).[27] Jackson seems to have had access to Comber's original document since he states that, in it, Comber actually refers to a note on a leaf of the Lincoln manuscript.[28] Moreover, in compiling his pedigree Comber must have had access to various other documentary sources, perhaps even private family papers that have now gone missing. Their disappearance is particularly disappointing, but the reported existence of Comber's note on the pedigree does at least confirm that the Lincoln manuscript continued to be associated with East Newton and that it probably remained here in the private possession of members of the Thornton family until Comber's time.

The history of the descent of the London manuscript is much less certain and only part of it can be patched together imperfectly. The only name shared by both Thornton manuscripts is that of the scribe. The absence of

[20] The main surviving examples of such miscellanies, where the works of mystical writers survive alongside ME romances, are the Vernon and Simeon collections (texts by Rolle and Hilton accompany the ME *Robert of Sicily* and *The King of Tars*), and Cambridge, University Library MS Ii.4.9 (Rolle's *Form* shares company with *Robert of Sicily*). But these examples are more apparent than real, given the pious nature of the 'romances' chosen for the three devotional miscellanies. And no attempt has been made by the compilers here to segregate 'religious' and 'romance' material.

[21] Stern (1976), 33–6.

[22] A useful model for the type of work needed before the accidental survival of some ME items in multiple copies can be used as a guide to an individual scribe's interest in his inherited material is provided by the recent exhaustive textual analysis of the extant copies of *Sir Degarre* conducted by Nicholas Jacobs (1984).

[23] For notice of Lawton's work see David Lawton, ed. (1982), 6 and 13; see also Hamel (1983).

[24] See McIntosh (1962). My account here relies heavily on some of the qualifications that McIntosh has himself raised in his own published work on ME dialects.

[25] This project has been undertaken by Professor Frances McSparran. I am indebted to Professor McSparran for discussing some of her research with me.

[26] For the importance of Brevint's relationship with Comber in the history of the Lincoln manuscript and its descent see the account in Keiser (1976). The questionable accuracy of the Comber pedigree is discussed in Keiser (1979), 159.

[27] The precise nature of the corrections to the pedigree is discussed by M. S. Ogden (1938), xi.

[28] Jackson (1875), ix, n. The 'flyleaf' referred to here has either been lost without trace from the Lincoln manuscript, or, more likely perhaps, Comber's note may have intended to describe f. 49v, now containing a Thornton birth record alongside other casual scribbles.

[29] Cf. Doyle in David Lawton, ed. (1982), 95.

[30] There has been some dispute over the dating and the identity of the Nettleton signatures, for which see Stern (1976), 207–8; however, the marginal scribbles that accompany the Nettleton name on f. 139v (unnoted by Stern) are written in a similar ink and, undoubtedly, by a sixteenth-century hand.

[31] The hitherto unnoticed fact that Frostt's name is written in red ink suggests that he may have played a part in completing the minor decorative features that now adorn the London manuscript. The haphazard way in which some of Thornton's texts were rubricated and decorated is discussed below.

[32] For the few known biographical details concerning the Nettletons and the Savile family see A. G. Watson (1969), esp. 7–9.

[33] Aveling (1963), 252, 300.

[34] The identification is based on the documentary evidence cited by M. S. Ogden (1938), xiii.

other Thornton names in the book, however, does not necessarily mean that it quickly passed out of the hands of the scribe's family.[29] Instead it may suggest that, for a time, the London manuscript lay around in a much more neglected and unfinished state than its sister volume. Nevertheless, there are at least two indications that this manuscript left the Thornton family some considerable time before it reached the security of the British Museum. One is that Thornton's name has been disfigured and partially erased on the two occasions where it appears in the book. This is likely to have been the work of a later 'non-Thornton' owner. The other is that, on f. 49r, a later reader, presumably also a new owner of the book, has written 'John Nettletons boke'. Again, on f. 139v, the name 'Nettylton' occurs three times and also 'Netylton'.[30] In addition, on f. 73v, a fifteenth-century hand has written 'Willa Frostt' in red ink in the head margin of the page. The identity of Frostt, his relationship, if any, to the Thornton family and the extent of his possible interest in the London manuscript remain unknown but open to some speculation.[31]

One of the two John Nettletons of Hutton Cranswick in the East Riding has emerged as the most likely later owner of the London manuscript.[32] Both Nettletons may have been interested in collecting manuscripts from Yorkshire religious houses and the elder Nettleton (will proved 1553) may even have passed his collection over to his son, the younger Nettleton of the same name (administration of his will granted 1597). In turn, the younger Nettleton became the most important single source for the collection of medieval manuscripts made by Henry Savile of Banke (1568–1617). The younger Nettleton is known to have supplied Savile with books from the monasteries of Byland, Fountains and Rievaulx, all of which are in close proximity to each other and convenient to Hutton Cranswick. Hutton Cranswick itself is only about twenty miles from East Newton so, if the circumstances were right, it is easy to see how an established local collector like Nettleton could have acquired the London manuscript directly from the Thornton family.

Although the younger Nettleton remains little more than a name, Fr Hugh Aveling's study of recusancy in the West Riding has revealed that, in 1570, one John Nettleton, a recusant schoolmaster, was ejected from Ripon grammar school and reference is made in the same study to a Henry Savile, gentleman, of Halifax, who was a recusant in 1580.[33] In his work on the manuscripts collected by Savile, A. G. Watson makes the suggestion that this may be a reference to the elder Savile. A tradition of recusant tendencies in the Savile family, plus their interest in collecting so many manuscripts from Northern religious houses, makes this suggestion particularly attractive. Furthermore, the apparent facility with which Nettleton obtained so many monastic books for Savile, directly or indirectly from these houses on their dissolution, might well be explained by Nettleton's own recusant tendencies. Even if Nettleton the recusant schoolmaster cannot be too closely identified with Nettleton the book collector, the latter figure must have had some close contact with adherents of the old religion.

If these contacts extended to the East Newton area then another possible link between the younger Nettleton and the Thornton family makes his eventual ownership of the London manuscript seem even more plausible. On 8 July 1607, Dorothea, wife of a Robert Thornton of Stonegrave, was under charge for recusancy.[34] It is probably also this woman's name that appears on ff. 265r and 266r in the middle of a sequence of Latin prayers in the Lincoln manuscript. There was a strong history of recusancy at Stonegrave,

especially among female members of the Thornton family.[35] Moreover, a great number of recusant families in sixteenth-century Yorkshire were probably still using and sharing much older devotional material for their own private reading.[36] But the number of these families is still small enough to allow the possibility that it was the later Thorntons' shared religious sympathies, as well as perhaps the promise of some limited financial gain, that helped persuade them to part with a collection of, by now, outdated literary curiosities to someone like Nettleton.

It would be gratifying to be able to complete a network of presumed recusant ownership for the London manuscript by finding some evidence that, in turn, the collection passed from Nettleton's hands into the library of Henry Savile of Banke. Savile was certainly not averse to owning fragmentary or unbound gatherings;[37] however any suggestion that he eventually acquired the London Thornton manuscript in some such condition can only be tentative. For example, the most likely entry in Savile's *Libri Manuscripti* that might seem to refer to the manuscript is no. 122 which reads, *Tractatus qui dicitur Cursor mundi (anglicè the Cursur of World) secundum cursum sacrae paginae. 4⁰.*. But Watson hesitantly identifies this as a possible reference to British Library MS Cotton Vespasian A.3. The Cotton manuscript bears no evidence of Savile's ownership and the identification seems to rest on the similarity of the wording of the title in this copy of *Cursor Mundi* (described in the manuscript as 'the Cursur of the World') and the English title of the poem quoted in Savile's catalogue. However, it is hard to see how else the words 'Cursor Mundi' could be translated into appropriate English. The wording of the heading itself has been taken from the prologue of the poem (l. 267), so the ascription of this book to Savile can only really rest on the late date at which the title was added in the margin of the Cotton manuscript.

Against this rather uncertain evidence can be set the more reasonable claims of the London Thornton manuscript. Thornton's book provides the only extant copy of *Cursor Mundi* that may show signs of Savile's ownership through having once belonged to John Nettleton. The first item in the collection is a copy of *Cursor Mundi* and, although this is the first of many items in this miscellany, it is from this opening text that the compiler of Savile's catalogue is likely to have taken the general descriptive title for the collection as a whole. Unfortunately, the opening folios of the Thornton *Cursor Mundi* are now missing and so there is no way of checking a 'Thornton' heading against the entry in Savile's catalogue, or, indeed, of checking whether the opening folios in the London manuscript did once contain the distinctive Savile inscription of ownership. Even if the manuscript was once in the Savile collection it must have disappeared as mysteriously as many other Savile volumes at the time of Savile's death.[38] Nothing further is known about the volume's whereabouts or its physical condition until 1879. In that year it was sent from an anonymous American source to J. Pearson, a London bookseller, perhaps of Pall Mall, and then sold to the British Museum where it has since remained.[39]

Recent History of the Manuscript

The London manuscript was examined by S. J. H. Herrtage shortly after the book was purchased by the British Museum. Herrtage describes how the

[35] For details of the incidence of recusancy at Stonegrave see Aveling (1966), 104, 189, 285, 411.

[36] Aveling's work on Yorkshire recusancy provides much supporting evidence that the medieval prayers and devotions used by the fifteenth-century gentry fitted in well with the circumstances of Catholic family life in the sixteenth and seventeenth centuries. For other post-Reformation readers who still had a taste for medieval devotional works see also Helen C. White (1942). It seems natural, therefore, to assume that something a good deal stronger than an interest in fifteenth-century literary relics made the Thornton family continue to treasure the Lincoln manuscript until Comber's time at East Newton (when, in Aveling's words, Comber and his mother-in-law, 'made the family and parish a model of High Church devotion'). See Aveling (1966), 358.

[37] For the useful example of a manuscript fragment that Savile kept loose within a cover see Watson (1969), Appendix 1, 74–7.

[38] For the disperal of Savile's library see the account in Watson (1969), 10–12.

[39] See S. J. Herrtage (1880), viii and notes on a modern flyleaf in the manuscript. I have been unable to trace any further details concerning the transaction, but thanks are due to the staff of the Students' Room at the British Library for their unsuccessful efforts to help fill in some of the frustrating blanks in the history of the manuscript.

fragmentary manuscript then (as now) consisted of 179 paper folios and 'four leaves of parchment, part of the original binding'. However by the time Herrtage's account of the manuscript was published in 1880 the book had been rebound by the British Museum and the folios renumbered 1–183 to take account of the vellum bifolia that acted as flyleaves at each end of the newly bound volume. Herrtage gives notice of the renumbering in a footnote but it is odd, and potentially confusing, that he uses the earlier, less satisfactory, foliation of the manuscript for his edition of the Thornton 'Charlemagne' romances. This peculiarity in the EETS edition, plus the fact that Herrtage's account of the manuscript was probably published simultaneously with the rebinding of the book, implies that the manuscript may have been in its pre-1880 binding when Herrtage first examined it.

The four vellum flyleaves in the London manuscript once formed part of a late medieval Breviary but their origins are otherwise completely unknown. Interestingly, however, the relatively unblemished appearance of these leaves contrasts sharply with the grubby and wormeaten appearance of the outer leaves of the paper manuscript that they were supposed to protect. This suggests that the flyleaves themselves were only added some time after the paper gatherings which make up Thornton's book had suffered substantial losses and some soiling at both ends. Moreover, although Herrtage considered these leaves to have formed part of the 'original' binding, he probably meant by this the pre-1880 binding. The habit of using fragments from medieval service books as flyleaves is certainly not a medieval one and is normally associated with the book-binding practices of the late sixteenth century and afterwards.[40] If a more intact version of the London Thornton manuscript was once described in Henry Savile's *Libri Manuscripti*, it follows that the earliest known binding of the book probably dates from some time after it was described by the compiler of Savile's catalogue. Unlike its sister volume at Lincoln, therefore, there is nothing to suggest when the gatherings that originally made up the London manuscript were first bound together.[41]

It is also unfortunate that the manuscript has been cropped so drastically. Whereas the pages of the Lincoln manuscript measure on average 291 × 210 mm, the folios of the London manuscript now measure on average a mere 275 × 200 mm. The cropping of the London manuscript has been so severe that on ff. 98–101 parts of the main text have been lost. More generally, the heads, bottoms and sides of the ruled pages have also been affected by the trimming, with the result that the items in the book, and especially those copied in double columns, have a far more cramped appearance than the similarly presented texts in the Lincoln manuscript. Whatever Thornton's original intentions, the smaller and more fragmentary London manuscript now looks like an inferior product. But the bulk of this drastic treatment must have occurred after John Nettleton entered his name in the manuscript since part of his inscription of ownership in the head margin of f. 49r has been shorn away. The cropping has also affected the first of the lyric fragments on f. 94v which were also added by a later, probably sixteenth-century, hand. It would seem likely, then, that the cropping itself must represent a fairly modern desire to tidy up a ragged volume.

The most serious effects of this over-zealous trimming is that it has probably removed much of the evidence upon which a physical collation of the manuscript could be based. This would include a sequence of quire and leaf signatures and also possibly, but not certainly, some additional catchwords to the ones that still survive on ff. 8, 32 and 73. In the Lincoln

[40] See, for example, N. R. Ker (1954), esp. ix.

[41] It is now generally accepted that, in 1832, F. Madden examined the Lincoln manuscript when it was in a medieval binding (before having the book rebound at his own expense). See Madden (1839), 1 and also the comments by Ralph Hanna III (1974), 1, and D. S. Brewer and A. E. B. Owen (revised ed., 1977), xvi, n. 2.

manuscript, by contrast, catchwords and signatures appear frequently. A. E. B. Owen examined the manuscript in 1974 when it had been dismantled for rebinding and he was able to use these marks to establish fixed points in gatherings **C**, **E** and **O** from which to calculate the original size of these and adjacent gatherings.[42] No legible signatures survive in the London manuscript; however certain marks in the bottom margins of ff. 15r, 16r, 17r, 18r, 19r and 20r do look like the remains of ascenders and may well be tiny fragments of signatures that have escaped the binder's knife. These few traces, then, and the three catchwords, are the most obvious practical guides to the manner in which the manuscript was originally assembled.

The most recent binding history of the manuscript has added little to our fund of knowledge about the book. In 1972 the London manuscript was again dismantled for its second modern rebinding. By this time the paper bifolia must have been in such an advanced state of decay that, despite earlier repairs to individual leaves, it was deemed necessary to mount each surviving folio separately as a singleton onto a modern stub.[43] This guarding process has preserved the manuscript intact but, unhappily, no record was kept of the condition of the volume when it was disbound. Now, of course, all opportunities for examining the remains of Thornton's original gatherings at first hand are irretrievably lost.

[42] See Owen's comments in Brewer and Owen (revised ed., 1977), xiii–xvi. For suggested corrections to Owen's proposed collation see Thompson (1982) and *thesis*, 23–6 (suggesting possible slight revisions to the collation of gatherings **C**, **M**, **N**, **Q**). In order to differentiate between the gatherings in each of Thornton's manuscripts I have used upper-case letters (**A–Q**) to identify quires in the Lincoln manuscript and lower-case letters (**a–i**) for the London manuscript. To avoid possible confusion, I have also used Roman numerals (**i–xv**) for the 'Thornton' watermarks, five of which are shared by both manuscripts.

[43] Mrs Stern's account of the manuscript was based on her examination of the manuscript in its 1880 binding, for which see Stern (1976), 27. I am extremely obliged to Mrs Stern for allowing me to read the brief notes that she made on the manuscript prior to 1972. In these she indicates that ff. 3, 8, 9, 32, 74, 76, 80, 81, 119, 125, 126, 134, 168, 179, 180 and 181 had already been pasted onto stubs before the 1972 rebinding.

Contents of the Manuscript

The contents of the London manuscript have been described many times by succeeding generations of scholars, often as part of the introduction to editions of some of the ME literary items the collection contains. See, for example, the brief accounts of the book in F. A. Foster (1916), 11–13; I. Gollancz and M. M. Weale (1935), vii–x; and M. Y. Offord (1959), xi–xiii. Most scholars are indebted, to a greater or lesser extent, to the earliest known published account of MS Additional 31042 in S. J. Herrtage (1880), viii–ix. This also formed the basis for the description of the collection in *Catalogue of Additions to the Manuscripts in the British Museum, 1876–1881* (1882), 148–51, which was itself revised by Karl Brunner (1913). The best recent descriptions of this part of Thornton's two-volume collection are those by Karen Stern (1976), 214–8; Gisela Guddat-Figge (1976), 155–63; and the unpublished account in Pamela Robinson's thesis (1972), 153–9.

In the following description I have given the manuscript titles of Thornton's items where these have survived. An asterisk (*) preceding such a title indicates that it has been taken from the *explicit* of the text in question. Where the text survives anonymously, or where it now begins acephalously in Thornton's copy, a modern title for the work is indicated in parenthesis. Items that were added in a later hand are preceded by the sign (+). Where an item has been frequently edited the most accessible editions are cited, especially those which are based on or contain useful textual references to the Thornton copy in question. For full bibliographical references see the *Select Bibliography* and the *List of Abbreviations*.

1   ff. 3ra–32rb

(From *Cursor Mundi*, ll. 10630–14933)

Beg. . . . Sche was + that was sone appon hir sene . . . (*amen*).

Wells, ch. VI [1]; *Index* 2153; *MED*, Plan, 35.

Ed. Richard Morris (1874–93); Sarah M. Horrall (1978– ; Thornton text to be included as an appendix in vol. 3, forthcoming). Eight other copies (see 49, n. 33).

Incomplete and fragmentary text written in rhyming couplets. Copied in double columns with narrative subsections indicated by MS headings and spaces left for future decoration (unfilled). Begins abruptly.

2   ff. 32rb–32vb

(Also from *Cursor Mundi*, ll. 17111–88; *A Discourse between Christ and Man*)

Beg.   Ihesu was of mary borne . . . (*amen amen amen Per charite amen amen Et Sic Procedendum ad Passionem domini nostri Ihesu Christi que incipit in folio proximo sequente secundum ffantasiam scriptoris*).

Index 1786; *Manual*, VII [2(b)].

Ed. Richard Morris (1876). Three other copies, in two of which this item survives as an independent poem; see 51 below.

Written in rhyming couplets. Copied in double columns. Separated from the previous *Cursor Mundi* passage by the one word *explicit* of item **1**.

3   ff. 33ra–50rb

*Passio Domini nostri Ihesu Christi

Beg.   Lystenes me I maye ʒow telle . . . (*amen amen per charite* and louynge to god þʳfore gyfe we R Thornton *Explicit Passio Domini nostri Ihesu Christi*).

Index 1907; *MED*, Plan, 62; *Manual*, V [303].

Ed. Frances Foster (1913–16, 1930). Eleven other copies and expanded version.

Incomplete text written in rhyming couplets. Copied in double columns with part of f. 41rb and f. 41v left blank (due to defective exemplar?). Decorative opening initial.

4   ff. 50r–66r

Distruccio Ierarusalem Quomodo Titus + vaspasianus Obsederunt + distruxerunt Ierusalem et vidicarunt mortem domini Ihesu Christi The Segge of Ierusalem Off Tytus and vaspasyane

Beg.   *Hic Incepit . . ./* In tyberyus tym that trewe Emperoure . . . (*amen amen amen Explicit la sege de Ierusalem R Thornton dictus qui scripsit sit benedictus amen*).

Index 1583; *MED*, Plan, 72; *Manual*, I [107].

Ed. E. Kölbing and M. Day (1932). Seven other copies.

Fragmentary text written in alliterative verse. Copied in single columns with text divided by passus divisions on ff. 54v, 57r, 60v, 63r. Decorative opening initial.

5   ff. 66v–79v

the Sege off Melayne

Beg.   Here Bygynnys . . ./ All worthy men that luffes to here. . . (. . . Bendis vp þaire engyne . . .).

Index 234; *MED*, Plan, 72; *Manual*, I [56].

Ed. S. J. H. Herrtage (1880); Maldwyn Mills (1973). Unique copy.

Fragmentary text written in twelve-line tail-rhyme stanzas (aabccbddbeeb). Copied in single columns with the rhyming pairs in each stanza linked by brackets, and the 'tail' line written in the right margin. Text divided on ff. 69v and 73r by passus/fitt divisions. Ends abruptly.

6   ff. 80r–81v

(Cantus to Our Lady: *O florum flos*)

Beg.   With humble hert I praye iche creature . . . (*amen Explicitt Cantus amen*).

Index 2168; *MED*, Plan, 97.

Ed. H. N. MacCracken (1913). One other copy (see 24–25).

Written in eight-line stanzas with a Latin refrain (ababbcbd). Copied in single columns with marginal rubrics indicating the stanza divisions. Final lines and *explicit* added in right margin of f. 81v.

7   ff. 82r–94r

Þe Romance Of Duke Rowlande and of Sir Ottuell of Spayne Off Cherlls of ffraunce

Beg.   Lordynges þat bene hende and ffree . . . (*amen per charite* Here Endes þe Romance of Duk Rowland + S*ir* Otuell of Spayne *Explycit* Sir Otuell).

Index 1996; *MED*, Plan, 69; *Manual*, I [57].

Ed. S. J. H. Herrtage (1880). Unique copy.

Written in twelve-line tail-rhyme stanzas (aabaabccbccb). Copied in single columns with the rhyming pairs in each stanza linked by brackets, and the 'tail' lines written in the right margin. Text divided on f. 84v by a fitt division. The word 'Charlles' is written in the side margin beside the *explicit* on f. 94r.

8   f. 94r

Passionis Christi Cantus

Beg.   *Hic Incipit quedam Tractatus Passionis Domini nostri Ihesu Christi in Anglicis/* Man to reforme thyne Exile and thi losse . . . (. . . appon my blody face . . .).

Index 2081; *MED*, Plan, 54; *Manual*, XVI [24].

Ed. H. N. MacCracken (1911). Five other copies (see also item **11** below).

Incomplete text written in eight-line stanzas (ababbcbc). Copied in single column with marginal rubrics indicating the stanza divisions. Ends abruptly (a false start by Thornton?).

9   f. 94v

        +(A short lyric fragment)

Beg.   *Exultit celum laudibus/* In bathelem in that fare sete . . . (. . . for he ys prens/ *Exultet celum lawdibus . . .*).

Manual, XIV [20].

Ed. Karen Hodder (1969). Cf. *Index* 1471

Copied in single column mainly in the head margin of the page by a 'post-Thornton' hand.

10   f. 94v

        + (Another short lyric fragment)

Beg.   Mare mod*er* cu*m* + se . . . (. . . þᵗ blyssyd chy . . .)

Manual, XIV [159].

Ed. Karen Hodder (1969). Cf. *Index* 2111

Copied in single column by a 'post-Thornton' hand. Only separated from the preceding lyric scrap by the Latin refrain of item **9**. Ends unfinished.

11   ff. 94v–96r

        *(*Passionis Christi*)

Beg.   Mman to refou*r*me thyn exile and thi losse . . . (*Explicit Passio Christi*).

Index 2081; *MED*, Plan, 54; *Manual*, XVI [24].

Ed. H. N. MacCracken (1911). Five other copies (see also item **8** above).

Written in eight-line stanzas (ababbcbc). Copied in single columns with brackets indicating the rhyme scheme and marginal rubrics indicating the passus divisions. Thornton's second, completed, version of *Passionis Christi Cantus*.

12   ff. 96r–96v

        (*Verses on the Kings of England*)

Beg.   *Willmo conquestor Dux Normannorum/* This myghty Willyam Duke of Normandy . . . (. . . and alle wales in despite of alle þaire myghte . . .).

Index 3632; *MED*, Plan, 56; *Manual*, XVI [100].

Ed. H. N. MacCracken (1934). Forty-two other copies of first redaction (see also A. S. G. Edwards, 1985); two other redactions.

Fragmentary text written in rhyme-royal with each stanza set apart from the others by a brief space and introduced by a heading indicating the name of the king with which it deals. Ends abruptly.

13   ff. 97r–97v

(*The Dietary*)

Beg. . . . Be noghte hasty nore sodanly vengeable . . . (. . . To alle in deferent recheste dyetarye).

Index 824; *MED*, Plan, 55; *Manual*, XVI [34].

Ed. H. N. MacCracken (1934). Fifty-six other copies (see also A. S. G. Edwards, 1985); two other related versions.

Fragmentary text written in eight-line stanzas (ababbcbc). Copied in single columns. Opens abruptly.

14   f. 97v

(A short Latin aphorism)

Beg. *Post visum risum . . . (. . . ne moriaris ita).*

Walther, II/3, 904 (72).

Four lines copied in single column of punctuated MS lines. Separated from the previous item by a brief space and by the marginal rubric used elsewhere to indicate stanza divisions.

15   f. 97v

(Another short Latin aphorism)

Beg. *lex est defuncta . . . (. . . Ius est incarcere tentum).*

Walther, II/2, 721 (95).

Two lines copied in single column and bracketed together as a pair. Separated from the previous item by a brief space and by the marginal rubric used elsewhere to indicate stanza divisions.

16   f. 97v

(A third short Latin aphorism)

Beg. *alterius lingue dic . . . (. . . vix est qui proprie possit habere modum).*

Walther, II/1, 101 (64).

Two lines copied in single column and bracketed together as a pair. Separated from the previous item by a brief space and by the marginal rubric used elsewhere to indicate stanza divisions.

17   f. 97v

a gud Schorte Songe of this dete This werlde es tournede up sodownne

Beg. To thynke it es a wondir thynge . . . (. . . Of the variaunce the whilke þat I now see . . .).

Index 3778; *Manual*, XII [94].

Ed. K. Brunner (1914). Unique copy.

Opening four lines of a fragmentary text? Copied in single column. Ends abruptly.

18   ff. 98r–101v

         (*The Quatrefoil of Love*)

Beg.   In a mornenyng of maye when medowes sall spryng . . . (. . . In a mornynge of may when medowes sall sprynge).

Wells, ch. VI [52]; *Index* 1453; *MED*, Plan, 68.

Ed. I. Gollancz and M. M. Weale (1935). One other copy.

Written in thirteen-line alliterating stanzas (abababababcdddc). Copied in single columns in pairs of punctuated lines with the tenth, eleventh and twelfth lines bracketed together, and the ninth line of each stanza written in the right margin.

19   f. 101v

         (*Prayer to the Guardian Angel*)

Beg.   Haile holy spyritt + ioy be vnto the . . . (*amen*).

Index 1051

Ed. K. Brunner (1914); Carleton Brown (1939). One other copy.

Written in rhyming couplets. Copied in single column of punctuated MS lines with each line containing a couplet.

20   ff. 102r–102v

         (Alliterating Paraphrase of Vulgate Psalm 50)

Beg.   *Miserere mei deus secundum magnam miserecordiam tuam*/ God þou haue mercy . . . (. . . all if I falle *in* fandynges fele . . .).

Index 990; *Manual*, IV [22].

Ed. J. Thompson (forthcoming). Unique copy.

Fragmentary text written in twelve-line alliterating stanzas (abababababcdcd). Copied in single columns of punctuated MS lines with the twelve lines in each stanza copied in pairs. Ends abruptly.

21   ff. 103r–110v

         (*Virtues of the Mass*)

Beg.   . . . *Iudica me deus* With Hole Hert and Entere . . . (*amen*).

Index 4246; *MED*, Plan, 56; *Manual*, XVI [87].

Ed. H. N. MacCracken (1911); ll. 145–76, ed. Jeanne Krochalis and Edward Peters (1975). Ten other copies.

Incomplete text written in eight-line stanzas (ababbcbc). The first seventy-one lines are copied in stanza units (the first of seven lines only and therefore incomplete?); a brief space between each stanza (ff. 103r–104r). The remaining text is copied in unbroken columns with frequent marginal notation. Marginal ascription to Lydgate on f. 103r (*Hunc librum qui dictavit Lydgate Christus Nominavit Iudica me deus . . .*).

22   f. 110v

a Carolle ffor Crystynmasse/ The Rose of Ryse

Beg.   The Rose es the fayreste fflo*ur* of alle . . . (. . . In plesaunce of þ*e* Rose so trewe).

Index 3457; *MED*, Plan, 101; *Manual*, XIV [436].

Ed. R. L. Greene (1935, 2nd ed., 1977). Unique copy.

Written in six-line stanzas (aaaabb) with a three-line burden (aab). Copied in a single column with the penultimate line in the burden and in each stanza added in the right margin. The heading is inserted in the side margins.

23   ff. 111r–119v

(*The Three Kings of Cologne*)

Beg.   . . . ffor Wynde or Rayne ffor Wate*r* or colde or hete . . . (*amen Explicit tractatus amen Trium magnum*).

Index *31 (*Supplement* *854.3); *MED*, Plan, 78; *Manual*, XVI [98].

Ed. H. N. MacCracken (1912). Unique copy.

Fragmentary item written in rhyme-royal. Copied in single columns of punctuated MS lines. Texts divided by MS headings on ff. 112v and 116r indicating passus divisions. The last twelve lines copied in the side margin of f. 119v. Begins abruptly. Originally began on the first of the two unnumbered stubs that now precede f. 111?

24   f. 120r–122rb

*Cantus Cuiusdam Sapientis . . . a lou*e*ly Song of wysdome*

Beg.   *Hic Incipit . . ./* Waste makes a kyngdome in nede . . . (*amen amen*).

Index 3861; *MED*, Plan, 103.

Ed. K. Brunner (1933). Two other copies (see 36).

Written in alternately rhyming eight-line stanzas. Copied in single columns on ff. 120r–120v and then in double columns on ff. 121ra–122rb. Marginal rubrics indicate stanza divisions.

25   ff. 122va–123ra

   A Song How þat mercy Passeth Rightwisnes

Beg.   By one foreste als I gan walke . . . (*amen Explicit Cantus amen*).

Index 560; *MED*, Plan, 88; *Manual*, VII [27].

Ed. K. Brunner (1914); Joyce Bazire (1985). Three other copies (see 37).

Written in eight-line stanzas with refrain (ababbcbd). Copied in double columns. Marginal rubrics indicate stanza divisions.

26   ff. 123ra–123vb

   a songe How mercy comes bifore þᵉ iugement Doo mercy Bifore thy iugement

Beg.   There es no creatoure but one . . . (*amen Explicit Cantus amen*).

Index 3533; *MED*, Plan, 101.

Ed. K. Brunner (1914). Three other copies.

Written in twelve-line stanzas with a refrain (abababbbcbc). Copied in double columns. Marginal rubrics indicate stanza divisions.

27   ff. 123vb–124vb

   A Songe how þᵗ mercy passeth alle thynge

Beg.   Be weste vndir a wilde wodde syde . . . (*Amen Explicit Cantus amen Explicit Cantus amen*).

Index 583; *MED*, Plan, 88.

Ed. K. Brunner (1914). Two other copies.

Written in twelve-line stanzas with a refrain (abababbbcbc). Copied in double columns with the final stanza crushed into the bottom margin of f. 124v. Marginal rubrics indicate stanza divisions.

28   ff. 125ra–163va

   *The Romance Of Kyng Richerd þe Conqueroure

Beg.   . . . Lorde Ihesu Criste kyng of glory . . . (*amen Explicit . . .*).

Index 1979; *MED*, Plan, 69; *Manual*, I [106].

Ed. K. Brunner (1913). Seven other copies (see N. Davis, 1969).

Incomplete and fragmentary text written in rhyming couplets. Copied in double columns with f. 160rb left blank (due to a defective exemplar?). Mechanical scribal error on f. 142r. Opens abruptly.

29   ff. 163va–168vb

   Ihesu Christi . . . the Romance of the childhode of Ihesu Criste þat clerkes callys Ypokrephum

Beg.   Here Bigynnys . . ./ Allemyghty god in Trynytee . . . (*amen*)

Index 250; *MED*, Plan, 48; *Manual*, V [311].

Ed. C. Horstmann (1885). Two other copies.

Written in twelve-line stanzas (normally abababcdcd). Copied in double columns. Part of f. 168vb left blank.

30   ff. 169r–176v

The parlement of the thre Ages

Beg.   In the monethes of maye when mirthes bene fele . . . (*amen amen* Thus Endes The Three Ages).

Index 1556; *MED*, Plan, 64; *Manual*, XIII [244].

Ed. M. Y. Offord (1959). One other copy.

Written in alliterative verse. Copied in single columns.

31   ff. 176v–181vb

A Tretys and god Schorte refreyte Bytwixe Wynnere and Wastoure

Beg.   Here Begynnes . . ./ Sythen that Bretayne was biggede and Bruyttus it aughte . . . (. . . To þe kirke of Colayne þr þe kynges ligges . . .).

Index 3137; *MED*, Plan, 83; *Manual*, XIII [243].

Ed. I. Gollancz (1920). Unique copy.

Fragmentary text written in alliterative verse. Copied in single columns until f. 180v and then, on ff. 181r–181v, the text is crushed into double columns. Ends abruptly.

Physical Make-up

Previous Attempts to Collate the Manuscript

There have been no less than three recent attempts to suggest a physical collation for the London manuscript. In 1976, Karen Stern suggested a partial collation for the first 57 folios based on her own examination of the manuscript in its 1880 binding.[1] But she had to conclude that 'it seems that the total collation of the manuscript is impossible without further information'. These tentative findings were revised by Sarah M. Horrall who, in 1979, made the first full-scale attempt to collate the book. Horrall's work was based on an account of the pattern which the watermarks seem to form and a new estimate of the nature and extent of possible physical *lacunae* in Thornton's collection. In this respect her research has established that the most problematic part of the manuscript is ff. 74–124 where the watermarks form no readily discernible pattern and where, with some uncertainty, Horrall concludes that the folios form six 'sections'.[2] In 1984 this was seen as an unsatisfactory solution to the problem by Ralph Hanna III who attempted to revise Horrall's collation for ff. 74–124. Hanna recognised more readily than Horrall that in a folio arrangement like Thornton's book each water-marked half-sheet must have once been conjoint with an unwatermarked half-sheet. Therefore in his suggested collation he readily admits the uncertainties caused by the fragmentary nature of the manuscript. He opts for the suggestion that ff. 74–124 once formed four quires, two of which seem characteristic of Thornton's tendency to construct large gatherings and two of which seem unusually short and fragmentary. This corrected account of Horrall's collation sorts more readily with some of the watermark patterns in Thornton's paper but it leaves unresolved several other important difficulties raised by the present fragmentary state of the London manuscript.[3]

The Collation

The suggested physical collation for the fragmentary London manuscript in its pre-1972 state is **ii** + ?; **a**? (ff. 3–8; a fragment of six leaves); **b**24 (ff. 9–32); **c**22 (ff. 33–53; wants xxii); **d**20 (ff. 54–73); **e**28? (ff. 74–97; wants v, viii, xxvi, xxviii); **f**36? (ff. 98–124; xix–xx stubs, wants vi–x, xxxv–xxxvi); **g**22 (ff. 125–143; wants xx–xxii); **h**26 (ff. 144–168; wants xxvi); **i**? (ff. 169–181; fragment of 13 leaves) + **ii**.

The processes of arriving at this complex collation are outlined below and in figs 1–10.

[1] Stern (1976), 27–31.

[2] The use of the term 'section' in preference to gathering or quire is ambiguous and confusing because the proposed collation does not further specify whether these 'sections' were originally composed solely of singleton leaves, or a mixture of singletons and bifolia, or of quires made up of bifolia, some of which have now gone missing and were presumably 'cancelled' by Thornton.

[3] Hanna's findings are based on a reinterpretation of the evidence which the runs of watermarked leaves seem to offer; but in his preferred collation he was eventually forced either to ignore or reject the evidence of some runs of paper in his description of ff. 118, 119, 75, 96. See Hanna (1984), 125–6, esp. n. 10.

The Evidence

Due to the detailed nature of the discussion needed to support this account of the manuscript, it seems best to describe in broad outline the main types of physical and textual evidence used here before examining the original make-up of each quire in turn. This approach has the additional advantage of allowing the usefulness of a new approach to the problem to be outlined and then demonstrated in three of the least problematic quires (**b**, **c** and **d**) before tackling the particularly troublesome middle section of the manuscript (ff. 74–124).

The best guides to the original make-up of the quires are the three surviving catchwords on ff. 8, 32 and 73.[4] These mark the logical extent of quires **a**, **b** and **d** and usefully limit the manner in which **c** can be described. However, the successful description of the remaining quires in the manuscript rests on two other factors. Firstly, a revised account is offered of the nature and probable extent of the *lacunae* in Thornton's badly damaged quires.[5] This account is based on the pragmatic dictum that, ultimately, hypotheses of losses to any fragmentary manuscript should never be greater than the minimum required by both physical and textual evidence. This is an important point since previous accounts of the fragmentary state of the manuscript have tended to place the highest premium on the very limited evidence provided by textual evidence, despite the fact that many of the fragmentary items under discussion now survive uniquely in the London manuscript. Fortunately, however, it is usually still possible to use a second source of evidence, in Thornton's paper itself, to suggest the minimum *physical* losses that have affected his original quires.

Both Thornton's manuscripts are folio arrangements and it would be especially helpful if it could be assumed automatically that all the gatherings in this two-volume collection were composed exclusively of watermarked bifolia. But both Stern and Hanna have pointed to the possibility that some of Thornton's paper stocks may have been unwatermarked sheets. In particular, Hanna has suggested that three unwatermarked bifolia still survive in the Lincoln manuscript.[6] Only one of these (ff. 108/117) is a clear example of an unwatermarked sheet; but even this outlandish survival is sufficient to make the task of collation all the more complicated as it is always possible that many other examples lurk undetected in the London manuscript. Nevertheless, the equally fortunate survival of so many sequences of watermarked half-sheets in the London manuscript minimises the difficulties raised by this possibility. Consequently, the task of collation must begin by continuing to match each of these watermarked half-sheets with their most likely unwatermarked conjoint leaves. An even more precise restriction can be imposed on any attempt to collate the manuscript by these means if the chain indentations in Thornton's paper are also used as a method for establishing the original conjugacy of the surviving leaves.

In 1954 Allan Stevenson described how an omnipresent feature of handmade paper is the indentation left by the paper mould.[7] The most obvious and best known is, of course, the watermark design itself, but other marks also always appear in laid paper and they too are watermarks of sorts. These are the ribs, made by fine laid wires, and the troughs or grooves, made by the chain wires in the original mould. Whereas chain lines are visible from both sides of the sheet, chain indentations occur only on the side of the sheet that was nearest to the actual mould during the manufacturing process. Once the

[4] Despite recognising the usefulness of these devices, the catchwords were ignored by Stern in her partial collation. See Stern (1976), esp. 31. Some greater problems are caused by the puzzling catchphrases which sometimes appear on both the recto and verso sides of many of the pages containing prose items in the Lincoln manuscript (these are not discussed by A. E. B. Owen in his account of the manuscript). Their survival may be some slight indication that Thornton occasionally copied his material onto sheets of paper *before* the sheets had been folded to form the bifolia in his quires. For discussion see *thesis*, 20–22.

[5] The three accounts of the fragmentary nature of the London manuscript offered by Stern, Horrall and Hanna all differ in some important respects and none of them is entirely convincing. See further the discussion below for details.

[6] These are ff. 51 and 52, 108 and 117, 296 and 299. However, ff. 51 and 52 are singleton leaves in a very fragmentary gathering (**C**). Owen's suggestion that they were probably once conjoint is based on unconvincing evidence (see further *thesis*, 23–24). In addition, watermark **xv** actually appears on f. 299, but this was unnoticed by Horrall and Hanna. Compare the account of the watermarks in Horrall (1980) and the description offered in the *Appendix*, below.

[7] It is fair to say that Stevenson's work has helped make the study of paper a sophisticated, reliable and respected source of information for the analytical bibliographer. For details see the references cited in the *Select Bibliography* (Stevenson, 1948–1967); and the accounts in G. Thomas Tanselle (1971); Stephen Spector (1978), 162, n. 4.

side of the sheet on which these indentations appear has been identified, we are in a position to distinguish between what Stevenson calls the 'right' side (mould side) and the 'wrong' side (rough or felt side) of the paper. Although these indentations appear in all medieval paper it is sometimes extremely difficult for the eye to distinguish between the mould and the felt sides of the sheet. Sometimes the distinctions may be obscured by the thinness of the paper, or, more usually, by the use of very fine chain wires in the original mould. Stevenson has also suggested that in some mills the paper seems to have been deliberately smoothed and polished before dispatch. In addition, general wear and tear and exposure of the paper to excessive damp for lengthy periods can also make the identification of the mould side a difficult or impossible task. While some of these factors have caused problems in the examination of the London manuscript, the general thickness of Thornton's paper means that on most of the leaves the chain indentations are still partially visible. They can best be identified using the method recommended by Stevenson: when the leaf in question is held below an undiffused light, and the eyes held parallel to the chain lines on the mould side of the paper, then a slight shadow marks the indentations.

Stevenson used chain indentations as an aid for settling problems of conjugacy caused by cancels and other sorts of page substitution in certain early printed books, and mainly in quarto and octavo formats. Since then, due chiefly to a suggestion by Theo Gerardy in 1980, a system of describing medieval paper with regard to the mould and felt sides has been formulated.[8] Gerardy's nomenclature distinguishes between paper that is *Abgewandt* (A) and *Zugewandt* (Z): if a sheet of paper is placed on a flat surface so that the watermark is right way up and on the left-hand side of the paper, and the mould side is visible, then it is *Zugewandt*. If the mould side is facing downwards, then the felt side is visible and the paper is *Abgewandt*.[9] In the recent important work of scholars like R. J. Lyall and Stephen Spector the identification of mould and felt sides has been seen to be of immense value for the symmetry principle of collation.[10] In a folio arrangement like the London Thornton manuscript, for example, not only did each watermarked half-sheet originally need to have a corresponding unwatermarked half-sheet in the other half of the gathering, but an A half-sheet must also have had a corresponding Z half-sheet. In the case of a leaf with watermark **X**, then, it is physically impossible for the correspondence to be anything other than *either* **X**A:−Z, *or* **X**Z:−A. There is one other complication that must be taken into account. Sometimes the watermarked bifolia became inverted before they were used and this inversion is now only apparent in the watermarked half-sheet (**X**A*; **X**Z*). Because there is no way of telling whether the unwatermarked half-sheet is itself inverted, the correspondences will *appear* to be **X**A*:−A, *or* **X**Z*:−Z. If this is taken into account, and we assume, for example, that an unwatermarked half-sheet (−A) appears in the first half of a gathering composed entirely of watermark **X** paper, then its watermarked conjugate in the second half of the gathering must be *either* **X**Z *or* **X**A*.

Given the present fragmentary state of the London manuscript, the value of this symmetry principle of collation is obvious. Logically, its only limitation is that it can only be used to settle matters of conjugacy where there is good evidence that more than half of the gathering in question has survived. This means that this approach is of no use in the discussion of the extensive *lacuna* at the beginning of the manuscript and of only very limited use in the estimate of the original size of gathering **i** at the end. But, elsewhere in the

[8] The same procedure can be used for describing watermark 'twins', for which see Stevenson (1951–52).

[9] I am deeply indebted to Rod Lyall for explaining Gerardy's system to me and for discussing his unpublished work on the analysis of medieval paper. Dr Lyall very patiently introduced me to the techniques used to identify chain indentations in medieval paper. At my request, he also undertook an entirely independent examination of the paper in both Thornton manuscripts. In the following discussion I rely heavily on Lyall's identification of the indentations on ff. 74–124; but, in every case where there remained some doubt about the identification after his initial examination, I have checked the manuscript again. The result is that I have confirmed Lyall's findings on all but two occasions (see n. 24 below). The suggested collation offered here is, of course, entirely my own work and responsibility, although at a later date Dr Lyall and I hope to develop some of the points made here in a more thoroughgoing analysis of the European origins of the paper used by Thornton and other Yorkshire scribes.

[10] See Spector (1978). A much-needed standard descriptive system to supplement Gerardy's A/Z convention has yet to be adopted; see Paul Needham (1982), 453. The account offered here is based entirely on Dr Lyall's elaboration of Gerardy's system.

collection, the evidence of the chain indentations in Thornton's paper imposes another much-needed restriction on the way in which the patterns of watermarked paper in Thornton's folio arrangement can be used to reconstruct the original size of his quires. On these occasions a *minium* requirement of any proposed collation must now be that it does not conflict with either the poles of symmetry established initially by the watermark patterns, or with the physical presence of the contours in the paper. This crucial restriction not only assists in the identification of the likely extent of suspected physical *lacunae* in the manuscript, but also, most importantly, it provides the evidence for determining the original cores of gatherings **e** and **f** and their probable composite nature.

Reconstruction of Thornton's Quires

Quire a? (ff. 3–8)

Less than half of the original quire has survived. By 1880, ff. 3–8 already formed six singletons while the catchword on f. 8 indicates that this was once the last surviving leaf of the quire. Textual evidence also suggests that the loss to the London manuscript at this point is likely to be extensive. The fragment of text preserved on these leaves is part of the Thornton copy of *Cursor Mundi*. His copy now begins abruptly with part of the description of the early life of the Virgin, followed by the poem's account of the birth, childhood and early ministry of Christ (corresponding to ll. 10630–14933 of the EETS edition of the poem).[11]

It would be helpful at this point if there could be greater certainty that the London Thornton manuscript was once described in Henry Savile's *Libri Manuscripti* since this would support the likelihood that the volume did once contain the opening section of *Cursor Mundi*.[12] By this reckoning (and by using Thornton's manner of presenting his text in double columns on ff. 3–32 and the EETS edition of the text as a rough guide) as much as 70–75 leaves of text may have gone missing from the beginning of the manuscript.[13] If these hypothesised losses are added to the leaves now numbered ff. 3–8, and Thornton's tendency to construct large gatherings is assumed, it is possible to argue for the almost total loss here of three large, probably unevenly sized gatherings. Although we can never now be certain that the London manuscript suffered exactly this kind of loss, the risk of such a loss is the kind of hazard that many other manuscripts have faced during their history, especially if they remained unbound for some time after they were originally copied.[14]

Quire b[24] (ff. 9–32)

Quire **b** seems to have survived relatively intact with the catchword on f. 32 indicating the last leaf of the original quire. The evidence of the chain indentations confirms that there is no apparent physical or textual loss here and that the gathering originally consisted of twelve bifolia comprised solely of paper with watermark **i** (fig. 1). Although it proved impossible to tell on which side of f. 20 the mould side occurs, logically this must be a Z leaf since ff. 20 and 21 seem to have once formed the central bifolium and f. 21 is a watermarked half-sheet appearing as **iA**.

[11] See further the discussion of the Thornton fragment, 49–55. Line references are to Richard Morris, ed. (1874–93). Morris was not aware of the existence of Thornton's fragmentary copy.

[12] Suggested, 7 above.

[13] A less attractive possibility is that the loss here might be restricted to the portion of *Cursor Mundi* that deals with the beginning of the fifth age of the world (i.e. the birth and early life of the Virgin described in ll. 9229–10629). By this reckoning, only about one thousand four hundred lines may be missing from the Thornton copy. Since Thornton normally managed to copy about one hundred and forty to one hundred and fifty lines on each leaf that has survived, this much smaller number of missing lines could probably have been accommodated comfortably on nine or ten more leaves, making the opening gathering at least **a**[16?].

[14] The most satisfactory explanation that can be offered to account for the fragmentary state of the middle section of the London manuscript is also that the gatherings that made up this part of Thornton's collection must have lain around unbound and susceptible to damage and rearrangement for a considerable length of time. See further the discussion below.

Fig. 1. Suggested collation for quire **b**

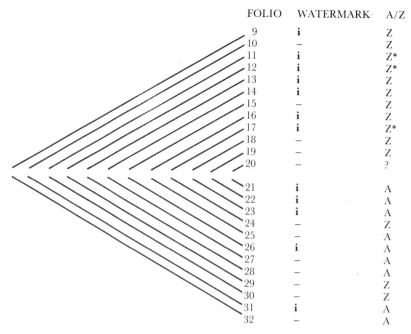

FOLIO	WATERMARK	A/Z
9	**i**	Z
10	–	Z
11	**i**	Z*
12	**i**	Z*
13	**i**	Z
14	**i**	Z
15	–	Z
16	**i**	Z
17	**i**	Z*
18	–	Z
19	–	Z
20	–	?
21	**i**	A
22	**i**	A
23	**i**	A
24	–	Z
25	–	A
26	**i**	A
27	–	A
28	–	A
29	–	Z
30	–	Z
31	**i**	A
32	–	A

Quire c²² (ff. 33–53; wants xxii)

Reference to other extant copies of *The Siege of Jerusalem* suggests that the manuscript lacks one leaf after f. 53. This probably contained the eighty-six lines of text necessary to complete Thornton's interrupted copy at this point.[15] The chain indentations in **c** confirm that it was a gathering of eleven bifolia comprised solely of paper with watermark **ii** (fig. 2). The missing leaf following f. 53 in **c** may well have contained a catchword.

[15] The estimated loss here corresponds to ll. 289–374 of *The Siege of Jerusalem*, for which see E. Kölbing and M. Day, ed. (1932), esp. vii, 16–21.

Fig. 2. Suggested collation for quire **c**

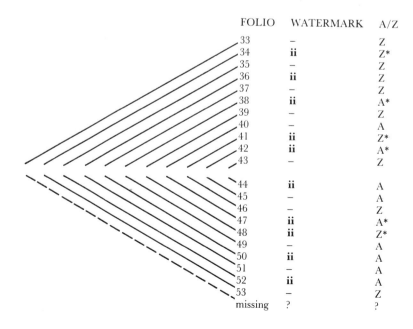

FOLIO	WATERMARK	A/Z
33	–	Z
34	**ii**	Z*
35	–	Z
36	**ii**	Z
37	–	Z
38	**ii**	A*
39	–	Z
40	–	A
41	**ii**	Z*
42	**ii**	A*
43	–	Z
44	**ii**	A
45	–	A
46	–	Z
47	**ii**	A*
48	**ii**	Z*
49	–	A
50	**ii**	A
51	–	A
52	**ii**	A
53	–	Z
missing	?	?

Quire d[20] (ff. 54–73)

Quire **d** has suffered no obvious textual loss and the catchword on f. 73 suggests that this was probably the last leaf of the quire. The original quire contained three types of watermarked paper (watermarks **iii**, **iv** and **v**). Although it is not always possible to identify the mould side of each half-sheet, the quire can be described as shown in fig. 3. Once this pattern has been retrieved from the paper it is clear that f. 54 can only be −A, f. 55 can only be −Z, and f. 56 can only be −A.

Fig. 3.   Suggested collation for quire **d**

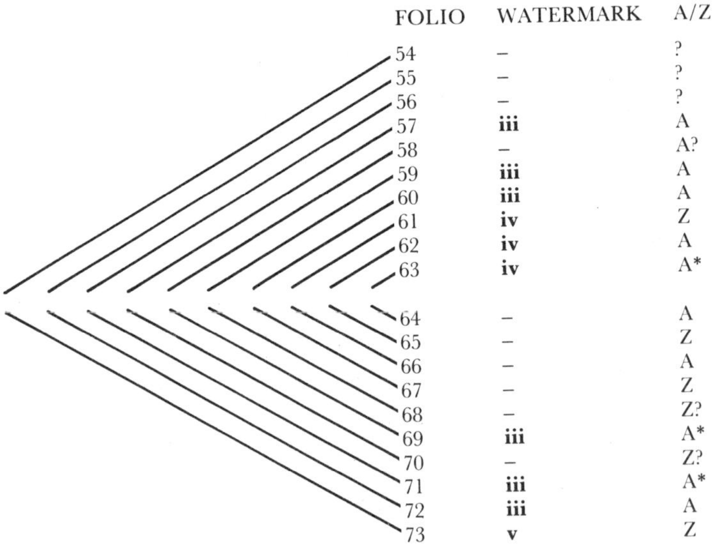

FOLIO	WATERMARK	A/Z
54	–	?
55	–	?
56	–	?
57	iii	A
58	–	A?
59	iii	A
60	iii	A
61	iv	Z
62	iv	A
63	iv	A*
64	–	A
65	–	Z
66	–	A
67	–	Z
68	–	Z?
69	iii	A*
70	–	Z?
71	iii	A*
72	iii	A
73	v	Z

Quire e[28?] (ff. 74–97; wants v, viii, xxvi, xxviii)

Textual evidence: Thornton's interrupted copy of *The Sege of Melayne* supports the assumption that some leaves are missing following ff. 77 and 79, although the extent of these textual *lacunae* is obviously open to doubt.[16] In addition, Stern, followed by Horrall and Hanna, argues that a leaf after f. 79 probably also contained the opening stanza of the ME Marian lyric on ff. 80r–81v. But this text (*O florum flos*) is now curiously 'sandwiched' in the manuscript between *Melayne* and *Duke Rowlande and Sir Ottuel*.[17] Interestingly, the Thornton copy of this inoffensive lyric also presents certain difficulties of interpretation which illustrate well important and sometimes neglected aspects of the dissemination of such material. Consequently, although a *minimum* physical loss of one leaf after f. 79 is indicated, it does not necessarily follow that that leaf need have contained any portion of the Marian lyric.

Reference to the *Index* shows that a copy of *O florum flos* is also extant on f. 366v of British Library MS Harley 3869. It is the obvious textual similarity of the Thornton copy and this item that has encouraged speculation concerning a missing first stanza in the Thornton text. However, the opening stanza of the Harley text (with no counterpart in the Thornton copy) is a seemingly self-contained authorial prayer to the Trinity.[18] This is immediately followed by another authorial prayer directed at the poet's intended audience and corresponding to the present opening stanza in Thornton's text.[19] The

[16] *Melayne* now survives uniquely in the Thornton copy. Although it is generally accepted that the ME poem is based on a lost French source, scholars have not been able to identify a possible analogue among other European treatments of the Charlemagne legend. See, however, H. M. Smyser's comments on this and on the probable clerical origin of *Melayne* in his unpublished thesis (1931), 202 ff. Compare also the varying comments on what the missing text following f. 79 might have contained by Herrtage (1880), x, and Maldwyn Mills (1973), 196.

[17] For an account of the probable circumstances in which this 'sandwiching' took place see below, 46–47.

[18] The text has remained unpublished. It reads:

Myght wisdom goodnesse of the
    Trinite
Mi naked sowle inspire with influence
The grace of that indyuidid unite
Where tresour is of eterne sapience
Forgyn my mouthe with the tongue of
    eloquence
For to discryue my souereyn ladi fre
This is my teem to hire excellence
O florum flos, O flos pulcherime

This particular stanza of *O florum flos* is the subject of a puzzling entry in *Supplement* 2168 which suggests that it once existed independently of the Marian lyric as the first stanza of a carol on the Trinity now extant in CUL MS Additional 7350 (see also *Supplement* 3328.5). My own examination of the Cambridge manuscript (a paper bifolium containing the four 'Bradshaw carols') has confirmed that this is not the case. Thanks are due to Mr A. E. B. Owen for his assistance during my unsuccessful attempts to trace the source of this strange error. For the text of the 'Bradshaw' carols see R. H. Robbins (1966).

[19] See H. N. MacCracken (1913), 60–63.

remaining sixteen stanzas consist of a mechanical anatomical eulogy bestowing blessings systematically on various parts of Mary's body. In the Harley copy the scribe inadvertently omitted eight complete stanzas from his original copy of the poem, but he scrupulously noted his mistake and eventually added the missing stanzas after he had copied the formal *explicit* for the text.[20] Of course, if the scribe had not noted his mistake the Harley copy would have shown signs of a textual *lacuna* without any actual physical loss in the manuscript. This may be close to the situation in the Thornton copy.

Thornton's text shows no obvious sign of being a fragment and H. N. MacCracken, who knew only this copy, printed the lyric as a complete poem. Indeed, Thornton's careful presentation of this item also suggests strongly that he considered his item complete as it now stands. On ff. 80r and 81v (i.e. on the first and last pages on which the lyric is copied) the first word in the opening line of each stanza has been highlighted with touches of red. More importantly, as Thornton transcribed the poem he also indicated the beginnings of twenty-one of the twenty-two stanzas which make up this version of the lyric. He did this by placing paraph signs ($\overline{x}$) as stanza indicators in the side margins.[21] This normally insignificant detail begins to assume some greater importance when it is realised that the only stanza in Thornton's copy of the lyric that lacks a paraph sign is the present opening stanza on f. 80r. Elsewhere in his copy Thornton's attention to detail even extends to the only other occasion when the first line of a stanza coincided with the first line of text on the page itself (f. 80v), but obviously there was no real need for him to add a stanza indicator on f. 80r to what he probably considered the opening stanza of his text. Consequently, because of this omission, it is as well to bear in mind that the missing leaf or leaves following f. 79 probably only contained the end of *The Sege of Melayne*. In the absence of any particularly compelling evidence to the contrary, *O florum flos* can be considered complete as it now stands on ff. 80r–81v.

The texts on ff. 96–97 show more obvious signs of being fragments. Thornton's copy of Lydgate's *Verses on the Kings of England* ends on f. 96v in the middle of a stanza, and his *Dietary* commences abruptly on f. 97r. Both these texts are extant in many manuscripts and reference to the *Index*, *Supplement*, and *Manual* suggests that these particular items were occasionally updated, revised, and expanded.[22] However, there is nothing in Thornton's copies or in his manuscript to suggest that these items are anything other than unexpanded versions. Instead it seems likely that following f. 96v about forty-five lines of *Verses on the Kings of England* were originally contained on a missing leaf. In addition, about seventeen lines of the Thornton copy of *The Dietary* seem to be missing. This copy of *The Dietary* is presented in unbroken single columns of text, but if we also take into account Thornton's slightly more spacious presentation of *The Kings of England* (a factor ignored by Hanna), then, as Horrall points out, this would be about the right number of lines to fill up the remainder of the hypothesised missing leaf. There is no obvious physical evidence in the manuscript to support an even greater loss.

The case for a textual *lacuna* following f. 97v is more problematic and the extent of any physical loss here is incalculable from textual evidence alone. Nevertheless, Thornton's presentation of his unique copy of a short lyric he entitles *This werlde es tournede up sodownne* would suggest that any impression that the poem is complete in itself (Horrall) is probably mistaken.[23] On f. 97v, before copying the four surviving lines of this item, Thornton was

[20] For full discussion of the Harley copy see *thesis*, 174–76.

[21] For this commonly found medieval punctuation mark see M. B. Parkes (1969), pl. 3 (ii). For Thornton's use of these marks in the Lincoln manuscript see M. F. Vaughan (1979), 7–9, esp. n. 16 and the discussion, 56–57, below.

[22] For full details see the bibliographical references in the description of these items. The complex textual histories of both texts remain virtually unexplored; but note A. Renoir's account of the third redaction of *Verses on the Kings of England* (Renoir, 1979).

[23] Thornton's heading here does indicate that he considered the poem to be a 'gud schorte songe' and the term 'short' might suggest that the poem need hardly have consisted of more than one or two stanzas. Nevertheless, the arbitrary way in which Thornton also used the term to describe *Wynnere and Wastoure* as a 'god schorte refreyte' means that the title is no guarantee that the poem on f. 97v was only a few lines long.

careful to add a fairly lengthy heading for the text. This occupies two lines on the page and fills just over a third of the space currently filled by the entire item. If it is maintained that the poem is complete as it now stands then the inordinate amount of attention given to this heading is puzzling and unprecedented elsewhere in Thornton's presentation of other short items in both manuscripts. Thornton even took the trouble to reserve space in the opening lines of this text so that a coloured capital could be added later. If this is a complete poem it is also the only occasion where Thornton has presented a four-line tag in such an elaborate way. It seems best to assume that at least part of this text (and possibly some other unknown material) was originally contained on a leaf or leaves following f. 97.

Physical evidence: The evidence of the chain indentations confirms that the batch of paper containing watermark **vii** on ff. 80–91 probably once formed the core of this large and fragmentary gathering.[24] The major problem in dealing with this paper is the considerable difficulty experienced in identifying the mould side on the unwatermarked half-sheets. As fig. 4 shows, this proved an impossible task on ff. 89 and 91 because the moulds on which this paper has been manufactured contained very fine chain wires that left particularly faint traces on the paper itself. This difficulty can be used to an advantage, however, since it is also very easy to distinguish the batch of **vii** paper from the sheets of paper manufactured on the watermark **vi** moulds on ff. 74–79 and 92–97. This is because of the heavier and more distinctive chain lines in the **vi** mould paper. This usefully confirms that f. 91, with its very faint impressions of fine chain wires, could hardly have been manufactured on a **vi** mould. As the chain indentations and the watermark pattern indicate, it is most likely to have been conjoint with f. 80.

Once the core of gathering **e** has been isolated, the problem that remains is one of matching each watermark **vi** half-sheet with its most likely unwatermarked conjugate. The difficulties here are made worse by the fact that textual *lacunae* of completely unknown extent follow ff. 77, 79 and 97. All of these *lacunae* involve watermark **vi** paper. In view of this uncertainty, the safest course seems to be to retrieve a consistent pattern from the physical evidence in **vi** mould paper that is not contradicted by the other scraps of evidence. When this important point is conceded a minimum loss of one leaf after ff. 77, 79 and 97 in gathering **e** suggests the probable shape of the original quire (fig. 5).

Quire f[36?] (ff. 98–124; xix–xx stubs, wants vi–x, xxxv–xxxvi)

Textual evidence: On f. 102v Thornton's copy of an alliterating paraphrase of Vulgate Psalm 50 ends abruptly while on f. 103r his copy of Lydgate's *Virtues of the Mass* begins acephalously. Hitherto it has been assumed that a single missing leaf could have accommodated the remaining lines of both these texts; but this assumption has been based on a mistaken estimate of the amount of text that is probably missing from the psalm paraphrase.[25] Once this is realised it is clear that there is no straightforward textual *lacuna* here.

The paraphrase of Vulgate Psalm 50 was originally written in a similar twelve-line alliterating stanza form to *Pearl*. Although the poem now survives uniquely in this copy, this is a systematic expansion of a twenty-verse psalm and it is likely that eight stanzas and eleven lines are missing from Thornton's copy. These lines were probably once contained on a single missing leaf.

[24] Cf. the rather more indecisive discussion in *thesis*, 200–202. Subsequent re-examination of ff. 80–91 confirmed that f. 85 is a Z leaf (not the A leaf that was originally assumed). I was also unable to find any evidence to support an identification of f. 91 (Dr Lyall originally identified this as a Z leaf). The difficulties arise here because these folios, and several others including Thornton's stock of **viii** (I) paper, seem to have been pressed very hard in the process of manufacture. The result is that the impression of the felt is left in the surface texture of *both* sides and even the corrugations of laid lines and indentations of chain lines have been pressed out.

[25] Stern, followed by Horrall and Hanna, assumed that the poem originally consisted of 19 stanzas and that 37 lines are missing from the Thornton copy. Comparison of Thornton's copy to the Vulgate text confirms that this ME paraphrase of Vulgate Psalm 50 lacks the remains of a twelfth stanza and eight (not seven) others. Stern's mistake here seems to have stemmed from the fact that she was following the conventional numeration in the Clementine Vulgate which subdivides the main text of Psalm 50 into nineteen verses. But the Vulgate text used by the author of the 'Thornton' paraphrase subdivided the text into twenty verses, the second of which is not indicated by the rubrication of the Clementine Vulgate. See the verse beginning *Et secundum multitudinem miserationum tuarum* in the Thornton text.

Fig. 4. Suggested collation for ff. 80–91

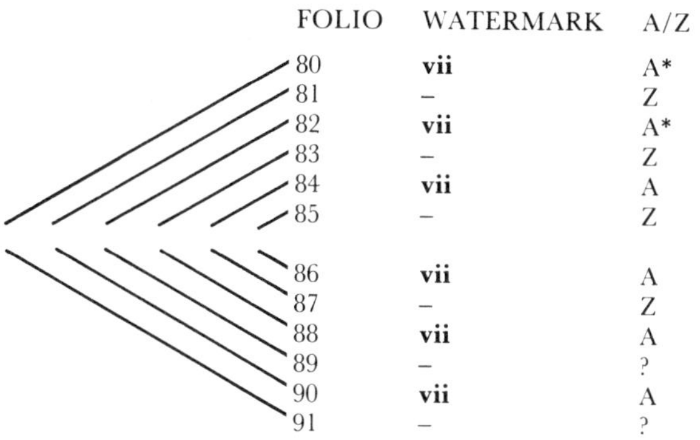

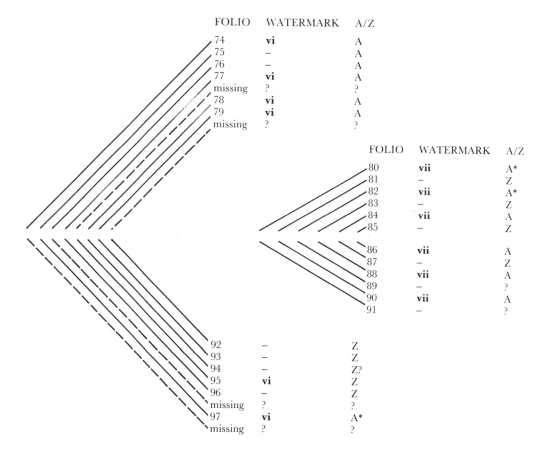

Fig. 5. Gathering **e** (ff. 74–97) reconstructed

Thornton's presentation of this item also gives some indication of the amount of space these lines would occupy if it is assumed that the missing lines were copied as consistently as the rest of the poem. For example, on ff. 102r–102v Thornton copied each twelve-line stanza onto six lines on his page (thereby grouping the metrical lines of the poem in pairs and giving the editors of the *Index* and *Manual* the false impression that the poem was written in six-line

[26] See the bibliographical references in the description of this text. Despite this economical presentation, it should be noted that Thornton was careful to distinguish each metrical line from its companion by punctuating his text with a form of the *punctus elevatus* (:). For the use of this device to indicate a major medial pause in a manuscript line see M. B. Parkes (1978), esp. 140.

[27] Herrtage (1880), ix, followed by the description in *Catalogue of Additions to the Manuscripts in the British Museum, 1876–1881* (1882), 150. Interestingly, the section in the manuscript beginning with the line *Moralisacio Sacerdotis . . .* (corresponding to ll. 145–176 in MacCracken's 1911 edition) has recently been edited without any indication that the text forms part of Lydgate's poem. See Jeanne Krochalis and Edward Peters (1975), 234–5. The oversight is hardly surprising since the copy in the London manuscript opens with no heading at the point where Lydgate turned from his prefatory comments and began to consider the importance of Psalm 42. The only heading occurs on f. 104r at a point corresponding to l. 145 of the poem. On f. 104r Thornton also abandoned his habit of copying the text in single columns with a one-line space between each eight-line stanza and commenced copying in continuous single columns. If he ever thought about this material 'editorially' then he too probably considered this ME compilation to be a series of closely related units rather than a single integral text. This may well have been close to Lydgate's own attitude towards the task of compiling the poem. See further the account of the 'joinery work' that created *Virtues of the Mass* and associated material in Derek Pearsall (1970), 258–9. For another comparison of the compiling interests of Lydgate and Thornton see 52–53.

stanzas).[26] Each stanza is also preceded by the beginning of the Latin phrase from the psalm that the following stanza will expand. Therefore, Thornton actually required a seven-line single column space to copy each complete stanza: on f. 102r he managed to copy five of these and the first eight lines of a sixth (40 manuscript lines), and on f. 102v he copied the remaining four lines of the sixth stanza, five complete stanzas, and the first line of a twelfth (39 manuscript lines). Assuming a similar layout on the missing leaf, Thornton would only have had room for about forty manuscript lines on the recto side of that leaf (i.e. the remaining lines of the twelfth stanza and another five stanzas), and on the verso he could then have copied the last three stanzas, or 21 manuscript lines. If he had added an *explicit* or left a space of some kind this would have reduced the remaining space still further, but it seems reasonable to allow that only about half the verso of the hypothesised missing leaf remained blank when he had completed his copy of the paraphrase of psalm 50.

Reference to MacCracken's edition of *Virtues of the Mass* (1911) and to the *Index* and *Manual* suggests that about fifty-seven lines are missing from the opening of Thornton's copy of Lydgate's text. However, on ff. 103r–110v Thornton consistently managed to copy only about thirty-eight to forty lines of this item onto each page. Despite important changes in Thornton's *mise-en-page* (which encouraged Herrtage and others to assume that the different sections of *Virtues of the Mass* were separate items in Thornton's collection),[27] Thornton never managed to copy more than 42 lines of text on any one page. So, even if the entire verso side of the hypothesised missing leaf was available for his use, Thornton could hardly have had sufficient space to copy another 57 lines of *Virtues of the Mass*. There are of course a number of possibilities, for example, Thornton may have copied Lydgate's text from a fragmentary or otherwise incomplete exemplar. Nevertheless, leaving aside questions concerning the probable nature of his Lydgate source for the moment, there does seem to be far too many lines missing from Thornton's items on ff. 102–103 to fit comfortably onto a single missing leaf after f. 102. On the other hand, there seems to be too few to fit conveniently onto two.

Finally, there is a distinct possibility that at least one leaf is missing following f. 124. The reason why this possible loss has remained unnoticed is because the evidence suggesting a *lacuna* has little to do with textual evidence in isolation, but is instead indicated by an important change in the manner in which Thornton presented his material on f. 124v. On ff. 123v–124v Thornton copied a short lyric entitled *A songe how þat mercy passeth alle thynge* as the last surviving item in a cluster of short didactic poems, the bulk of which are presented in double columns. However, on f. 124v he obviously had to crush the final twelve-line stanza of *Mercy passeth alle thynge* into the damaged bottom margin of the page. Thornton's space here was so limited that he had to start writing two metrical lines to every single manuscript line, thereby squeezing the final stanza into six crowded lines in his margin. Initially, this action might suggest that Thornton was reluctant to start a fresh page (or perhaps even a new gathering) when he had only a few lines of text left to copy. A possible precedent for this reluctance might be Thornton's presentation of the final stanza of *O florum flos* which was copied in the side margin of f. 81v. Nevertheless, this explanation is made less likely by the fact that Thornton also used a different black ink to copy the last few lines of text on f. 124v than that used for copying the rest of the poem (or for that matter most of the other items in the manuscript, with the exception of a short 'filler'

itcm on f. 101v).[28] This implies that some time after Thornton had completed the items on ff. 120–124 he probably had to return to f. 124v to add the final stanza in the bottom margin.

On this particular occasion, however, there is no textual evidence to suggest that this final stanza (now also extant in the earlier copies of the lyric in the Vernon and Simeon manuscripts) is anything other than an original and integral part of the poem.[29] Therefore there remains the remote possibility that Thornton's original exemplar was defective at this point and that at a later date he found a fuller version of the poem and used it to make good his own defective copy. However it seems much more reasonable to assume that Thornton originally copied the final stanza of the poem (and perhaps other unknown material) onto a leaf that has now gone missing after f. 124. Some time later he returned to the unbound gathering containing this cluster of lyrics and found that this leaf was so badly damaged that, in order to preserve *Mercy passeth alle thynge* intact, he had to recopy the final stanza into the nearest available blank space on f. 124v. Any other material on this hypothesised missing leaf (or leaves) was either completely lost or recopied elsewhere in his collection. Following f. 124, therefore, we may have another example in the problematic and fragmentary middle section of the London manuscript where at least one leaf has now gone missing.

Physical evidence: A pole of symmetry can be established in the paper containing watermark **viii** (I) by assuming that f. 110 and the unnumbered leaf that once followed it (now indicated in the manuscript by a surviving stub) once formed the central bifolium of gathering **f**. This hypothesis is supported by the continuous sequence of watermarked half-sheets on ff. 104–108 and the need to match this sequence with a similar series of unwatermarked half-sheets. The evidence of the chain indentations suggests that the core of this gathering can be extended without much difficulty to include ff. 103 and 116. However, as fig. 6 indicates, there is then more watermark **viii** (I) paper at the end of this reconstructed core than there is at the beginning. Fortunately, this coincides with a point in the manuscript where an uncertain textual *lacuna* has already been assumed. The evident physical loss before f. 103 has to be accounted for either by the suggestion that Thornton originally copied the acephalous item that begins on this folio (*Virtues of the Mass*) in a gathering that was already fragmentary, or else by the assumption that several other items have now disappeared completely from the manuscript.

If ff. 103–119 offer a first fixed point in **f** there is some evidence that the core of paper in this reconstructed quire can be extended to include f. 120 as another half-sheet that was manufactured on a watermark **viii** (I) mould. F. 120 was produced on a mould with very fine chain wires and this has caused problems since the indentations left by these wires are not sufficiently pronounced to enable positive identification of the mould side of the leaf.[30] By fortunate accident, however, the ribs and chain lines on f. 120 are distinguishable from similar marks on ff. 98–102, 121–124 which were made by watermark **vi** moulds. On these latter folios, the chain lines were made by much heavier chain wires and, consequently, the chain indentations themselves are much more pronounced than the very much fainter marks left by the finer chain wires in the watermark **viii** (I) moulds. This feature of **vi** paper has already aided in the reconstruction of the core of **vii** paper in gathering **e**. Therefore, although it would be impossible to distinguish an unwatermarked half-sheet of **viii** (I) paper from a similar sheet of **vii** paper,

[28] The short 'filler' on f. 101v is the *Prayer to the Guardian Angel*. For the economical manner in which the items on ff. 98r–102v have been presented and their links with Thornton's four 'songs' on mercy on ff. 120r–124v see 39–40, figs. 11–13.

[29] For text and bibliographical references see 17.

[30] See n. 24 above.

Fig. 6.   Suggested collation for ff. 103–20

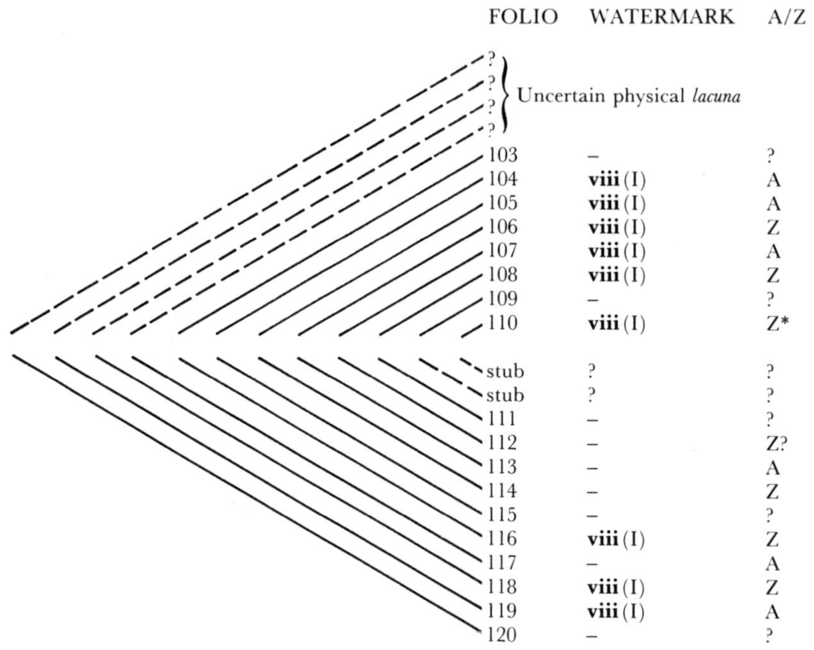

FOLIO	WATERMARK	A/Z
?		
?		
?	Uncertain physical *lacuna*	
?		
?		
103	–	?
104	**viii** (I)	A
105	**viii** (I)	A
106	**viii** (I)	Z
107	**viii** (I)	A
108	**viii** (I)	Z
109	–	?
110	**viii** (I)	Z*
stub	?	?
stub	?	?
111	–	?
112	–	Z?
113	–	A
114	–	Z
115	–	?
116	**viii** (I)	Z
117	–	A
118	**viii** (I)	Z
119	**viii** (I)	A
120	–	?

it is possible to distinguish batches of both kinds of paper from sheets manufactured on the **vi** mould.[31] In quire **f** it seems best to assume that, in common with the leaves that were originally conjoint with ff. 117–119, the conjugate of f. 120 has also gone missing before f. 103.

The need to match the few remaining leaves of **vi** paper with their most likely conjugates and the evidence of the chain indentations both suggest the collation offered in fig. 7. If this description of gathering **f** is accepted, then the physical loss following ff. 102 and 124 would appear to have been much greater than the minimum suggested by textual evidence alone. Following f. 102 it now seems likely that the remaining lines of the paraphrase of Vulgate Psalm 50 partly filled a half-sheet that was once conjoint with f. 121, but this has now gone missing along with four half-sheets of **viii** (I) paper before f. 103. In the following chapter I shall try to establish why these particular leaves were especially vulnerable in this particular quire as part of the discussion of Thornton's own practical compiling activities. In addition, following f. 124, the physical evidence suggests a loss of two leaves from the end of this large gathering. One of these leaves probably contained the final stanza of *Mercy passeth alle thynge* (first version) which Thornton may have recopied on f. 124v. So, here again, this damage seems to have occurred while Thornton was still working on his larger collection. The remaining space on these missing leaves may also have contained other material, or the last leaf may even have been a blank that Thornton himself removed just as he seems to have done elsewhere in his collection.[32]

[31] In order to make a further distinction between **vi** paper and the paper manufactured on **vii** and **viii** (I) moulds, an attempt was made to measure the distances between the chain lines in the unwatermarked folios on ff. 74–124. These measurements produced no conclusive evidence since the variations in the distances involved were so slight.

[32] See also the discussion of gathering **h** below. In the Lincoln manuscript, in gatherings **C**, **K** and also possibly in **M**, Thornton appears to have cancelled the final probably blank leaves in his original quires. See the account in D. S. Brewer and A. E. B. Owen (revised ed., 1977), xiii–xvi, supplemented by *thesis*, 23–36.

Fig. 7.   Gathering **f** (ff. 98–124) reconstructed

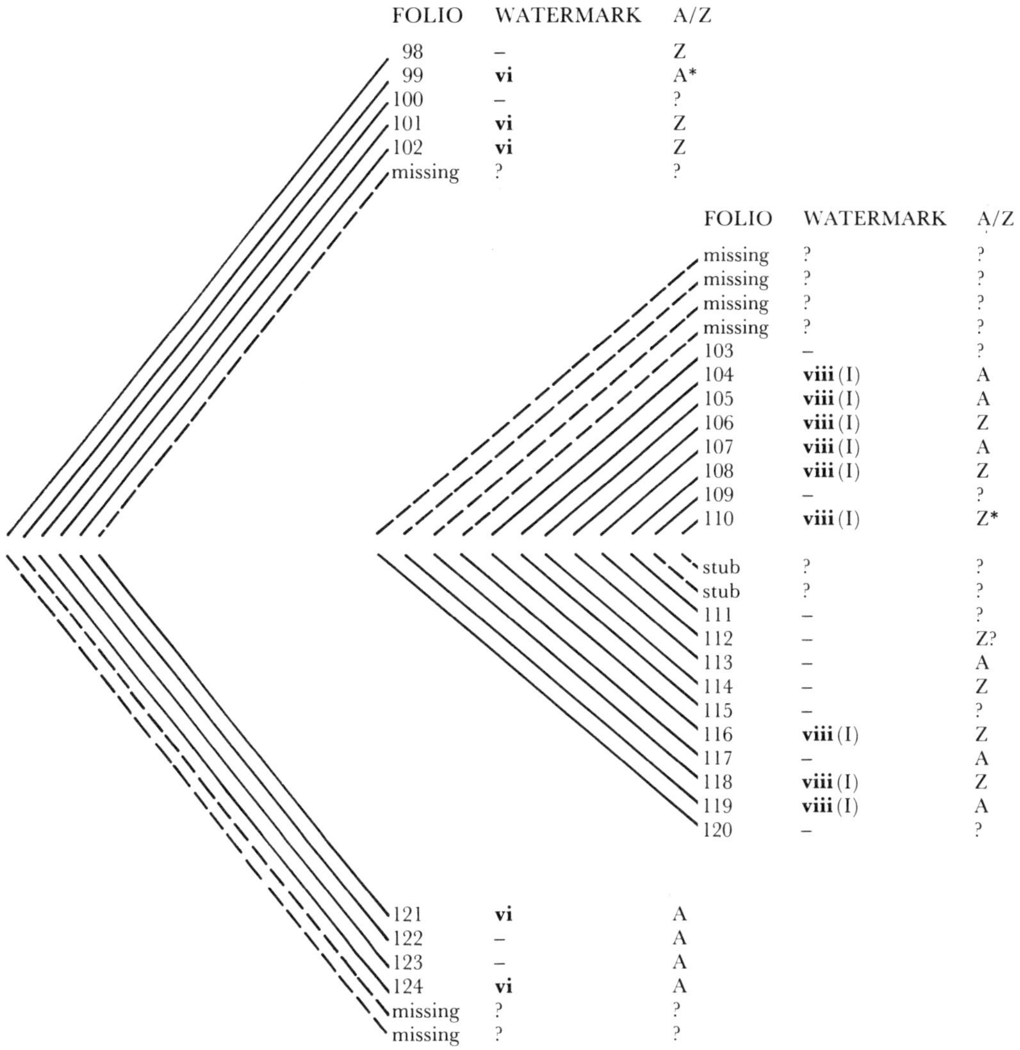

FOLIO	WATERMARK	A/Z
98	–	Z
99	**vi**	A*
100	–	?
101	**vi**	Z
102	**vi**	Z
missing	?	?

FOLIO	WATERMARK	A/Z
missing	?	?
missing	?	?
missing	?	?
missing	?	?
103	–	?
104	**viii**(I)	A
105	**viii**(I)	A
106	**viii**(I)	Z
107	**viii**(I)	A
108	**viii**(I)	Z
109	–	?
110	**viii**(I)	Z*
stub	?	?
stub	?	?
111	–	?
112	–	Z?
113	–	A
114	–	Z
115	–	?
116	**viii**(I)	Z
117	–	A
118	**viii**(I)	Z
119	**viii**(I)	A
120	–	?

121	**vi**	A
122	–	A
123	–	A
124	**vi**	A
missing	?	?
missing	?	?

Quire g²² (ff. 125–143; wants xx–xxii)

The Thornton copy of *Richard Coeur de Lion* is abruptly interrupted after f. 143v. Despite the complex textual history of this item, reference to the other extant copies of this ME romance supports the assumption that the manuscript lacks three leaves after f. 143.[33] These probably contained just over 500 lines of text. The assumption of this loss is supported by the evidence of the watermark patterns and the chain indentations (fig. 8).

[33] See the account in K. Brunner (1913), esp. 251.

Fig. 8.   Suggested collation for quire **g**

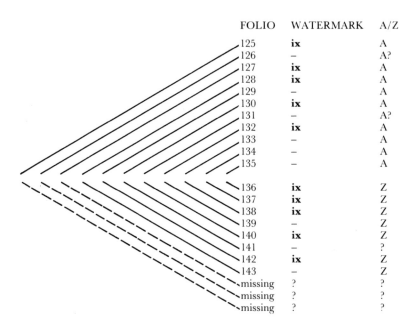

FOLIO	WATERMARK	A/Z
125	**ix**	A
126	–	A?
127	**ix**	A
128	**ix**	A
129	–	A
130	**ix**	A
131	–	A?
132	**ix**	A
133	–	A
134	–	A
135	–	A
136	**ix**	Z
137	**ix**	Z
138	**ix**	Z
139	–	Z
140	**ix**	Z
141	–	?
142	**ix**	Z
143	–	Z
missing	?	?
missing	?	?
missing	?	?

Quire h[26] (ff. 144–168; wants xxvi)

Horrall's collation assumed that f. 144 was originally a singleton leaf that Thornton added to a quire of eleven bifolia consisting of ff. 125–143. She also argued that ff. 145–168 form another gathering of twelve bifolia and that this seems to be intact. This identification of f. 144 does present problems and seems due to Horrall's reluctance to concede that a physical loss might have occurred here for which no textual evidence has survived.

The Thornton copy of *Richard Coeur de Lion* occupies ff. 125r–163v. It seems highly improbable that, halfway through the task of copying this text, Thornton should have added just one singleton leaf to the gathering containing the opening lines of his text when the remaining lines were copied into a second gathering. Moreover, if f. 144 was originally an added singleton, it is unusual (and under most circumstances would seem impossible) that it should have survived intact when the final leaves of the original gathering have themselves gone missing. It seems best to adopt the description of f. 144 offered here. Quire **h** contains the remaining lines of *Richard Coeur de Lion*. In the space remaining Thornton added *Ypokrephum* which he completed with space to spare on f. 168v. *Ypokrephum* is now followed on f. 169r, in a new gathering, by *The Parlement of the Thre Ages* which begins intact. But when Thornton originally completed his copy of *Ypokrephum* he was probably left with a final blank leaf in **h** following f. 168. That leaf was once conjoint with f. 144 and may even have contained a catchword. At some later stage, however, it was either deliberately removed or else lost without trace from the original gathering. The chain indentations in ff. 144–168 support the description of the original quire offered here (fig. 9). It should be noted that f. 152 is now a fragment in the manuscript.

Fig. 9.   Suggested collation for quire **h**

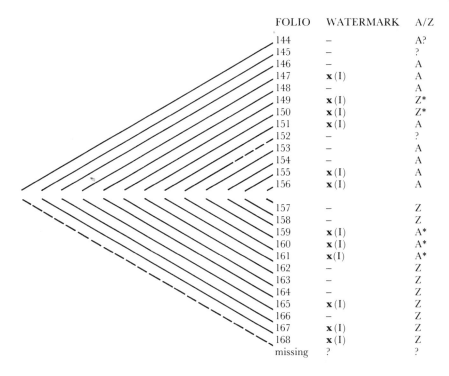

FOLIO	WATERMARK	A/Z
144	–	A?
145	–	?
146	–	A
147	**x**(I)	A
148	–	A
149	**x**(I)	Z*
150	**x**(I)	Z*
151	**x**(I)	A
152	–	?
153	–	A
154	–	A
155	**x**(I)	A
156	**x**(I)	A
157	–	Z
158	–	Z
159	**x**(I)	A*
160	**x**(I)	A*
161	**x**(I)	A*
162	–	Z
163	–	Z
164	–	Z
165	**x**(I)	Z
166	–	Z
167	**x**(I)	Z
168	**x**(I)	Z
missing	?	?

Quire i? (ff. 169–181)

The Thornton copy of *Wynnere and Wastoure* ends abruptly on f. 181v and most scholars have followed Gollancz's original suggestion that not much of this unique surviving copy of the poem is likely to be lost.[34] This does not sort well with the watermark evidence. Horrall uses the run of watermarked leaves here to suggest that five leaves are missing at the end of the poem, but without attempting to reconcile the apparent discrepancy between the textual evidence and the more important physical evidence. Reference to Thornton's normal scribal practices elsewhere, however, does help to clarify the puzzling situation at the end of the London manuscript.

In both manuscripts Thornton sensibly preferred to copy his alliterative texts using a single-column writing space. In the London manuscript all of *The Parlement of the Thre Ages* (ff. 169r–176v) and most of *Wynnere and Wastoure* are presented using this same predictable format. Nevertheless, on f. 181r Thornton suddenly commenced copying the long lines of *Wynnere and Wastoure* in double columns. This totally uncharacteristic practice significantly alters the visual appearance of the text so that the lines are crushed together on the page, regardless of Thornton's obvious efforts to maintain some kind of distinction between them and present a legible copy. Therefore, the sudden deterioration in his presentation of this poem might also indicate that the space remaining in the gathering Thornton was using was much more limited than the watermark evidence suggests. Assuming a minimum textual loss of one leaf following f. 181, it seems most likely that Thornton was copying *Wynnere and Wastoure* into a gathering that was *already* fragmentary.[35]

[34] Gollancz (1920), ii.

[35] A possible precedent for this kind of fragmentary gathering is provided by gathering **C** in the Lincoln manuscript where at least half of the gathering is missing but where there is no apparent textual loss. This would suggest that Thornton sometimes used defective gatherings (i.e. quires that did not consist exclusively of bifolia) as he added some of his material to the collection. For the probable circumstances in which gatherings **A–C** were added to the Lincoln manuscript see Thompson in Derek Pearsall ed. (1983), 114–7 and also the discussion in the concluding chapter below.

Fig. 10.   A possible collation for ff. 169–81

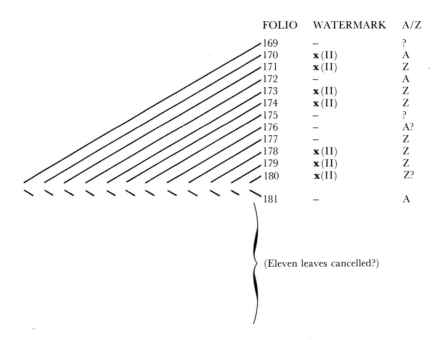

FOLIO	WATERMARK	A/Z
169	–	?
170	**x**(II)	A
171	**x**(II)	Z
172	–	A
173	**x**(II)	Z
174	**x**(II)	Z
175	–	?
176	–	A?
177	–	Z
178	**x**(II)	Z
179	**x**(II)	Z
180	**x**(II)	Z?
181	–	A

(Eleven leaves cancelled?)

The evidence of the chain indentations here is of very little use. They simply serve to confirm that the physical *lacuna* in this manuscript is far greater than Horrall has supposed. Assuming a folio arrangement, and no disarrangement of leaves before the text was copied, the evidence suggests a *minimum* loss of eleven leaves (fig. 10).

Compilation Procedures in the Manuscript

The physical collation suggested for the London manuscript in the previous chapter allows the contents of the miscellany to be grouped in the following series of small sub-sections:

(1) ff. 3–32, consisting of two gatherings (**a** and **b**) and containing a fragmentary extract from *Cursor Mundi*;

(2) ff. 33–97, consisting of three gatherings (**c**, **d** and **e**) and containing an amorphous cluster of material, some of which is fragmentary;

(3) ff. 98–124, consisting of a single extraordinarily large and very fragmentary gathering (**f**) and containing a similarly varied collection of short items;

(4) ff. 125–168, consisting of two gatherings (**g** and **h**) and containing two items that Thornton described as 'romances' – these are his fragmentary copy of *Richard Coeur de Lion* and *Ypokrephum*;

(5) ff. 169–181, consisting of a single very fragmentary gathering (**i**) and containing *The Parlement of the Thre Ages* and the remaining lines of *Wynnere and Wastoure*.[1]

This arrangement can be used to support the view that Thornton originally copied some of the motley collection of items that eventually formed part of the London manuscript into separate units of one or more gatherings. Usefully, this is a procedure that can also be said to lie behind the gradual compilation of several of the items in the Lincoln manuscript, but there the practical processes of compilation have reached a stage where larger clusters of texts find themselves in 'romance', 'religious', or 'medical' sections.[2] Nevertheless, within the various units or sections into which Thornton's two-volume collection can now be divided, it is also important to attempt to identify the types of compiling activities that may have taken place before Thornton copied his material. Inevitably, due to the limited nature of our present knowledge about the states in which Thornton received his exemplars, a grey area must remain where it is sometimes impossible to distinguish Thornton's efforts from those of earlier compilers and scribes. Because of this difficulty, the disorderly and unsettled nature of the material in the London manuscript often seems to offer a surer grip than the rather 'better-organised' Lincoln manuscript. On this occasion at least, the unfortunate defects in the

[1] The serious fragmentary state of **i** means that the status of this final 'section' in the manuscript must remain quite uncertain. See, however, the recent discussion of *The Parlement* and *Wynnere and Wastoure* as part of Thorlac Turville-Petre's attempt to provide a literary-critical context for the latter poem as 'the earliest datable poem of the Alliterative Revival' (Turville-Petre, 1977, 1–6, esp. 5).

[2] See *thesis*, 18–153 where the basic argument offered is that it is important not to overstress Thornton's personal responsibility for the creation and maintaining of this tri-partite division.

London volume can be used to some advantage. For this approach to be effective, however, it is necessary to work outwards from the scraps of physical and textual evidence available in the composite and fragmentary middle section of the manuscript (gatherings **e** and **f**) so that some of Thornton's more practically-motivated compiling activities in his second smaller collection can first be brought back to light.

The physical make-up of the London manuscript not only highlights the fact that Thornton compiled his collection from a series of irregularly-sized gatherings but it also suggests that he assembled some material in sequences of unbound gatherings which were susceptible to considerable wear and tear, and perhaps even some disarrangement, before his collection reached its present shape and size. Some of the physical *lacunae* in the London manuscript seem to have existed before Thornton had completed the task of copying all his items into unbound gatherings. Several of these losses were possibly blanks that Thornton removed. Others are more serious and involve textual losses at the beginnings and ends of quires that could have occurred at any time while the gatherings remained unbound. But these assumptions still may not account for the fact that so many leaves have gone missing from the *inner* leaves of gatherings **e** and **f**. While there need not be an obvious explanation for this peculiarity in the London manuscript, the problem does encourage closer examination of the internal organisation of material in both gatherings. Here, the fact that these exceptionally large and fragmentary gatherings are themselves composite, with the cores of each made up from a different stock of paper than the outer leaves, helps to uncover several stages in Thornton's compilation of his items.

The four short lyrics on ff. 120r–124v in gathering **f** provide a convenient starting-point for this discussion because, to the modern reader at least, these items dealing with the related themes of wisdom, mercy and judgement seem to form a distinctive literary grouping in the London manuscript. Moreover, the 'Thornton' *incipits* and *explicits* for this material suggest that their intended readers were encouraged to recognise that the lyrics form a closely related sequence of four 'songs'. Now reference to other copies of the same or similar texts can provide a much-needed context from which to estimate the general late medieval reputation of these short items.

A louely song of wysdome is the first and longest of the four songs and has had a particularly interesting textual history. The Thornton copy consists of thirty-eight eight-line stanzas and, despite the fact that Karl Brunner knew of two longer manuscript versions of the same material, he chose to edit the Thornton copy as an independent poem in its own right.[3] Brunner also published separately the much longer version of the poem that forms part of a shared cluster of didactic items in Cambridge, University Library MS Ff.2.38 and Magdalene College Pepys MS 1584.[4] This was printed with the title of *The Proverbs of Salamon*. As the poem stands in this longer version it consists of ninety eight-line stanzas, twenty-one of which also appear in the Thornton copy: but in the shorter version these twenty-one stanzas are also presented in a different order and are intelligently supplemented by seventeen other stanzas not present in the two Cambridge copies. Because of this feature, Brunner considered the Thornton version to be a meaningful and complete revision of a much longer poem. The seventeen added stanzas deal with very commonplace and elementary didactic topics such as the dangers of the seven deadly sins, the transitoriness of earthly glory and riches, the wickedness of a false tongue and the need for good works. This suggests that

[3] See Brunner (1932), 191–95; (1933), 178–99.

[4] For further discussion of the didactic sequence that includes *The Proverbs of Salamon* and is shared by MSS Ff.2.38 and Pepys 1584 see J. R. Kreuzer (1938), 78–85 and the recent comments in Frances McSparran and P. R. Robinson (1979), vii–viii, xvi.

at least one reviser of the longer *Proverbs* text was concerned to expand further the more generalised instructional elements already in the poem.

The second song in the 'Thornton' sequence is written in twenty eight-line stanzas. Other copies of the poem (*A song how þat mercy passeth rightwisnes*) are also extant in National Library of Wales Deposit MS Porkington 10; Lambeth Palace MS 853; and West Sussex Record Office Chichester, Cowfold Churchwarden's accounts.[5] The Lambeth manuscript is especially interesting since the text forms part of a conflated sequence of short didactic poems that have been copied as prose and which also includes a copy of the third item in the 'Thornton' sequence (*A song how mercy comes bifore þe jugement*).[6] This third item is the shortest in the 'song' sequence, consisting of eight twelve-line stanzas. Other copies of the poem can be found in BL MSS Harley 1704 and Additional 39574. However it is particularly striking that, in both the Lambeth manuscript and Thornton's collection, two obviously thematically related items should be found in such close proximity to each other and in the company of a sequence of short items, mainly in verse, and dealing with such familiar moral themes as the transitoriness of the earth and earthly things, the need for penance, and the necessity for the repentant sinner to have God's mercy rather than absolute justice.

It is not hard to find similar lyric clusters in other miscellanies. The fourth song in the 'Thornton' sequence (*A song how þat mercy passeth alle thynge*) is also extant in both the Vernon and the Simeon manuscripts.[7] On both occasions a copy of this lyric is the opening item in similar extended sequences of short didactic poems. The order of these short items in both collections is identical, except that in the Simeon manuscript the twenty-seven items shared with the Vernon sequence have been supplemented by two further short poems.[8] In his study of the relationship of these sister collections, A. I. Doyle has discussed how the didactic sequence of twenty-seven items in the Vernon manuscript forms a final manuscript section. Like the other four sections Doyle identifies in this collection, it seems likely that the task of obtaining exemplars and selecting and organising the material in the final section must have taken place at some stage prior to the actual copying of the material itself. The appended material in the Simeon sequence shows how, even though a lengthy didactic sequence had already been created in a carefully planned way, the sequence itself was always capable of being expanded by the addition of further items.

It is also intriguing that in the Simeon sequence (but not in the Vernon sequence) the *explicits* for thirteen of the first fourteen short didactic items describe these texts as 'songs'. This bears an obvious resemblance to the use of the same term to describe the material in a similar didactic sequence in Robert Thornton's collection and suggests that the present context of this material in the London Thornton manuscript is hardly unusual. Thornton himself probably inherited the idea of grouping these texts as 'songs' from an exemplar that already contained a similar didactic sequence. Once the likelihood of this is realised, the first of the 'Thornton' songs (*A louely song of wysdome*) might even appear to have been tailor-made for this particular sequence by an earlier compiler who was perhaps also responsible for the original ordering of the other songs in the sequence. The examples of the Vernon and Simeon collections imply that the idea for short verse sequences on commonplace moral and didactic themes is normally likely to have been clerical in origin. The sequences that were created and circulated in this way towards the end of the fourteenth and throughout the fifteenth centuries were

[5] See Auvo Kurvinen (1972) and Joyce Bazire (1982). Both scholars show how this text too was subject to editorial interference through revision and updating. Bazire concludes that the surviving copies, 'though they may have many features in common, demonstrate how a poem could "develop" in the course of transmission, both oral and scribal'. Note now also Bazire (1985).

[6] The Lambeth 853 sequence contains thirty-four ME items, of which all but one are in verse. These consist of six Marian lyrics; eight poems written in praise of Christ's name; four dealing with the transitory nature of the earth; five dealing with the related themes of judgement, mercy and penance; seven offering instruction in appropriate moral behaviour for the pious layman; and four teaching the fundamental tenets of the Christian faith. See the edition by F. J. Furnivall (1867) and description of the manuscript in M. R. James (1930–32), 809–11.

[7] Bodleian Library MS Eng. poet. a.1 and British Library MS Additional 22283 respectively. For descriptive accounts see the appropriate library catalogues and the useful account in Gisela Guddat-Figge (1976), 145–51, 269–79. These huge sister-volumes were probably compiled from a range of textual combinations in earlier exemplars by scribes working in a Cistercian house in the last decades of the fourteenth century. The most important studies of the relationships of these manuscripts to each other include M. Serjeantson (1937), K. Sajavaara (1967), A. I. Doyle (1974) and separate contributions by Doyle and R. A. Lewis in M. Benskin and M. L. Samuels (1981), 265–82, 251–64. Dr Doyle is preparing the introduction for a facsimile edition of the Vernon manuscript that is due to be published by Boydell & Brewer Ltd in 1986.

[8] These are a poem in praise of telling the truth (*Index* 4135) and a morning prayer of thanksgiving to the Trinity (*Index* 1369). The other twenty-seven short items shared by both the Vernon and the Simeon collections can be characterised as follows: ten deal with the topics of Divine love, judgement and mercy; six deal with the transitory nature of the world; four praise Mary; three discuss general moral and ethical principles; two deal with the lessons to be learned from English history; and

two instruct the reader in fundamental elements of Christian faith. See the edition by C. Horstmann and F. J. Furnivall (1892, 1901).

[9] Numerous scholars are working in this area; for the best preliminary account of the crucial role played by the regular clergy in English religious houses in the creation, preservation and transmission of a huge range of vernacular material see Dr Doyle's unpublished thesis (1953). In the Lincoln manuscript, the limited available evidence certainly points to a clerical provenance for 'Thornton' clusters of religious lyrics, Rolle-related material, and unascribed items in the collection by Walter Hilton and others. In his thesis Doyle makes the point that, by Thornton's time, this material had passed from its original owners to become 'a ready-made answer to the appetites of the newly enlarged spiritually conscious public' (1, 48).

probably compiled from texts that were themselves originally written, revised and gathered together using the resources that were most readily available in many of the great religious houses of the period. The four 'Thornton' songs do not seem to demonstrate Thornton's own compiling instincts, but rather seem to indicate the availability for his use of exemplars emanating from these houses and also available for dissemination among devout and literate readers with an interest in such didactic literature.[9]

The most obvious indication that the 'Thornton' song exemplar may have contained more than just the four short lyrics on ff. 120r–124v is the probability that two leaves have been lost from the London manuscript following f. 124. These seem to have been the final outer leaves of gathering **f** and they were hardly blank cancels since Thornton seems to have attempted to make good a textual loss here by recopying the final stanza of the fourth song into the bottom margin of f. 124v. Other material originally derived from the same exemplar may have been recopied elsewhere in Thornton's collection. At any rate, Thornton need not have copied all the items in this exemplar on just these pages. In this context, careful examination of the other items in gathering **f** helps provide further information about the probable circumstances in which Thornton copied his four song texts and compiled this section of his collection.

At first sight the present context of the 'Thornton' songs seems to reinforce the impression that the material on ff. 120r–124v forms a small but exclusive grouping in the London manuscript. The four songs on the final leaves of gathering **f** bear no obvious thematic or stylistic similarity either to the item that immediately precedes them in **f** (*The Three Kings of Cologne* on ff. 111r–119v) or to the item that follows in quire **g** (the romance of *Richard Coeur de Lion* on ff. 125r–163v). But gathering **f** is defective, consisting of a fragmentary batch of watermark **viii** (I) paper inserted into a smaller batch of watermark **vi** paper. Most of the song texts are copied onto **vi** paper, and, when the other items that have been copied onto the same paper at the beginning of the quire are examined, they generally appear to share the same didactic preoccupations as the four songs. Moreover, there seems to be some evidence in the manner in which Thornton presented these other items (which need not necessarily have come from the same exemplar, of course) that the gathering itself has been subject to considerable disarrangement during the course of its long history. An important point that must be recognised at the outset is that the order in which Thornton's items now appear in **f** is not necessarily the order in which he originally copied them.

The texts on ff. 98r–102v (i.e. in the present opening leaves of quire **f**) can certainly be said to act as thematically appropriate supplementary reading for the intended audience of the 'Thornton' song sequence. In *The Quatrefoil of Love* (ff. 98r–101v) the central figure is Mary and she is the intermediary through which mercy is obtained by the penitent sinner seeking grace. Appropriately, *The Quatrefoil*, with its complex thirteen-line alliterating stanza form, is followed immediately on f. 101v by a short penitential *Prayer to the Guardian Angel* written in rhyming couplets. This simple prayer is another minor indication of the general awareness of and the genuine need for the range of practical devotional ME texts that were made available in a variety of different forms to the devout lay person who wished to work actively for the remission of his sins.[10] In turn, this text is followed on f. 102r–102v by the ME paraphrase of Vulgate Psalm 50. The Lincoln manuscript contains a copy of the Latin text of the same psalm on ff. 258r–258v and, from the

appearance of other versions elsewhere in the fifteenth century, there is considerable evidence to suggest that the psalm itself was a favourite choice of poets, translators, commentators, scribes and readers.[11] In particular, the literary-didactic appeal of the psalm to lay readers was probably the direct result of the importance and availability of Vulgate Psalm 50 in late medieval prayer-books. In most *Horae*, for example, the psalm not only finds a place in the Psalter but is also one of the Seven Penitential Psalms.

The fact that all three of the didactic items on ff. 98r–102v have been presented in a particularly unusual and cramped lay-out also suggests that the close thematic comparisons that can be made here should be matched by a closer look at the possible implications of the striking visual peculiarities of Thornton's presentation. In this respect the appearance of Thornton's copy of *The Quatrefoil of Love*, and the short prayer on ff. 98r–101v has already evoked some critical discussion. Sarah Horrall, following an earlier suggestion by Dieter Mehl, suggested that ff. 98–101 originally formed a 'gathering' of two bifolia and this seems to reinforce the impression that the material in these folios may also once have formed a separate 'booklet'.[12] Reference to the chain indentations of ff. 98–101 shows that it is physically impossible for Horrall's description to be correct, and for the booklet theory to work here, these leaves must consist of, at best, one bifolium and two singletons. Once a more convincing collation is adopted by the process outlined in the previous chapter, the same types of physical evidence that Mehl and Horrall used in isolation can be reinterpreted and used to suggest a reason why gathering **f** in the London manuscript is so fragmentary.

It is interesting that all recent descriptions of these leaves have chosen to ignore the similarities between the physical appearance of ff. 98–101 and f. 102. Yet it is on all these folios that the results of the severe cropping that the manuscript has had to endure can be seen at their most serious. In marked contrast to the surrounding folios, the excessive trimming has shorn away almost all the original side margins on ff. 98–102 with the result that all three items copied here look as though they have been copied right to the edge of the pages. Thornton certainly presented these particular items differently from most of the other material in his collection and this serves to alert the modern reader that, as he copied these texts, he was trying to make careful use of a very limited amount of space.

The consistent and economical presentation of the paraphrase of Vulgate Psalm 50 was discussed in the previous chapter, and the same general point can be made about the copy of *The Quatrefoil* on ff. 98r–101v. Nevertheless, despite the crowded appearance of this text on his page, where the first eight lines of each thirteen-line stanza are written in pairs, Thornton was always careful to punctuate his text and thus indicate the line divisions by his use of the *punctus* and the *virgula suspensiva*. He also copied each of the rhyming couplets in his *Prayer to the Guardian Angel* on f. 101v in a single line on his page, but again indicated the metrical division between each line using a form of the *punctus*. Therefore, the texts on ff. 98r–102v show every sign of having been added to Thornton's collection as 'fillers': they provide outstanding examples of cases where Thornton's evident desire always to present material in the most legible format possible was compromised by the limited amount of available blank space on which to copy them. The result is a series of five crowded leaves which seem to have formed the opening leaves of gathering **f** but exhibit all the signs of having been the final leaves in the gathering that Thornton actually filled with material.

---

[11] For a summary account of the different surviving ME versions of Vulgate Psalm 50 see *Index* 1961, 3755, 2157, 1591, 355, 1956, 990; and *Manual*, IV, 12, 15, 17, 18, 19, 21, 22.

[12] Mehl (1968), 260; Horrall (1979), 103. The generally ragged and soiled condition of ff. 98–101 also contrasts very unfavourably with the relatively unblemished condition of the last leaf of the previous gathering (f. 97 in gathering **e**) and the first surviving leaf of the watermark **viii** (I) insert (f. 103 in gathering **f**).

The economical use of watermark **vi** paper on ff. 98–102 provides another useful point of comparison with the similarly economical use of the same paper for Thornton's 'songs'. This is indicated by a curious change in writing format on ff. 120r–124v. On ff. 120r–120v, on what appears to have been the final leaf of the inserted batch of **viii** (I) paper in **f**, Thornton copied the opening lines of the first 'song' using a single-column format. The remaining material in the sequence is copied on **vi** paper, and in a similar ink, but in double columns. Elsewhere, such abrupt changes in Thornton's presentation of his items seem to have been prompted by the practical exigencies of his informal methods of book production. The evidence on ff. 98r–102v and 121r–124v would therefore seem to suggest that when Thornton filled the outer leaves of gathering **f** he was very aware that the space available for his material was severely limited. By contrast, on f. 120, when he added the opening lines of his first song, Thornton's presentation implies that he was simply interested in filling up the remainder of the single-column writing space that he had previously ruled for his batch of watermark **viii** (I) paper (ff. 103–20).

Acting on the assumption that the distinctions that have been drawn between the two stocks of paper in gathering **f** are valid, the available scraps of evidence would suggest that several 'production stages' are responsible for the present state of this large fragmentary gathering.[13] These are represented by figs. 11, 12 and 13.[14] Originally, ff. 121–24 seem to have formed the opening leaves of a gathering consisting of six bifolia (ff. 121–24, 98–102); ff. 103–20 formed an entirely separate quire composed originally of at least twelve bifolia. In stage I Thornton copied the opening lines of the first of his four songs on mercy and judgement in single columns on the last leaf of a gathering that already contained *The Virtues of the Mass*, *The Three Kings of Cologne* and probably *The Rose of Ryse*. He then changed to a more economical format and copied the remaining song items in double columns on ff. 121–24. The last stanza of the fourth song was originally copied on the first of two leaves that have now gone missing after f. 124. Finally, Thornton filled the second half of this small gathering with other thematically appropriate items, including *The Quatrefoil*, and the alliterating paraphrase of Vulgate Psalm 50.

In stage II the rapid deterioration of these unbound gatherings must have started when Thornton eventually returned to these items. Presumably because he was aware that he was in imminent danger of losing more material from an already defective gathering of **viii** (I) paper (ff. 103–20), Thornton protected the remainder of his gathering by refolding his smaller quire of **vi** paper so that ff. 98–102 and 121–24 formed an envelope for ff. 103–20. At the end of stage II, ff. 103–20 became a fragmentary insert in gathering **f**. By this time the four leaves before f. 103 (originally the outer leaves of the smaller gathering) had already gone missing and a further leaf following f. 102 (another outer leaf) had also gone. Coincidentally, Thornton's action in refolding his paper had the result of juxtaposing a, by now, fragmentary paraphrase of Vulgate Psalm 50 on f. 102 with a damaged copy of *Virtues of the Mass*, beginning with Lydgate's treatment of *Judica me Deus* on f. 103. The formation of this sequence has created its own difficulties since several early accounts of the manuscript actually considered that the texts on ff. 102 and 103 form part of a single composite item.[15]

Thornton's rearrangement of his quires does not appear to have halted the continued deterioration of the newly-created composite gathering. At some stage, the outer leaves at the opening of the gathering (i.e. ff. 98 and 99)

---

[13] The following chapter will discuss how one of these 'production stages' – the decoration of the material in the watermark **viii** (I) insert – shows signs of having been completed *before* the items in this large and composite gathering settled finally into their present order in the London manuscript.

[14] Thornton's rearrangement of paper in this gathering, and also elsewhere in the London manuscript, should be compared to his similarly unorthodox use of refolded gatherings in the Lincoln manuscript. See my essay in Derek Pearsall, ed. (1983) and *thesis*, esp. 49–56 (rearrangement of quire **I**); 116–118 (quire **N**) also now Keiser (1984).

[15] The problem seems to have originated with Herrtage's 1880 account. He writes: 'On lf. 102 follows a prayer in verse, most of the verses beginning with a Latin line; on lf. 103 it is called a "psalme"; "Take this psalme", & c.; and on lf. 104 begins a morality . . . to which the "psalme" forms a kind of introduction' (ix). See also my discussion of the Thornton copy of *Virtues of the Mass*, 28 above, and n. 27.

Fig. 11.   Thornton's compiling activities in gathering **f**: stage I

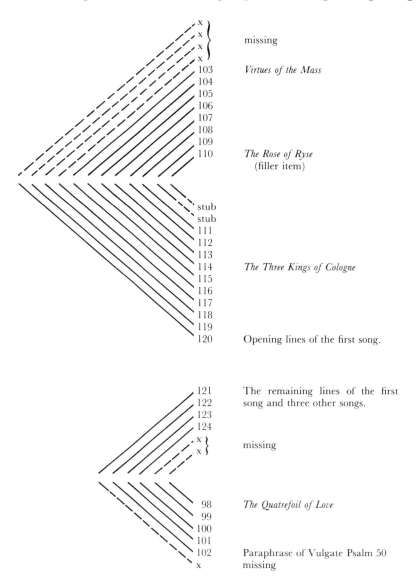

sustained considerable damage from dirt and dampness. Even more severe damage to their conjoints at the other end of the gathering probably led to the complete disappearance of the final leaves in **f** from the collection. When Thornton finally returned to **f**, perhaps this time to assemble it alongside his other unbound quires, he probably found that he was in imminent danger of losing the leaf following f. 124. It was at this stage that he rescued the last stanza of *Mercy passeth alle thynge* and added it in the most suitable remaining space on f. 124v. At the same time he may have added his *Prayer to the Guardian Angel* in the same ink and in the very brief remaining space on f. 101v.

Fig. 12.   Thornton's compiling activities in gathering **f**: stage II

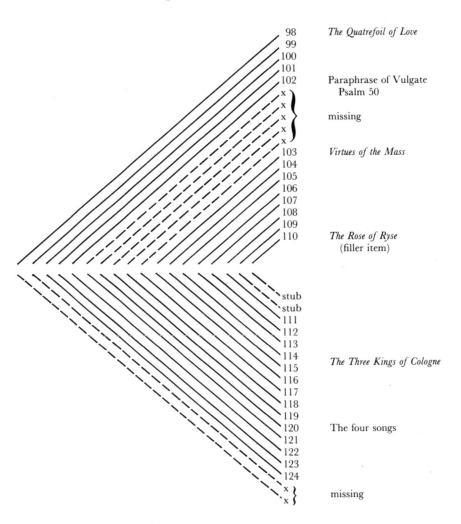

98	*The Quatrefoil of Love*
99	
100	
101	
102	Paraphrase of Vulgate
	Psalm 50
x ⎫	
x ⎪	
x ⎬	missing
x ⎪	
x ⎭	
103	*Virtues of the Mass*
104	
105	
106	
107	
108	
109	
110	*The Rose of Ryse*
	(filler item)
stub	
stub	
111	
112	
113	
114	*The Three Kings of Cologne*
115	
116	
117	
118	
119	
120	The four songs
121	
122	
123	
124	
x ⎫	missing
x ⎬	
x ⎭	

This hypothetical reconstruction of the stages by which one of the fragmentary composite gatherings in the middle section of the London manuscript was constructed prompts further analysis of the other large gathering in the same section of Thornton's miscellany (gathering **e**). The varied collection of material copied here consists of the final lines of *The Sege of Melayne* on ff. 74r–79v; the short Marian lyric *O florum flos* on ff. 80r–81v; *Duke Rowlande and Sir Ottuel* on ff. 82r–94r; Lydgate's *Passionis Christi Cantus* (two versions, f. 94r; ff. 94v–96r), his *Verses on the Kings of England* (ff. 96r–96v), his *Dietary* (ff. 97r–97v); and three Latin aphorisms and the opening lines of the fragmentary song *This werlde es tournede up sodownne* on f. 97v.

In this gathering it is obvious that the Thornton Lydgate items form another very distinctive literary sequence. This material seems to reflect the Bury monk's own wide-ranging interests in devotional, moral, historical and didactic themes: in *Passionis Christi Cantus* Lydgate urges sinful man to stand before an image of the crucified Christ and to think well on Christ's original suffering and sacrifice; in his *Verses on the Kings of England* Lydgate teaches the reader the moral lessons inherent in the history of English kingship; while, in

Fig. 13.   Thornton's compiling activities in gathering **f**: stage III

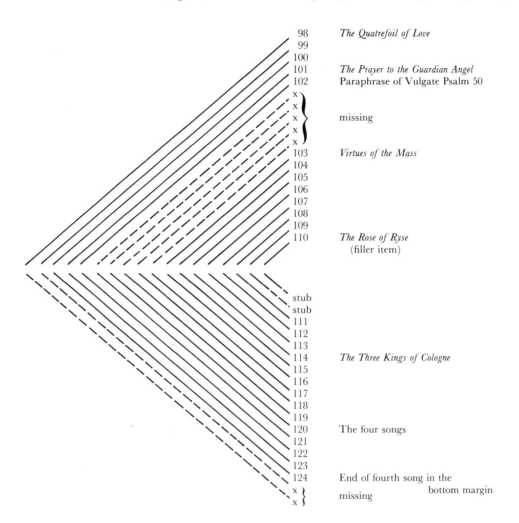

98 *The Quatrefoil of Love*
99
100
101 *The Prayer to the Guardian Angel*
102 Paraphrase of Vulgate Psalm 50
x
x
x missing
x
x
103 *Virtues of the Mass*
104
105
106
107
108
109
110 *The Rose of Ryse*
  (filler item)
stub
stub
111
112
113
114 *The Three Kings of Cologne*
115
116
117
118
119
120 The four songs
121
122
123
124 End of fourth song in the
      bottom margin
x
 missing
x

his *Dietary*, he instructs his reader not only how to eat well but also how to live a life of moral rectitude. Therefore it is hardly surprising that these items, dealing with human, moral and social behaviour, should form a sequence in the London manuscript. They obviously reflect literary-didactic interests that are not unique to Thornton or Lydgate, but which seem the fundamental didactic preoccupations of the later middle ages. In the absence of evidence to the contrary, it seems most reasonable to assume that Thornton copied these short Lydgate items from a similar sequence in his exemplar and that he merely formed part of a much wider audience of literate and devout readers for whom such material was written and compiled. The real question seems to be whether the Thornton Lydgate exemplar contained any other items that Thornton also copied in his collection. Closer examination of the texts on f. 97v would suggest that this is a distinct possibility.

The last lines of *The Dietary* are followed immediately on f. 97v by three short Latin aphorisms which comment briefly on the transitory nature and corruptibility of man.[16] These are followed by *This werlde es tournede* which

[16] These provide a minor example of the late middle age's delight in epigrams which were both mnemonic and practical. Mrs Stern (1976), 212, aptly makes the point that the sentiments expressed here are not unlike those in the Latin originals of Lydgate's own *Duodecim Abusiones*. They must have been topics which were dear to the hearts of other ME versifiers as well since the second Latin tag on f. 97v (complaining that the law is dead because the hand of the judge is greased) can also be found incorporated in a macaronic complaint poem in the clerically-owned British Library MS Royal 17.B.17. See the text in C. Horstmann (1896), 65.

[17] This fragment too can profitably be compared to other short poems either by Lydgate or written in the Lydgate style. It might even be said that the first lines of Lydgate's *So as the Crabbe Goth Forward* are little more than a satirical reworking of the sentiments expressed more straightforwardly in *This werlde es tournede*. The Lydgate satirical poem begins:

þis worlde is ful of stabulnesse,
þer is þerinne no varyaunce;
But trouthe, feyth, and gentylesse . . .

(ll. 1–3)

See the edition by H. N. MacCracken (1934), 464–7.

[18] Compare the descriptions of similar sequences in ns. 6 and 8 above.

[19] Pearsall (1970), 204–6.

[20] In this context, Rosemary Woolf's description of two general types of fifteenth-century miscellanies (the 'poetical' collections of works by single authors and the 'privately-owned' anthology) serves to make Thornton's compiling actions a little more comprehensible. See Woolf (1968), 375–6. The London manuscript best fits Woolf's category of 'the privately-owned anthology'; but most of the anthologising processes that were creating 'selected works' collections by Lydgate and related authors would appear to have been going on already in Thornton's exemplars.

deals with the mutability of the earth.[17] The theme of all these short scraps is one that was close to Lydgate's own heart, and, since the similarity of the ink in which all the scraps on f. 97v were copied would suggest that they were added at the same time as *The Dietary*, it is likely that Thornton was simply inheriting someone else's didactic sequence. The single folio that seems to be missing following f. 97 presumably contained the continuation of *This werlde es tournede* and may even have contained other thematically similar material that is now completely lost.

The hypothetical reconstruction of Thornton's rearrangement of ff. 98–102 and 120–24 to enclose what at one stage appears to have been an independent quire (ff. 103–20) suggests an intriguing new context for the didactic material in **e**. Originally, the items on f. 97 may have been set beside a quire whose opening leaves contained Lydgate's *Virtues of the Mass* as well as perhaps some other related items that are now missing (fig. 11). The last leaf of this quire also contained the opening lines of the first of the four songs on the theme of mercy and judgement. This combination of material is very suggestive, especially since the four song items on ff. 120r–124v would seem to be the logical extension of the didactic sequence on ff. 94v–97v. If the Thornton *incipits* and *explicits* are any indication of the type of literature he thought he was copying at this point, then these four 'songs' would appear to share some link with Lydgate's *Passionis Christi Cantus* and, even more obviously, with *This werlde es tournede* which Thornton describes as 'a gud schorte songe'. Indeed, reference to the Simeon song sequence is helpful here since it suggests that a short poem on the transitory nature of the earth is precisely the kind of text that the Thornton song exemplar might be expected to have contained.[18] It is also interesting that, in his study of Lydgate's verse, Derek Pearsall found it useful to consider in detail the striking stylistic similarities between some of Lydgate's didactic poetry and the cluster of short items in the lyric sequence shared by the Vernon and Simeon manuscripts.[19] These comments might equally well apply to the thematically and stylistically similar song sequence in the Thornton collection. It seems quite possible that it was Thornton himself, acting as scribe and book compiler, who actually disrupted a sequence of songs on the themes of mutability and mercy which may even have come to him in a batch of texts that also included a sequence of short poems by Lydgate. Even if it is not possible to explain fully Thornton's motives here, they seem to have been prompted more by his desire to use up the remaining blank leaves in his half-completed gatherings than by any desire to preserve the order in which the texts appeared in his exemplar.[20]

The present context of Lydgate's *Virtues of the Mass* is also of some interest since this is the only other Lydgate item in Thornton's entire collection, and yet it too seems to have become detached from the continuous sequence of short 'Lydgate' texts on ff. 95r–97v. When ff. 103–20 are examined with these thoughts in mind, then, within gathering **f**, there seems to be an example of a second gathering which Thornton may have rearranged as he incorporated it in his collection.

Thornton's possible compiling actions are outlined in fig. 14. In stage I, I suggest that ff. 103–20 once formed a gathering where ff. 120–120a were the central bifolium and the stub following f. 110 (110b) and f. 110 formed the outer bifolium. At an early stage Thornton copied *The Three Kings of Cologne* onto ff. 110ar–119v. This action filled the first half of the original gathering. When this task was completed f. 120 remained blank, as did the second half

Fig. 14.   Thornton's compiling activities in gathering **f**:
two possible preliminary stages

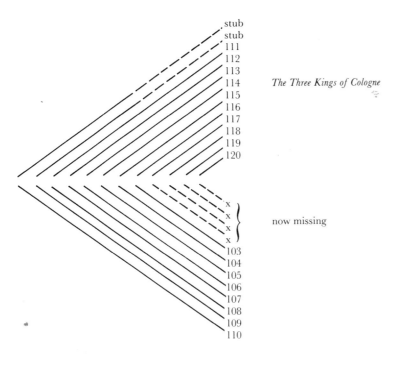

The Three Kings of Cologne

now missing

STAGE ONE

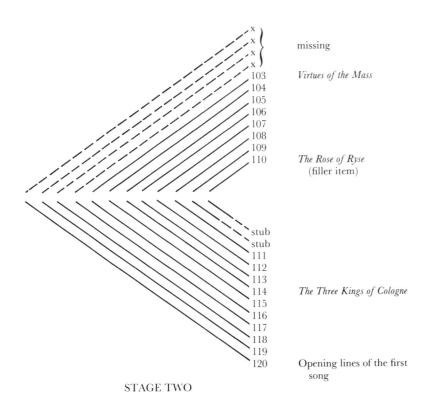

missing

Virtues of the Mass

The Rose of Ryse
(filler item)

The Three Kings of Cologne

Opening lines of the first
song

STAGE TWO

of the gathering. Thornton may have received his Lydgate exemplar at a relatively late stage in his book-producing activities. By this time the second half of the gathering containing *The Three Kings of Cologne* still remained blank, as did the second half of gathering **e** (ff. 74–97). If Thornton originally wanted to ensure that the Lydgate poems in his source were kept reasonably close together, yet he still wanted to use up the valuable remaining spaces in his half-filled gatherings, then all he had to do was refold the gathering containing *The Three Kings of Cologne* so that the *first* half of the refolded gathering remained blank. Thornton then copied *Virtues of the Mass*, and possibly other unknown material, into the refolded gathering before turning to gathering **e** to continue copying his Lydgate items. When gathering **e** was filled (and by this time Thornton was copying the song sequence from his source) he turned back to his rearranged gathering and added the opening lines of the 'first' song on f. 120r. For a time the only remaining space in the refolded gathering occurred on f. 110v, but at some stage even this was used up to crush *The Rose of Ryse* into the collection as a 'filler' text. It was possibly only after this complex of practically-motivated activity that the items on ff. 103–20 settled into their present sequence.

Thornton's actions in gathering **f** would appear to be those of a scribe-compiler who is in the final stages of assembling partly-filled gatherings into a fixed but not totally unalterable sequence. It may also have been for this reason that he seems to have chosen to copy items from his Lydgate exemplar into a gathering (**e**) that already contained the remaining lines of one Charlemagne romance, a short Marian lyric, and the complete text of a second Charlemagne romance. Both *The Sege of Melayne* and *Duke Rowlande and Sir Ottuel* are now extant only in the London manuscript and their thematic and textual relationship to each other has always been a matter of controversy. S. J. Herrtage, following a suggestion made by Gaston Paris, argued that *Melayne* was written and intended as an introduction for *Ottuel*, while Maldwyn Mills has argued more recently that the points of similarity shared by both Charlemagne romances are probably coincidental and that Thornton may have been responsible for the close proximity of both items in his collection.[21] Neither scholar attempts to explain the circumstances that led to the 'sandwiching' of *O florum flos* between the two romances.[22]

The outer leaves of gathering **e** consisted of eight bifolia of watermark **vi** paper into which was inserted a core of six bifolia of watermark **vii** paper to make up a composite quire. Of course this could have happened at any time after the paper had been manufactured, but it must have happened before Thornton added his copy of *Ottuel* to his collection since this text begins on f. 82r in **vii** paper but ends on f. 94r in **vi** paper. On the other hand, it may be more than just coincidence that the remaining lines of *Melayne* in gathering **e** are copied solely on paper containing watermark **vi** and that *O florum flos*, the intruder lyric, at present occupies the opening leaves of the batch of **vii** paper at the core of this composite gathering (see fig. 5 in the previous chapter). Given the obtrusive nature of *O florum flos*, it is attractive to assume that Thornton was responsible for expanding a quire that once consisted exclusively of **vi** paper with an insertion of **vii** paper. *Melayne* was copied in the first half of the original gathering, but, before copying *Ottuel*, Thornton expanded the gathering by inserting ff. 80–91. If the insert already contained *O florum flos*, then this would explain the present unexpected and quite illogical sequence of material at this point in the London manuscript.

Once this hypothesis concerning Thornton's compiling activities is accepted

[21] Compare Herrtage (1880), x, and Mills (1973), 196–7.

[22] However see the tentative comments on this by Stern (1976), 29–30, n. 19.

there is here the first indication of a delay of some kind between the time when Thornton copied *Melayne*, the time when he inserted the batch of paper containing *O florum flos*, and the time when he returned to the newly-expanded gathering to add *Ottuel*. This type of delay is suggestive of the uncertain conditions under which Thornton was working for at least part of his career as book compiler and it was presumably due to some similar uncertainty that the sequence of Lydgate items in the same gathering begins with a 'false start' on f. 94r. On this folio Thornton carefully copied the *explicit* of *Ottuel*, followed closely by his *incipit* and opening lines of *Passionis Christi Cantus*. The ink used for the Lydgate item seems different from the ink used for the main text of *Ottuel* and it would appear that the items on f. 94r were copied at different sittings. Moreover, on f. 94v it is impossible to escape the impression that something unusual must have happened as Thornton continued transcribing *Passionis Christi Cantus* since he abandoned this first copy and left about half of f. 94v blank before commencing to copy Lydgate's poem for a second time. A later hand subsequently filled part of the space on f. 94v with two carol fragments but, despite this activity, an embarrassing gap still remains on the page. There seems to be no obvious explanation to account for this completely unprecedented 'second start' in Thornton's copy of Lydgate's poem.[23]

Elsewhere in the London manuscript it is also possible to gain some limited impression of Thornton's practically motivated methods and motives. In gatherings **g** and **h**, for example, Thornton's characterisation of *Richard Coeur de Lion* (ff. 125r–163v) and *Ypokrephum* (ff. 163v–168v) as 'romances' in his *explicit* of the first text and *incipit* of the second on f. 163v seems a good indication that he was prepared to accept that these two texts formed a satisfactory 'romance' grouping in the London manuscript. The main evidence that suggests that Thornton was personally responsible for this grouping is the very obvious change of ink on f. 163v which coincides with the end of one item and the beginning of the other. *Richard* is copied in a noticeably darker ink than *Ypokrephum* which, in turn, is written in a poor-quality ink that has faded more than most other inks in the entire Thornton collection. This supports the idea of yet another time lapse before Thornton returned to a partly filled gathering – this time it was gathering **h** – and proceeded to copy *Ypokrephum* in this apparently self-contained 'romance' unit within his larger collection.[24]

The use of red ink in the presentation of *Ypokrephum* indicates another important stage in Thornton's production of this unit of material. Throughout his collection Thornton seems to have made a point of returning to his texts to add various decorative details in red ink. Unusually, however, on ff. 167r, 167v, and again on f. 168r, he has made good other minor defects in *Ypokrephum* using the same red ink. The result is that the reader's eye is unavoidably drawn equally to both the important decorative features of the text and also to some otherwise insignificant corrections. While this is, in itself, an indication of the haphazardly informal way in which Thornton could 'freshen up' as well as rubricate a faded text, it is also significant that *Ypokrephum* is the only Thornton text that has been treated in quite this way. In addition, it seems most important that the part of the *incipit* which describes the text as a 'romance' has also been added in red as a later addition to a phrase in the side margin of f. 163v. This phrase once simply read 'Ihesu Criste'. The original marginalia is written in the same faded ink as the main text and was probably derived from an exemplar. But it seems

[23] In a brief note describing this false start, Mrs Stern suggested that the reason for Thornton's unusual behaviour here was because 'the scribe recognized, as he copied it, an important religious text, and decided to give it greater prominence' (Karen Hodder/Stern, 1969, 379). But the few signs that remain – and it must be admitted that there are very few – suggest that the repetition of the opening lines of *Passionis Christi Cantus* on f. 94v was quite unplanned and probably hastily executed. For the argument that the repetition of material here was more likely to have been the result of some kind of technical miscalculation on Thornton's part see *thesis*, 231–7.

[24] Thornton's treatment of the 'romances' in gatherings **g** and **h** might well be compared to his treatment of similar 'romances' in the Lincoln manuscript where a saint's life, a miracle of the Virgin, an antimendicant satire and a series of political 'prophecies' all appear in a much larger 'romance unit' (gatherings **A–K**). See further my essay in Pearsall, ed. (1983). One possible reason why the Thornton copy of *Richard Coeur de Lion* has remained stranded in the London manuscript is because the defective text has never been repaired in the way in which Thornton originally intended. For the patchwork necessary to complete this romance see the concluding chapter below.

[25] It is clear, however, that the ME author of *Ypokrephum* was attempting to use the ephemeral delights of a lively narrative style for the didactic purpose of celebrating the virtues of obedience and mercy in this story of the childhood of Christ. The Thornton copy is the only one where the poem is called a 'romance', but, in British Library MS Harley 3954 (one of two other surviving copies of the poem) *Ypokrephum* follows a partially illustrated copy of *Mandeville's Travels* and is itself followed by a poem describing the efficacy of hearing mass. In the other copy (MS Harley 2399) *Ypokrephum* is preceded by pen trials, accompanied by heraldic marks, and followed by *How the Wise Man Taught His Son*. See further C. Horstmann, ed. (1878), 101–10, 111–23 (Harley copies); (1885), 327–39 (Thornton copy).

[26] This may even support the view that Thornton was more aware of and more interested in juxtaposing two stylistically different 'siege' romances than he was in stressing any of the 'Charlemagne' features that might link the two tail-rhyme romances now permanently separated by *O florum flos* in the London manuscript.

[27] The claim has been countered effectively by Stern (1976), 201–4.

[28] This very simple conversion (created by ruling parallel lines in the centre of the pages in question) takes place on ff. 98v, 161r, 211r in the Lincoln manuscript. Compare the situation described in n. 43 below.

likely that the present title for the poem (now written mainly in red but incorporating the original marginalia) has been added to the text as an afterthought. Thornton's designation of *Ypokrephum* as a 'romance' seems a determined effort on his part to create in his reader's mind some limited sense of continuity, despite the unlikely pairing of the blood-thirsty *Richard* with a story about the childhood of Christ.[25]

The combination of religious and romance material in gatherings **c** and **d** has already suggested a much stronger sense of thematic continuity to some scholars of the London Thornton manuscript. The items in question are Thornton's incomplete copy of *The Northern Passion* on ff. 33r–50r; *The Siege of Jerusalem* on ff. 50r–66r; and the opening lines of *The Sege of Melayne* on ff. 66v–73v. It can be argued that this material forms part of a recognisable historical sequence which is not only textually linked to the next gathering with which *Melayne* is shared (gathering **e**) but also shares some thematic link with the opening section of the manuscript containing the Thornton *Cursor Mundi* extract (in gatherings **a** and **b**). Nevertheless, the available evidence also shows that it is easy to overstress Thornton's presumed interest in, and personal responsibility for, the creation of this sequence.

After Thornton copied *Melayne* on the remaining leaves in gathering **d** he may have been generally aware that his actions meant that he was juxtaposing a Charlemagne siege romance with another siege text. His short title 'the Sege off Melayne' is written in the head margin of f. 66v in Thornton's hand, but the title itself seems to have been added rather casually in the only available space left after Thornton had copied the main text of this item. This is in marked contrast to the relatively formal layout of both the *incipit* and *explicit* of *The Siege of Jerusalem* on ff. 50r and 66r respectively. Since Thornton seems to have considered *Melayne* as an adjunct of some kind to the existing material in **c** and **d**, it is even possible that his title for this siege romance was influenced by the few words of French in the formal *explicit* of *The Siege of Jerusalem* on the previous page in his collection.[26] Leaving this speculation aside, the noticeable variation in Thornton's script on ff. 66r and 66v (which encouraged Herrtage to claim in 1880 that *Melayne* and *Ottuel* were copied in a different hand from *The Siege of Jerusalem*)[27] also suggests that *Melayne* was copied at a different time and probably from a different exemplar than the one used for *The Siege of Jerusalem*.

Thornton's presentation of *The Siege of Jerusalem* provides one more scrap of potentially useful information about the probable nature of the exemplar used for this text. On f. 50r Thornton commenced copying the long lines of the alliterative poem on the same page in which he had previously completed his copy of *The Northern Passion*. This is the only page in Thornton's entire collection where he took the trouble to rule the *first* part of a page for a text to be copied in double columns (this frame ruling is now filled with the last few lines of *The Northern Passion*), and the second part for a text in single columns (now filled with the opening lines of *The Siege of Jerusalem*). Presumably then, at the time when he ruled his page, Thornton *already* knew that the transition from *The Northern Passion* to *The Siege of Jerusalem* was going to take place at this point in his collection. Of course he need not necessarily have had the same kind of advance information elsewhere in his collection, or on the few occasions when Thornton adjusted the ruling on his page to allow for the much simpler changeover from a single-column to a double-column writing space.[28] But on f. 50r there remains the distinct possibility that Thornton's importance as a book compiler at the core of the London manuscript was

that of a scribe who was preserving rather than creating a thematic sequence that he found in one of his sources. In gathering **c** the juxtaposition of *The Northern Passion* and *The Siege of Jerusalem* stresses for Thornton's readers the continuous nature of the links between Christ's life and Passion and the repercussions of these events on the lives of both Christian knights and wicked Jews.[29]

The juxtaposition of *The Northern Passion* in **c** and *Cursor Mundi* in gatherings **a** and **b** is also based on very obvious historical principles, this time originating in the Scriptures. The fragmentary Thornton copy of *Cursor Mundi* finally ends on f. 32v with a colophon which announces that the Passion will follow. His text then omits the Passion section found in other copies of *Cursor Mundi* and most of the remainder of the poem's lengthy account of world history from Creation to the Day of Judgement. On f. 33r, in **c**, *The Northern Passion* makes good this apparent deficit in what appears to be a premeditated sequence of texts dealing with events in the life of Christ.[30] Scholars have long been aware of the existence of this sequence.[31] Now, however, closer examination of the rather uncertain reputation of the Passion section in *Cursor Mundi* among its late medieval audience can provide important supplementary information about the varied prehistory of the poem and the probable extent of Thornton's own rather practically-motivated activities as he copied and arranged this material in his collection.[32]

Throughout the history of the transmission of *Cursor Mundi* (now extant in the Thornton copy and in eight others),[33] the Passion section appears to have been a particularly dissatisfying section of the poem. The Thornton copy omits the section entirely, apparently encouraging readers to divert to *The Northern Passion*. In the mid-fourteenth-century copies of the poem in British Library MS Cotton Vespasian A.3, Göttingen University Library MS theol. 107r, and also in Thornton's copy (as well as in the exemplars behind these copies) the Passion section was 'updated' or 'reinforced' by the addition of a short, originally self-contained poem known as *The Discourse between Christ and Man* where the risen Christ reminds sinful man of His Incarnation and Passion. In MS Cotton Vespasian A.3 the Passion section was also 'patched' and updated in the fifteenth century by two extracts from the ME *Southern Passion*.[34] Finally, in the copy of *Cursor Mundi* in British Library MS Additional 36983 (c. 1442), the Passion section is entirely replaced by a ME version of *Meditationes Vitae Christi*.[35] This latter item has already been shown to have had a tremendous influence on Passion narratives: in *The Southern Passion*, for example, the ME poet seems to have evolved for himself a simplified version of the dramatic and deictic mode that he found in *Meditationes*:[36] interestingly, *The Discourse between Christ and Man* is another example of a particularly unrestrained and dramatic style of Passion narrative.[37] In the light of this catalogue of scribal or editorial interference in *Cursor Mundi*, therefore, the omission of the Passion section from the Thornton copy can be explained in part by the assumption that someone had rejected this part of *Cursor Mundi* because they had already read and preferred the much livelier and more attractive account of the Passion in *The Northern Passion*.

There is also good evidence to support the idea that the drastic editorial 'cut' in the Thornton copy was influenced by the change from octosyllabic couplets to septenary lines when the text of *Cursor Mundi* turns to consider and describe the Passion. This is the most remarkable metrical feature of the poem but it is not hard to find examples of similar long lines being used

[29] Note the way in which, in defiance of history, but true to the pious lessons to be learned from ingenious historical parallels, the *incipit* and opening lines of *The Siege of Jerusalem* link the Roman conquest of Jerusalem with the life, Passion and miracles of Christ. The unusual care which has been taken with the decoration of the opening initials of both *The Northern Passion* and *The Siege of Jerusalem* helps to forge another close link between these two poems. See the following chapter for details.

[30] The London manuscript is not the only one where *The Northern Passion* is the preferred Passion narrative in a verse collection. The poem is preserved in two manuscripts of the *Northern Homily Cycle* for this reason. Elsewhere, selected passages from *The Northern Passion* was also taken to help expand this cycle at a later date. The text of *The Northern Passion* was itself subject to considerable internal revision and adaptation during the course of its history. For some sense of this see F. Foster (1916), 1–13, 47–80.

[31] Frances Foster's account (Foster, 1916, 12–13) has formed the basis for all subsequent discussion of the Thornton sequence.

[32] In a forthcoming study I plan to offer a more detailed discussion of the status of *Cursor Mundi* as an 'open' ME text than is possible here. See also *thesis*, 261–337.

[33] *Index* 2153 lists ten surviving manuscripts, but the reference to McGill University MS 142 should be deleted; see Michael Sargent (1974). For a listing of the *Cursor Mundi* manuscripts and an extremely useful bibliography see the edition of the Southern 'version' of *Cursor Mundi* being prepared by Sarah M. Horrall (1978, in progress). Professor Horrall is at present preparing a revised stemma for the nine surviving copies of the poem and I am extremely grateful to her for a copy of her notes on the textual affinities of the Thornton fragment. These confirm the close textual relationship of the Thornton copy to the fragment in Bodleian Library MS Fairfax 14 that was first noted in *Catalogue of Additions to the Manuscripts in the British Museum* (1882), 148–51. Horrall's work also suggests that the Southern copies of this Northern poem are all derived from an exemplar best represented among Northern copies

by Göttingen University Library MS theol. 107r.

34 See *thesis*, 276–86 and the brief comments in C. Horstmann (1881), lxvii; Carleton Brown (1911); M. Görlach (1974), 128.

35 Ed. J. M. Cowper (1875). See the discussion in *thesis*, 290–306. The literary taste shown in MS Additional 36983 suggests that the original compilers of this version of *Cursor Mundi* also had access to *The Prick of Conscience*, an English version of Deguileville's *Pèlerinage de l'âme*, and even perhaps *Handlyng Synne*. They did not copy these texts *in toto*, but, instead, small parts of these lengthy ME compilations were used to 'update' sections of the *Cursor Mundi* narrative which were felt to be deficient.

36 See B. D. Brown (1927), lxxviii–xcii. For the enormous influence *Meditationes* had on many other Passion narratives see Elizabeth Salter (1974, 1981).

37 For example, it is entirely typical of the exclamatory style in which the poem was written that Christ implores man to:

Bi-hald and se my blodi side,
þat for þi luue es opend wide;
Put in and grape, mi suete freind,
Take vte mi herte bituix þi heind;
þen mai þu wid þin eien se
Hu truli þat i loued ai þe

(Göttingen text, ll. 17139–44)

For an excellent discussion of this style of writing in ME meditative literature in general see Pamela Gradon (1971), 300–13.

38 The best-known examples are the ME *Ormmulum* and *The South English Legendary*. It is also probable that the use of two very distinctive metrical forms in *Cursor Mundi* was in imitation of the use of a similar technique in other poems by earlier Anglo-Norman compilers. For examples see M. D. Legge (1963), 77.

39 Derek Pearsall has charted the origins and decline of the ME septenary line in some detail. In particular, he notes that *The Tale of Gamelyn*, written in septenary couplets, seems to have been discarded as 'unfashionable' by most fifteenth-century romance readers. Its survival is due solely to its interpolation as The Cook's Tale in more than twenty *Canterbury Tales* manuscripts. See Pearsall (1977), esp. 144.

elsewhere in other ME teaching texts.[38] In particular, the septenary line is a characteristic of much thirteenth-century didactic verse where clerical writers obviously considered both couplet and quatrain arrangements of the line to be especially functional and uncluttered metrical forms for the purposes of religious instruction. Inevitably, however, one of the great disadvantages of using regular septenaries is the deadening effect that they can have on a narrative. Eventually, a much looser line developed and what had originated as a prestigious metrical form degenerated to the level of doggerel.[39] By Thornton's day, therefore, texts written in septenaries may sometimes have been out of favour. More particularly, this loss of literary status for the Passion section of *Cursor Mundi* obviously had serious and direct implications for the reception of this part of the poem by its audience. A fashion-conscious book-producer, for example, seeking the best texts for a prospective customer's consumption, was hardly likely to prefer the formal and restrained account of the Passion in *Cursor Mundi* if he had access to any one of the large number of more attractive Passion narratives which were also in circulation a century after *Cursor Mundi* was first compiled. Similarly, a pious collector like Thornton, who may not have had access to quite such a wide range of texts, may well have considered what had originally been a stylised metrical feature of this lengthy world history to be irreverent and inappropriate, more suited to a ballad than to a narrative about Christ's death. Consequently, it may well have been a medieval reader's conservative instincts, and strong sense of propriety, that resulted in the removal of the offending Passion section from two extant copies of *Cursor Mundi*.

Thornton's *Cursor Mundi* extract first breaks off at the important narrative intrusion corresponding to l. 14933 in all the extant Northern copies. However the 'originality' of the colophon appearing at this point in Thornton's copy must be qualified by its undoubted similarity to the narrative intrusion which it is intended to replace. This can best be seen by setting an appropriate sample of *Cursor Mundi* next to the Thornton text. The lines read:

For fast it draus te þe nede	ffor faste now neghes to þe nede
For his to suffir passiun.	ffor to suffre his passyoun
For-þi to speke of þat ransum	Anothir boke spekes of þat rawnsoune
þat richer es þan erd or heuene,	ffor now I thynke of this make ende
Or all þat manes witt mai neuene,	And to þe passyoun will I wende
For-þi me think þat nu es gode	Anothir boke to bygynn
þat we speke sumquat of þe rode.	And I may to my purpose wynn
And alsua of þat ranssuning,	And þat I it till ende may brynge
þat for vs gaf iesus, heuene king,	I beseke oure heuen kynge
And resun es we vr rime rume,	Als I this till ende hafe broghte
And set fra nu langer bastune.	He grante me grace þat me dere boghte
Crist and his moþer do me spede!	Till his honoure and haly kirke
þat i vnworþi es to rede,	He leue me space this werke to wirke
And of his will me send his grace	Amen amen that it swa bee
Of witt and will, and þar-to space,	I pray 3ow alle 3e praye for mee
þat i it rede wid sli lu[u]ing	þat takes one hande þis begynnynge
I may it wele till end bring,	he brynge me vnto gode endyng
To lu[u]ing of god and halikirke	Amene.
To manes note als forto wirke.	(Thornton copy, f. 32r)
(Göttingen text, ll. 14913–33)	

The main additions in the Thornton copy are, firstly, that there is talk of turning to 'another book' and making an end of this one, and, secondly, that the Thornton narrator prays for grace in his undertaking and asks his readers to pray for him also in his new beginning. This new information has been woven together with textual material that already formed part of an important narrative intrusion in *Cursor Mundi*.

However Thornton did not proceed directly to the Passion narrative in another book as the colophon on f. 32r promises. Instead, having omitted the account of the Passion in *Cursor Mundi*, the remaining space in gathering **b** is filled with material corresponding to ll. 17111–17188 of the poem. These lines contain *The Discourse between Christ and Man*, the short lyric written in octosyllabic rhyming couplets that has also become embedded (in a longer composite version) in MS Cotton Vespasian A.3 and the Göttingen copy of *Cursor Mundi*. Besides these copies, *The Discourse* was copied as an independent poem in MSS Takamiya 15 (*olim* Sotheby's, 10 December 1969; lot 43), and in a Hopton Hall manuscript that is now missing.[40] In the Cotton and Göttingen manuscripts *The Discourse* follows on appropriately enough at the most logical point in the poem (i.e. directly following the description of the Passion); but this kind of textual accretion in some *Cursor Mundi* copies and not in others is entirely typical of the way in which this lengthy verse compilation continued to grow and change throughout the later middle ages.[41] Moreover, by closer examination of important changes in the way in which the Göttingen copy presents the Passion section and the accompanying *Discourse*, it is possible to suggest some very practical reasons why *The Discourse* also survives in the Thornton copy while the Passion section and the remaining lines of the poem dealing with biblical history to the Day of Judgement do not.[42]

The presentation of *Cursor Mundi* in three of its earliest copies, and, incidentally, in the EETS edition, tends to obscure the fact that the Passion section is written in septenaries. In these texts the longer septenary lines are split at their natural caesura and presented in double columns like the rest of the narrative, giving the casual reader no visual indication of the striking metrical change that takes place at l. 14937. However, in its three fifteenth-century Southern copies, and in the earlier Göttingen copy (c. 1350), the Passion section is the only portion of the narrative that is copied in single columns of long lines. Once this has been completed all these copies return to presenting their text in double columns. But the Göttingen copy is also the only extant manuscript that recommences copying *Cursor Mundi* in double columns with *The Discourse* text (plate 35). Therefore, the peculiarities in the Thornton copy of the poem might, in part, also be explained by assuming that a compiler-scribe came to the Passion section in an exemplar with the same layout as the Göttingen copy, saw that it was written in single columns, decided to omit that section (possibly because it looked like an intruder text written in an uncongenial verse form), and turned the pages of his source until he found where the text recommenced in double columns with *The Discourse*.[43]

If Thornton was that medieval 'editor' then we can say as a preliminary that his reason for copying *The Discourse* may have been practically motivated. Once he had chosen to omit the Passion section of *Cursor Mundi* from his copy Thornton was left with a self-contained manuscript unit in which part of f. 32r and all of 32v remained blank. From f. 31vb Thornton may even have 'stretched' his *Cursor Mundi* text so as to make it go further. Rather than leave

[40] I am indebted to Professor Takamiya for providing me with information about his manuscript and drawing my attention to the reported existence of the poem in the Hopton Hall manuscript (described in *HMC*, ninth report, 1884, Appendix, 384).

[41] For an attempt to chart the protean structure of *Cursor Mundi* in its various surviving copies see *thesis*, Appendix 3, 460–67.

[42] Thanks are due to Dr Haenel and the staff of the Universitäts-bibliothek, Göttingen for allowing me to consult the copy of *Cursor Mundi* in their care.

[43] The scribe of the Göttingen copy was also quite unprepared for the change to a single-column format to copy the Passion section of *Cursor Mundi*. In this copy, ff. 100v–114v, which now contain the Passion narrative, were originally ruled for a text to be copied in double columns. Despite the fact that the scribe may have inherited the change in layout from his source, his own decision to use single columns for the Passion section was not automatic but rather forced him to reject the frame rulings that had previously been drawn when the gathering was completely blank.

ff. 32rb–32v unfilled, therefore, he seems to have decided to use the most appropriate material available to him to fill the last leaf of gathering **b**. He found this material in his *Cursor Mundi* exemplar. Nevertheless, despite the limited sense of visual continuity given to the reader by Thornton's presentation of this material using a double-column format, the inevitable result of this meddling with his copy of *Cursor Mundi* is that *The Discourse* is now illogically 'sandwiched' between a colophon which promises the reader that the story of Christ's Passion will begin in 'another book' and a text which begins in a new gathering and actually fulfils that promise. If, as is generally assumed, the items in the opening section of the London manuscript have been carefully organised to form a continuous historical sequence, then *The Discourse* should logically appear *after* and not before the account of Christ's death in *The Northern Passion* in the next gathering.

There are also signs on f. 32v that Thornton went to some trouble to provide yet another signpost for his readers, directing them from his first manuscript unit containing the *Cursor Mundi* extract to a second one beginning with *The Northern Passion*. He copied a fairly standard *explicit* for *The Discourse*, but he then followed this with another explanatory colophon. This reads:

> *Et Sic Procedendum ad Passionem domini nostri Ihesu Christi que incipit in folio proximo sequente secundum ffantasiam scriptoris.*

At first sight, the use of the term *ffantasiam scriptoris* is quite puzzling. According to R.E Latham's *Revised Latin Word List* (1965), the meaning of *fantasiam* could range from 'whim' to 'imagination' but its sense was generally derogatory. This makes Thornton's words read rather like an apology. Moreover, reference to the rather wider range of meanings that the vernacular term 'fantasie' could have had in the later middle ages suggests that Thornton probably intended the word to be used in a much more appropriately precise way than might at first be assumed. In the language of medieval scholastic psychology and literary tradition the word 'fantasie' was used as a technical term to describe one of the five inward 'bodily wits':

> þe office of þe fantasie. . . is forto forge and compowne, *or to sette to gedir in seemyng, þingis whiche ben not to gedir, and whiche maken not oon þing in kynde* (my italics).[44]

[44] Taken from *The Donet* by Reginald Pecock, ed. Elsie V. Hitchcock (1921), 10.

The word was also in common literary usage by the fifteenth century. Lydgate used the term, in a form derived from the OF *fantasier*, in his *Fall of Princes*. In the prologue to that poem (ll. 22–28) he describes the role of writers:

> Thyng that was maad of auctours hem beforn,
> Thei may off newe fynde and fantasie,
> Out of old chaff trie out ful cleene corn,
> Make it more fressh and lusti to the eie,
> Ther subtil witt and ther labour applie,
> With ther colours agreable off hewe,
> Make olde thynges for to seem newe.[45]

[45] Taken from H. Bergen, ed. (1924).

The phrase *fantasiam scriptoris* in the London Thornton manuscript reveals something of its potential significance for the book's intended readers when interpreted in the light of these two statements. Lydgate was offering a colourful description of the processes by which older literary material was assembled by later medieval writers to produce a 'new' literary text, while

Thornton was outlining the practical activities of a much less ambitious kind of compiler. But, in their own ways, both these men were also attempting to account for the varied and complex processes of conflation and juxtaposition of material that characterise not only their respective achievements as individual craftsmen but also the literary interests and achievements of their age.[46]

In other equally important respects the two colophons accompanying the Thornton *Cursor Mundi* extract may be quite misleading. The fact that both appear in the present opening section of the London manuscript might imply to the present-day reader some sense of confidence on Thornton's part that he was sure that he could follow on in a 'new book' with a different Passion narrative. Any such confidence someone like Thornton may have felt here is especially surprising since, elsewhere in his manuscripts, there are many indications that his exemplars often came to him in an unpredictable way, and that he did not always have access to all the material he might have wished to copy and compile together in his collection. Of course, Thornton's 'confidence' only appears as confidence if it is assumed that he copied the opening sequence of items in the manuscript in the order in which they now appear. Several other minor physical details in the London manuscript suggest too that, in discussing the relationship between gatherings **a–b** and **c–e**, it is again possible to suggest something of the stages in which the material in these gatherings was drawn together from 'þingis whiche ben not to gedir and whiche maken not oon þing in kynde'.

The transition from the end of the first section of the London manuscript (f. 32v) to the beginning of a new one (f. 33r) is marked by a deterioration in the condition of the first leaf of the second section. On f. 33r the opening page of *The Northern Passion* in gathering **c** is grubbier and the ink more faded than on f. 32v in **b**. Often this kind of deterioration can be explained by the fact that separate, and not always textually self-contained gatherings lay around unbound for a period before being compiled together to form a single book. It has also been argued that the grubby condition of outer leaves of gatherings that now form integral parts of larger collections may support the hypothesis of 'booklet' circulation of the items in them.[47] In the particular case of Thornton's collection, and the soiled condition of f. 33r in gathering **c**, it seems most likely that, for a time, this leaf simply formed the outer leaf of a separate section and that the addition of *Cursor Mundi* marks an important *later* stage in the gradual assembly of the material for this particular Thornton book. This assumption is supported by Thornton's relatively more ambitious decorative plans for *Cursor Mundi* (discussed in the next chapter). As he copied this poem he already seems to have decided that it should stand at the head of a collection of gatherings that had already been gathered together at an earlier stage in his career. These scraps of detail are of limited value in isolation but they can be used to support the theory that, when Thornton copied the two colophons at the end of his extracts from *Cursor Mundi*, he was actually expanding his collection by appending new material to an existing core made up of *The Northern Passion* and *The Siege of Jerusalem*. Therefore his 'confidence' when writing these colophons and dealing with the Passion narratives to which he had access seems that of a man who already had 'another book' containing the story of the Passion and who clearly preferred that version to the one he found embedded in *Cursor Mundi*.

The Göttingen text of *Cursor Mundi* yields up one final possible clue, and a further puzzle, about the likely state of the exemplar that Thornton used for

[46] The scholastic theory of *compilatio* that lurks some way behind the definitions discussed here is described in M. B. Parkes (1976), and Alastair J. Minnis (1979).

[47] For the criteria used to identify the 'booklet' see P. R. Robinson (1980). It is becoming increasingly apparent that the 'booklet' was a pragmatically useful mode of production as well as sometimes being a relatively cheap means of marketing written material to an audience who could not afford more expensive books.

48 For John as author see Hupe's comments in the EETS edition (ed. R. Morris, 1893, 187*–89*). Strangely, Hupe, in his strenuous efforts to disprove the theory that John commissioned and owned the Göttingen manuscript, writes that the manuscript, 'shows no ornaments at all'. The Göttingen manuscript is, in fact, profusely decorated (see the following chapter for details).

49 This is confirmed by the following revised collation of the Göttingen manuscript (cf. the slightly different description offered by Horrall, 1978, 19–20): **a–f**12 (ff. 1–72); **g**2 (ff. 73–4); **h–o**12 (ff. 75–158); **p**12 (ff. 159–169, wants xi–xii).

50 An early reader of the Göttingen manuscript appears to have been irritated and unsettled by this section of the narrative. A lengthy marginal note appears on f. 103r, most of which consists of meaningless scribbles. In the opening lines, however, the anonymous and obviously confused reader complains, 'John how shuld I tryst yow?' He accuses John of being 'of þe newe lernyng' and complains further about not understanding John's meaning, saying that 'it is not as þai do say'; but it is not clear to whom 'they' refers. The writer appears to be referring to John of Lindbergh, whose name appears in the colophon on f. 114v and who is presumably being held responsible in some way for the compilation of the Passion section on ff. 100v–114v in this copy.

51 This might conveniently explain why only vestiges of the narrative intrusion that ends the Passion section and names John as owner of the poem survive in just two other copies. Presumably this, or some similar personal reference to the owner's name, would have been dropped in many copies because most scribes felt reluctant to interrupt their copying of the text with what could easily be seen as an irrelevant personal *ex libris* tacked on to the end of a separate manuscript unit in their exemplar.

52 This hypothetical situation is made more feasible, perhaps, by the fact that Professor Angus McIntosh has established that two dialectally different exemplars lie behind the Göttingen copy. McIntosh pinpoints the changeover from one exemplar to the other to a point corresponding to ll. 10995–10997 on f. 75r in the manuscript (i.e. near the beginning of the first leaf in

his copy of the poem. On f. 114v in the Göttingen manuscript the last lines of *Cursor Mundi* to be presented in single columns (ll. 17087–110) form an extended narrative intrusion between the Passion section and the beginning of *The Discourse* (plate 35). The first part of this intrusion is also extant in MS Cotton Vespasian A.3. Here ll. 17087–98 inform the reader that the story of the Passion is complete and offer up a pious prayer for God's grace. Indeed, the 'Thornton' prayer for God's grace and the request that future readers should pray for him now that part of his writing task is completed in the colophon of f. 32r are both sentiments shared with the original author of ll. 17087–98. Therefore, the way in which the Thornton colophon seems to have been constructed using some of the words, phrases and ideas taken from the narrative intrusion that introduced the Passion section in the poem (ll. 14913–33) makes it attractive to assume that other ideas and words were borrowed from another intrusion that once concluded that same section in an earlier source.

And perhaps there is another very practical reason why Thornton seems to have abandoned his copy of *Cursor Mundi* after he had copied the short *Discourse* text. In the Göttingen text, the general prayer for grace that concludes the Passion narrative is followed by the more personal prayer request of one John of Lindbergh. Ll. 17099–110 read:

> And speciali for me ʒe pray
> þat þis bock gart dight,
> Iohn of lindbergh, i ʒu sai
> þat es mi name ful right.
> If it be tint or dune a-way,
> treuli mi trouth i plight,
> Qua bringes it me widuten delay,
> i sal him ʒeild þat night.
> And qua it helis and haldis fra me,
> treuli i ʒu tell,
> Curced in kirc þan sal þai be
> wid candil, boke, and bell.

Here John identifies himself as the man who caused this book to be 'arranged', but it is not clear whether he is talking as the owner of the Göttingen manuscript itself, or whether he is talking as an earlier owner, or perhaps even as the original author of the poem.[48] Nevertheless, it is also fair to say that this colophon reads exactly like the *ex libris* that might be found at the beginning or end of any privately-owned volume. This is puzzling since these comments occur at a central point in *Cursor Mundi* and, in the Göttingen copy, the text runs on for another fifty-five folios. Moreover, unlike the Thornton colophon, John's words do not coincide with the end of an identifiable manuscript unit where their function as a concluding statement of ownership might make some more sense.[49] Strangely, but similar to the experience of readers of Thornton's copy, the readers of the Göttingen text are given the distinct impression that they have come to the end of a unit of material. But, unlike Thornton's book, the Göttingen copy does not direct the reader to a second 'book' or 'volume'.[50]

If there is a rational explanation for this apparent peculiarity in the Göttingen text then it may have something to do with the way in which certain copies of *Cursor Mundi* circulated in the later middle ages. The colophon in the Göttingen copy makes it clear that John expected a variety of readers to borrow his book, and also to return it. Some of these readers could

also have been scribes who used John's book as an exemplar. If this was the case, then, in turn, it may have been in the exemplar that lies behind the Göttingen copy that John of Lindbergh's colophon made most sense. That exemplar could easily have consisted of more than one 'book' or manuscript unit.[51] John's colophon also acts as a reminder of how easy it would be in these circumstances for portions of *Cursor Mundi* to get lost or damaged or separated from other sections of the poem.[52] Although it remains pure speculation, Thornton's failure to complete his copy of *Cursor Mundi* may well have been due to the fact that his exemplar originally consisted of more than one manuscript unit and that he only ever had access to the first part of this encyclopaedic and lengthy ME compilation of biblical history.[53] Therefore, here, as elsewhere in the London manuscript, the nature and extent of Thornton's own compiling activities remain ill-defined but they may well have been dictated to him in the main by the states of his sources and the practical conditions in which he was working.[54]

gathering **h**). For the linguistic evidence see McIntosh (1975), 230, n. 1. I am extremely grateful to Professor McIntosh for explaining at length the linguistic implications of some of his findings in a private communication.

[53] It is also hard to resist the possibility that the Northern source from which the Southern 'version' of *Cursor Mundi* is derived, now best represented by the Göttingen copy, also consisted of several manuscript sections. One of these may have ended near the point corresponding to ll. 23905–08. Here the narrator promises to move on from this account of the Day of Judgement to deal with his loosely-appended sequence of material in praise of Mary, 'ellis quare/Quen i am comen to better space'. All the Southern copies end at this point with a concluding colophon, although their Northern source can be shown to have once contained the Marian material. Nevertheless, a final manuscript unit, containing the missing Marian material could easily have been lost or stolen or mislaid some time before a Southern scribe-editor translated the poem into a new dialect.

[54] The 'religious' unit in the Lincoln manuscript also provides several examples of material that can be shown to have circulated in various disarranged, incomplete and fragmentary forms throughout the fifteenth century. Consider, for example, the extremely complex textual history of material like the twelve Rolle-related items (ff. 192r–196v); the ME translated versions of St Edmund's *Speculum Ecclesie* and related texts (ff. 197r–209v); Hilton's *Scale of Perfection* (an anonymous extract from chapter 44 of Book one, containing the celebrated Holy Name passage survives on ff. 229v–230v); the disarranged fragmentary ME *Gratia Dei* compilation (ff. 237r–250v); or *The Prick of Conscience* (an extract survives on ff. 276v–277r). For full details see *thesis*, 66ff.

Analysis of the few decorative features in the Thornton manuscripts has played a very minor part in previous discussions of Thornton's achievement.[1] This is hardly surprising since the slight decoration in both miscellanies often seems drab and insignificant when considered alongside similar details in other more *de luxe* productions of the period, and there is certainly little in Thornton's collection to interest the scholar seeking the vivid colours, the richness and variety that is usually associated with late medieval illumination.[2] Nevertheless, when seen in a different context, the decoration – and intended decoration – of both the Lincoln and the London manuscripts can provide potentially useful information about the preparations and decisions Thornton was making and about his expectations and hopes for his completed collection as he continued to copy and prepare certain texts for inclusion in it.

The attention of the modern reader is immediately caught by the ways in which red ink has been used to add some colourful decorative features in both Thornton's manuscripts. Red ink is regularly used to colour the letter-forms of the simple decorative capitals which appear with varying frequency, but which are scattered nonetheless throughout the London manuscript and in the 'romance' and 'religious' units in the Lincoln manuscript.[3] Red ink is also employed to varying degrees to point out headings, *incipits* and *explicits*, for highlighting narrative details and, particularly in the opening lines of an item, to draw attention to details of versification or punctuation.[4] In a limited sense, therefore, these frequent appearances of red ink contribute to any sense of coherence or uniformity of treatment that the reader might sometimes be inclined to find in Thornton's heterogeneous two-volume collection. But there is little that is new or surprising in this. Many such features belong to what M. B. Parkes has called, 'the general repertory of punctuation that emerged during the course of the Middle Ages'.[5] Moreover, Thornton's use of these devices seems quite informal since no single consistently applied system of punctuation emerges from his collection as a whole.[6] Sometimes the colourful appearance of a 'Thornton' text may even be a good general guide to the way in which the same text was punctuated in his source: Some of the Latin items in the Lincoln manuscript

[1] But see the brief comments by Karen Stern (1976), 209–10 and E. G. Stanley (1978). I am extremely grateful to Dr Kathleen Scott for her comments on an earlier version of this chapter.

[2] For typical examples see J. J. G. Alexander (1978). The most useful survey of secondary elements of decoration in fifteenth-century English manuscripts remains Margaret Rickert (1940).

[3] Quire **Q**, containing Thornton's copy of *Liber de Diversis Medicinis* is the only quire unit in Thornton's entire collection that is exempt from this colourful decorative treatment; see Thompson (1982).

[4] See previous chapters for examples of Thornton's use of the marginal rubric (π) to indicate important narrative sub-divisions such as a new stanza, paragraph or strophe. These marks are sometimes added in red but more often in black.

[5] Parkes (1978); see too the casual, often indiscriminate, use of punctuating devices among other fifteenth-century ME compilers discussed by Pamela de Wit in her unpublished thesis (1977).

[6] Despite this comment, the infrequent appearances of devices such as the *littera notabilior*, the *punctus* or the *virgula suspensiva* in Thornton's collection were clearly designed to assist readers to follow the text. But in the London manuscript it is also noticeable that Thornton uses the *punctus* and the *virgula suspensiva* very sparingly. The

are the most densely rubricated items in Thornton's entire collection and part of the reason for this seems to have been that their sources were similarly well-punctuated. Despite the additional possibility that their parent copy may have been even more colourful and more richly decorated, Thornton still seems to have attempted to reproduce as faithfully as he could the actual sequence of coloured capitals that he found in his exemplar.[7]

It is very hard to escape the impression that much of the rubrication and decoration in his books is Thornton's own work. Throughout both books there is nothing to suggest that any strict division of labour existed between the tasks performed by a scribe and the tasks which, under other more organised conditions, might well have fallen to a professional rubricator. Instead all the evidence points to the intimate involvement of at least one decorator with minor tasks that must also be associated with Thornton. In the London manuscript, for example, Thornton seems to have returned to gathering **h** to make good the textual deficiencies in his copy of *Ypokrephum* using the same red ink with which the text is also decorated. His hand can be detected at work as both rubricator and scribe in the *incipit* for this 'romance' (f. 163v), as well as in the even longer *incipit* for *Vita Sancti Christofori* in the 'romance' unit of the Lincoln manuscript (f. 122v), and on other occasions where at least part of the *incipits*, *explicits* or headings have been presented in red.[8] Elsewhere in both manuscripts this kind of information was simply added by Thornton in the same ink as the main text. In quire **g** (London manuscript) and **M** and **N** (Lincoln manuscript) Thornton has even used red ink to draw the frame rulings for his items.[9] This idiosyncrasy too would suggest that Thornton's roles as both scribe and rubricator frequently interchanged with little or no warning. The task of decoration, like the task of gathering up and copying his items, would appear to have been a gradual and at times haphazard process.

Some clearer sense of the chaotically inconsistent manner in which some items were decorated can be gained by examining gatherings **f**, **g** and **h** in the London manuscript more closely. The first of a lengthy sequence of green letter-forms suddenly appears on f. 104v in the text of the *Virtues of the Mass*. From ff. 104v–120r these green letter-forms alternate with the red ones that are more usually found in Thornton's items. From ff. 121r–143v a continuous sequence of red capitals briefly reappears. But then the sequence of alternating green and red capitals begins again on f. 144v, halfway through *Richard Coeur de Lion*. This alternating sequence continues until f. 168v. Ff. 104–20, 144–68 are the only occasions where green-coloured capitals appear in either of Thornton's manuscripts and their existence obviously disrupts the sense of visual continuity that is built up, however precariously, by the frequent use of red capitals elsewhere in the London manuscript.[10] When these few minor details are combined with the information concerning the gradual compilation of the material in these gatherings (discussed in the previous chapter) then a good case can be made for saying that the alternating sequence of red and green capitals was simply an early attempt to decorate some of his gatherings which Thornton later abandoned.

Gathering **f** originally seems to have been created from two separate quires. One of these consisted of ff. 103–20 and now contains the *Virtues of the Mass*, *The Rose of Ryse*, *The Three Kings of Cologne* and the opening lines of *A louely song of wysdome*. It is only on these folios that the alternating sequence of green and red capitals appears in **f**. Thornton appears to have decorated ff. 103–20 at the time when they formed an independent quire of twelve

punctus appears by itself in his presentation of the three short Latin aphorisms, his *Prayer to the Guardian Angel*, his paraphrase of Vulgate Psalm 50 and occasionally in his copy of *The Three Kings of Cologne*. Both the *punctus* and the *virgula suspensiva* are used in his cramped copy of *The Quatrefoil of Love*. By contrast, these devices appear frequently throughout Thornton's prose items in the Lincoln manuscript where they serve to provide the reader with shorter sense-units of text. They also proliferate in the alliterative *Morte* where Thornton regularly added the *punctus* in black ink to mark the medial pause in the lengthy metrical lines of the poem. Here someone, again probably Thornton, returned to the text and added additional devices (normally examples of the *virgula suspensiva*) in red ink and at exactly the same medial points.

7 For details see *thesis*, 56–66, 340–41.

8 These other occasions all occur in the Lincoln manuscript. For example, Thornton consistently used red ink to write many of the *incipits* and headings, *explicits*, and even some of the marginalia, in the series of items he ascribes to Rolle on ff. 192r–196v. All but three of the well-known 'Thornton' Rolle ascriptions are added in red and some (not all) of these may even represent an editorial afterthought on Thornton's part. See further *thesis*, 82–86.

9 Thornton's persistence in drawing red frame rulings, despite the unfortunate blotching effect on some of his pages, seems strikingly obstinate and inappropriate: in gathering **M**, Thornton must have been particularly interested in his experiment since he was using these colourful writing-frames at the same time as he was changing inconsistently from a single-column to a double-column writing format. Cf. the brief comments on the red frame rulings by A. E. B. Owen in D. S. Brewer and A. E. B. Owen (revised ed., 1977), xv.

10 In the London manuscript the only other occasion where a coloured capital has not been added in red is on f. 9v. Here a blue capital suddenly appears for no apparent reason in the middle of Thornton's *Cursor Mundi* fragment. Touches of blue and green also form part of the secondary decoration of the coloured capitals on ff. 19r and 19v in the Thornton copy of *The Life of Alexander* (the opening item in the

Lincoln manuscript). For other decorative features which distinguish these particular capitals in Thornton's collection see *thesis*, 342–44.

bifolia (fig. 11, previous chapter). This was *before* he refolded a second smaller quire (ff. 121–4; 98–102) to enclose ff. 103–20 (fig. 12, previous chapter). The remains of that smaller quire are now decorated with a continuous sequence of red capitals. But the surviving scraps of evidence would suggest that some of the decoration in this composite gathering had already taken place before the items in **f** had settled in their present order. At this earlier stage Thornton probably had no single or clear idea about how he eventually wanted to decorate his completed collection.

The alternating sequence of coloured capitals in quire **h** (ff. 144–68) but not in quire **g** (ff. 125–43) or **i** (ff. 169–81) is also useful as evidence. The visual isolation of **h** in this rather odd way implies that Thornton was encouraged to go back to **h** (but not **g**) simply because he completed the decorative work here, and also perhaps in **f**, at the same time as he was attempting to 'freshen up' his rather faded copy of *Ypokrephum*. The fact that the opening initial of *Ypokrephum* on f. 163v is the only capital in Thornton's entire collection where half the letter-form has been coloured in green and the other half in red seems another good indication of the excessive attention Thornton paid to this text as both scribe and decorator.

Two other opening initials have also been singled out for a rather different kind of special attention in the London manuscript. On f. 33r the opening capital of *The Northern Passion* has been decorated with a skilfully executed drawing of an encircling plant.[11] At one point, the entwining foliage overlaps the actual letter-form before forming the roundels that fill the first column of the fourteen-line space that Thornton originally left blank at the head of this page before commencing his copy of the text. These roundels are variously occupied by a drawing of a king, a grotesque and three acorn-like sprays. In addition, a woodwose with a pig's snout and beard has been drawn in the top margin but has not been incorporated into the main design.[12] On f. 50r the opening initial of *The Siege of Jerusalem* has been equally skilfully decorated, but this time it is solely the main body of the letter-form that has been overlapped by encircling foliage while male and female human profiles decorate the outer stem of the letter. The initial on f. 50r is dominated by a grotesque face with pointed ears and malevolent features which bear an obvious resemblance to the pig-like features of the grotesque on f. 33r. This similarity, and the fact that these are the only two decorative capitals in the London manuscript that have been executed with this kind of attention to detail and obvious technical skill, makes it seem likely that both are the work of the same artist.

[11] Even under ultra-violet light it proved impossible to make sense of the word that now appears in the middle of the blank space remaining in the second column on f. 33r.

[12] See also the description in Karen Stern (1976), 208–9.

It is also relevant to note that the actual letter-forms of both these decorative initials as well as the decorative details themselves have been added in the same black ink that Thornton used to copy the main text of *The Northern Passion* and *The Siege of Jerusalem*. The remainder of the decorative capitals in both these items, and throughout the rest of the London manuscript, consist of the simple coloured capitals discussed above, with no attention paid to any additional internal or external decorative penwork. As Thornton copied *The Northern Passion* on f. 33r he also seems to have taken special care to leave the top half of his page blank, presumably because at this early stage he had already decided that the opening lines of the item he was about to copy merited special decorative treatment or perhaps a lengthy heading. This may have been Thornton's own idea. But, since the opening initials for both *The Northern Passion* and *The Siege of Jerusalem* have been added in black ink, it is also conceivable that the idea of providing some type of

heading or decoration for this material came from an exemplar. Thornton probably only had limited access to this source, so the decorative opening capitals themselves may well have been added in an *ad hoc* manner at the same time as the texts were being copied and while that exemplar was still available. The other simpler, but more colourful, decorative features in both texts were then added later. *The Northern Passion* was never given a formal heading in Thornton's copy.

The competence with which the decorative details have been added on ff. 33r and 50r in the London manuscript is matched by similarly confident artwork in the Lincoln manuscript, but here the overall decoration of the book has proceeded to a much more advanced stage.[13] With a few exceptions, the decorative capitals in the Lincoln manuscript consist of red letter-forms with additional internal decorative scrolls or foliage added as patterned in-filling. These have usually been executed in a mauve ink that is now badly affected by discolouration. Sometimes the coloured capitals are actually inhabited, most often by an animal or by a simply drawn human figure, and these too are normally added in the same faded mauve ink. On many occasions the decorative penwork has even been extended to the inner margins of Thornton's pages where stylised flourishes act as external decoration for the coloured letter-forms. In particular, gatherings **D–F** (containing Thornton's copy of the alliterative *Morte Arthure* and the opening of *Octavian*) are profusely decorated with borderwork that consists of naturalistically drawn acanthus ornament into which is incorporated representations of grotesques, dragons, natural wildlife, household pets, and, on f. 93v, even a scroll containing Robert Thornton's own name.[14] Obviously the penmanship shown here bears comparison to the similar work in the London manuscript. This would seem to mark the artist at work in Thornton's collection (probably Thornton himself) as someone whose resources were perhaps limited, but who showed considerable ingenuity and skill in his use of the materials that were at hand as the collection was gradually assembled.

There are also signs that some of Thornton's most ambitious decorative plans have not been completed and that the present opening items in both manuscripts have been 'frozen' at an unfinished production stage through which none of the other items would have had to pass. In the Lincoln manuscript nine large blank spaces remain in Thornton's copy of the ME prose *Life of Alexander* and it appears likely that, as he copied this item from his exemplar, Thornton originally reserved these spaces for illustrations of some kind to accompany his text. The survival of brief marginal notes means that it is even possible to deduce the probable subject matter for two of these intended illustrations. On f. 7r Thornton wrote *rex equitans* in the side margin beside an unfilled gap eleven lines in height, and on f. 26r he added the words *Regina regalibus cum duabus astantibus* in the margin beside a gap of thirteen lines.[15] Presumably both these notes were intended as instructions or reminders to the artist who was eventually intended to illustrate the text, and they both seem to have been added as Thornton copied the Alexander item from his exemplar. Moreover, reference to Thornton's text at the points where these unfilled gaps occur confirms that the space on f. 7r could have been filled most appropriately with a picture of Alexander astride his horse, while the illustration on f. 26r could have provided Thornton's readers with a visual impression of Talyfride, Queen of the Amazons, on her first appearance in the narrative.[16] But it is difficult to speculate much further concerning the nature of Thornton's other intended illustrations, especially since he may

[13] The same general point is made with more detailed discussion than is possible here in *thesis*, 338–409.

[14] Another useful sign of Thornton's proprietorial attitudes to his material is the appearance of a 'Thornton' rebus in the internal decoration of a coloured capital on f. 23v in the Lincoln manuscript. See also M. S. Ogden (1938), viii–ix, n. 4. In this case it seems particularly appropriate that the identity of the scribe's family should be alluded to at the point in the narrative where Alexander, the hero of the ME romance biography on these pages, is himself getting married.

[15] The latter is wrongly transcribed in J. Westlake (1913), 65, n. 3.

[16] Intriguingly, the minor decorative details in ten of the inhabited initials in Thornton's Alexander item already seem to have been 'tailored' to suit the accompanying narrative. See the comments in n. 14 above and also *thesis*, 365–9.

[17] The only other extant illustrated ME Alexander text is *Alexander B* in the sumptuously decorated MS Bodley 264 (for which see the facsimile edition in M. R. James, 1933). But a lengthy colophon in the Bodley manuscript makes clear that the ME text is an interloper and only survives in this *de luxe* context because it fills a supposed omission in the French *Roman d'Alexandre*. For discussion of the illustrations in *Alexander B* see W. W. Skeat (1878), xix–xx; the revised description in F. P. Magoun (1929), 9–11; D. J. A. Ross (1963), 57; L. Lawton in Derek Pearsall ed. (1983), esp. 48. In both his published and unpublished work, Dr Ross has described how certain favourite subjects frequently recur in a variety of forms in what he terms the late antique picture cycle. For details see further Ross (1963, 1971, 1978). Dr Ross very kindly answered several other queries about the Alexander picture cycles and Thornton's intended illustrations in a personal communication.

[18] These may have been added by a 'post Thornton' hand, see 3, n. 13. In addition, it says much for the flexibility of the subject matter of these sketches that they might equally well be said to be a later reader's attempt to illustrate the celebrated episode in the alliterative *Morte* where Arthur fights the giant of Mont St Michel.

[19] Other general studies have shown that it was the availability as much as the suitability of compositional models that often determined the types of decorative illustration in certain manuscripts. See D. J. A. Ross (1952); M. Alison Stones (1976); Elizabeth Salter and Derek Pearsall (1980), esp. 103–5; Lesley Lawton in Derek Pearsall, ed. (1983), esp. 45–50 and refs.

[20] Only four of these headings can be matched by similar headings at exactly the same narrative points in other extant copies of *Cursor Mundi*. But the idea of subdividing the episodic narrative in this way, if not the actual headings, was probably inherited from a similarly presented exemplar.

[21] See the description in N. R. Ker (1977), 539–40.

[22] For discussion of the Cotton and Göttingen manuscripts see 49–55 and also *thesis*, 388–94.

have derived the idea for illustrating his text, but not, of course, the means to do so, from an illustrated Alexander exemplar.[17] Nevertheless, with the minimum of adaptation, the experimental and roughly drawn ink sketches, eventually added on ff. 52r and 52v in gathering **C**,[18] could have provided a later artist with stock images of chivalric combat in a section of the collection where an item dealing with these themes would appear to require this type of illustration.[19]

The unfinished decorative state of Thornton's Alexander item would appear to be matched by the similarly incomplete state of Thornton's copy of *Cursor Mundi* in the London manuscript. As Thornton copied this opening item in double columns he also subdivided his text into smaller 'chapter' units by adding separate headings in the columns of text at obvious narrative breaks.[20] Nineteen of these survive, but on nine occasions they have been accompanied in the same column by spaces that seem to have been left for a cluster of illustrations to be added at some later date. Due to the fragmentary nature of the Thornton copy of *Cursor Mundi* it is not certain that these blank spaces were the only occasions in the text where Thornton eventually intended to add further decoration of some kind. Therefore the plans for illustrating this opening item may have been even more ambitious than the evidence in this fragment would suggest. Moreover, a brief survey of other surviving copies of *Cursor Mundi* suggests that Thornton was not the only late medieval book-producer who intended to illustrate this lengthy biblical history. For example, the particularly fragmentary and disarranged mid-fourteenth-century text in the Royal College of Physicians in Edinburgh is another surviving copy where spaces seem to have been reserved in the narrative for illustrations that have never been completed.[21] By contrast, in the roughly contemporary British Library MS Cotton Vespasian A. 3. (c. 1340), spaces that were left in the text were eventually filled with genealogical diagrams or other visual summaries of the lengthy descriptions in the narrative at these points. In addition, the manuscript contains simple black ink drawings of the four streams of Paradise (f. 7v), Noah's ark (f. 12v), the division of the world by Noah's sons (f. 13v), the tower of Babylon (f. 14v) and a very roughly drawn sketch of the tablets of Moses (f. 36v). All these details have been added at appropriate points in the narrative, but they have had to be added in the margins since, unlike Thornton, the Cotton scribe made no advance planning for his text to be illustrated. In this context it is noticeable that all the drawings in the Cotton manuscript appear in the early part of the text and that the last marginal drawing is the rushed sketch on f. 36v. This may indicate that the scribe's enthusiasm for decorating the margins of his lengthy narrative waned considerably after only six attempts.

Göttingen University Library MS theol. 107r (c. 1350) provides the fourth and most lavish example of the impulse to illustrate *Cursor Mundi* in the later middle ages.[22] This copy contains nearly ninety richly decorated initials where the decoration of the letter-forms normally extends into the margins of the page to form a colourful decorative border. Many of the illuminated initials are inhabited by animal or human forms and, on at least fourteen occasions, this decoration depicts scenes that are also described in the *Cursor Mundi* narrative at these points. Of course these may have appeared in an even earlier illustrated *Cursor Mundi* exemplar, and certainly the Göttingen copy would have been all that someone like Thornton would have needed to provide a potential model for his own intended illustrations. However, the scenes that illustrate the Göttingen copy were chosen by an artist whose

choice was influenced as much by personal whim and the availability of suitable compositional models as by the presumed existence of a *Cursor Mundi* picture cycle in his source. All the episodes illustrated by him are stock religious scenes and it is easy to see how the artist in the Göttingen manuscript, or any other well-equipped medieval illustrator, could have created for himself an appropriate *Cursor Mundi* 'picture cycle' from contemporary Bible illustrations.[23] Inevitably, the only real restrictions on the scribe, artist, or book compiler who wanted to illustrate *Cursor Mundi* were the practical conditions in which their books were being produced. These uncertain conditions, which varied so much over the period in which this lengthy verse compilation continued to circulate, seem to provide the most likely explanation for the fact that such a relatively high proportion of extant copies of *Cursor Mundi* have been prepared for illustration but so few illustrated copies have survived. Therefore, in any final assessment of Thornton's attitudes and achievements as decorator and book producer, some notice must also be taken of the changing circumstances in which he was copying his items, rubricating them, and sometimes preparing them for even further decoration.

The desire to illustrate a ME literary narrative is itself particularly rare. For example, it is only in the fifteenth century that extended programmes of illustration were being developed for texts like Gower's *Confessio Amantis*, or Lydgate's *Troy book* and his *Fall of Princes*.[24] In most cases, the signs are that there were commercial reasons for this development, and, in some cases, the unfinished state of a manuscript intended for illumination seems to be an indication of an unsuccessful business speculation.[25] But the circumstances in which Thornton was producing his books would appear to have been somewhat different from the conditions in which other more *de luxe* English illuminated manuscripts were produced. Unlike many of these books, the Thornton manuscripts do not seem to have passed into the hands of professional craftsmen working in illuminators' workshops, but instead seem to have been decorated haphazardly and gradually while the task of gathering items together was still continuing. In the case of his copies of *The Life of Alexander* and *Cursor Mundi*, Thornton's main contribution may simply have been that he left blank spaces in his copies where illustrations appeared in his exemplars. But the act of reserving these spaces in the first place, accompanied at times by clear indications of the subject matter that was to be added at these points, is itself indicative of Thornton's confidence in his ability to ensure that his items would be illustrated. Regardless of the nature of his exemplars, his personal desire was to enhance the visual appeal of both books for future readers. In both cases, it seems likely, too, that, as Thornton copied these texts and confidently prepared them for future illumination, he was already aware that they were destined to form the opening items of two quite distinct volumes.

Thornton's *Life of Alexander* and his *Cursor Mundi* now head their respective collections, but this is no indication that these were the first items that Thornton copied for each book. Indeed, practically the reverse may be closer to the case. In the London manuscript Thornton appears to have copied his *Cursor Mundi* extract into a self-contained manuscript unit (gatherings **a–b**) which was then physically appended to an existing thematic sequence that once began with *The Northern Passion* in gathering **c**. In the Lincoln manuscript gatherings **A–C** containing Thornton's *Life of Alexander* form an 'Alexander' unit that eventually seems to have updated a collection that, for a time,

[23] H. Buchthal (1971), 9ff. has already suggested that, because of the ready availability of biblical illustrations to many illuminators, details from these scenes were used wholesale for the creation of unrelated secular picture cycles. It is not inappropriate to speculate that it would have taken very few examples of this type of compositional model to provide eminently suitable material for the intended illustrations in both the Thornton *Cursor Mundi* fragment and also in his copy of *The Life of Alexander*. Elsewhere, Lesley Lawton cites British Library MS Harley 1766 as a particular case where an extensive picture cycle was constructed from a few frequently repeated figure-types. See Lawton in Derek Pearsall, ed. (1983), 45–6, n. 26.

[24] For general discussion see Salter and Pearsall (1980) and Lawton in Derek Pearsall, ed. (1983), 41–69.

[25] A useful example here is Corpus Christi College, Cambridge, MS 61 for which see the discussion of the intended illustration in J. H. Fisher (1976) and M. B. Parkes and Elizabeth Salter (1978).

26 Part of this compiling sequence was originally suggested by G. R. Keiser (1979), 178, but see also my comments in Derek Pearsall ed. (1983), esp. 116–7 and 123 and the discussion of the chronology of Thornton's compiling efforts in the concluding chapter.

27 Future historical evidence might well be forthcoming concerning Frostt and his interest in the London manuscript. But the elementary nature of the minor decorative details that have been completed in the London manuscript makes it seem unlikely that he was ever commissioned by Thornton on a professional basis.

28 See Scott (1968). J. J. G. Alexander (1972) offers an interesting account of the similarly varied career of another English illuminator.

29 Professor John Friedman is currently working on the topic of fifteenth-century book production in York. But, among the entries in the register of Freemen for York between the years 1327 and 1473, there are already good indications that book production in the city, and in particular the decorating of books, was a specialised and organised business. Among the freemen who specified their trade can be counted 38 parchment makers, 1 stationer, 35 scriveners, 6 book binders, and, most importantly, 13 limners. See the edition by F. Collins (1897), quoted by G. R. Keiser (1979), 165. The nature and quality of the work undertaken by the York limners is unspecified but, in a slightly different context, Dr Scott has already suggested that 'One cannot anticipate the sort of book which an illuminator might have decorated, and the researcher cannot preclude a search of less attractive manuscripts simply because the artist was known to work on luxury books' (Scott, 1968, 196).

30 Madden seems to have examined the Lincoln manuscript in a medieval binding, but there is no evidence to suggest that this was added by Thornton rather than by some other medieval craftsman. Moreover, the binding of the Lincoln manuscript need not have called a halt to Thornton's plans for the eventual illustration of its opening item, despite the fact that it is sometimes assumed, wrongly, that medieval manuscripts were not illuminated after they were bound (see, for example, Graham Pollard, 1937, 14). D. J. A. Ross, among others, has shown that, in the examples he has seen, 'books were

probably opened with the alliterative *Morte* in **D**.[26] It now seems likely that one of the reasons for taking such care to decorate the capitals in gatherings **D–F** (Lincoln manuscript) and the opening initials in **c** (London manuscript) was because, at one time, Thornton assumed that these gatherings and the items in them, were going to head two separate thematic sequences in his collection. At the later stage, when he decided to add new manuscript units to his existing sequences of gatherings (thereby effectively supplanting the original opening items in each of his manuscripts), it was only to be expected that he should prepare these new opening items for a decorative programme that was potentially more elaborate than anything he had previously attempted.

It is also important to note that the decoration of the London manuscript is at a far less advanced stage than that of the Lincoln manuscript. Despite the suspicion that Thornton originally started to decorate the London manuscript using both red and green inks, most of the simple coloured capitals have been added in red, while the earlier slightly more ambitious attempt has been abandoned. However, some doubt about Thornton's personal responsibility for adding all these red letter-forms certainly seems justified when it is realised that in the top margin of f. 73v the name 'Willa Frostt' has been written in red ink. This provides the only clear example in either of Thornton's books where someone other than Thornton has used red ink. Therefore, it seems natural to associate Frostt's name, as well as Thornton's, with the eventual decoration of the London manuscript. In this manuscript at least, Frostt may well have completed some of the decorative features that were originally planned and partially executed by Thornton himself.[27]

Due to the ambitious nature of his plans for full-scale programmes of illustration for each manuscript, it is even possible that Thornton once considered specially commissioning a professional craftsman for the specific purpose of decorating his opening items. But much work remains to be done before we can talk with any assurance about the range of formal and informal tasks that were undertaken by fifteenth-century English provincial workshops to which book-producers like Thornton might have had access. Nevertheless, in her work on one mid-fifteenth-century illuminating-shop and its customers in London, Kathleen Scott has reconstructed a convincing picture of a workshop where two illuminators were prepared to work on a range of different kinds of commission for their various customers.[28] It is possible that similar commercial ventures were operating in other important centres such as fifteenth-century York.[29] Therefore we cannot automatically rule out the possibility that Thornton had access to a local shop, however small and informal, where he might have expected to find available the necessary facilities with which satisfactorily to complete the intended illustrations. His original plans for the finishing of his two books may well have included a visit to an illuminator's workshop as well as a visit to the book binder's.[30]

There are many possible reasons why this proposed visit did not take place. The most obvious is that, despite his ambitious plans, Thornton eventually found that he could not afford to pay for the services of a professional illuminator. However, the likelihood that William Frostt was left to complete quite minor decorative features in the London manuscript suggests another possibility. Thornton may well have died before he could complete all the production stages for the items in his two-volume collection. If this was the case, then Thornton may have delayed sending either his

Alexander item or his biblical history to be decorated until it was too late. Whatever his original intentions when he copied these items, Thornton's mortality or his limited financial resources, rather than any lack of suitable facilities in fifteenth-century Yorkshire, may well have determined that both his manuscripts were left in their present seemingly 'unfinished' states.

usually bound and not still in sheets or quires when they reached the illuminator' (Ross, 1952, 67). See the comments supporting Ross and suggesting too that some fifteenth-century scribes and printers could act as their own binders in Curt F. Bühler (1960), esp. 81–2.

Conclusion

The discussion elsewhere in this study, and especially in the previous chapter, has suggested that the networks of compiling procedure and the relationships between the two Thornton manuscripts are not nearly so obvious and straightforward as has hitherto been assumed. The collection of texts in the Lincoln manuscript now forms a separate book and may have existed as such in Thornton's day because of his efforts. It may even seem a 'better-organised' and more 'finished' collection than its smaller sister volume in London. But present appearances can be deceptive. Thornton's two-volume collection represents the efforts of a book producer with limited and often unpredictable aims and resources. Furthermore, at the earliest stages in the history of many of the quires in both manuscripts, Thornton can now be shown to have had a tendency to copy some of his material into originally self-contained manuscript units. One potential advantage of this informal production practice was that it could make 'work in progress' immediately available to local readers at the same time as an aspiring book producer continued to gather together more material for a larger collection.[1] Another possibility was that it allowed the compiler to keep some of his options open until a considerable amount of suitable material had become available for his use. In the case of the London manuscript, Thornton's collection seems to have been built up gradually from these units with additional material later inserted where space remained in earlier partly-filled quires or in newly-created composite gatherings. More generally, it was presumably also by a similar, gradual and not always entirely haphazard process, that the diverse material in Thornton's entire collection continued to accumulate.[2]

This preliminary assessment of the genesis of Thornton's impressive two-volume collection clearly invites closer analysis of the five types of watermarked paper shared by both manuscripts (containing watermarks **i**, **ii**, **iii**, **v**, **vi**).[3] The scattered distribution patterns of these shared stocks of paper, when seen in the context of a variety of other types of supporting physical and textual evidence, provide useful confirmation of the view that Thornton did indeed work on material for both manuscripts simultaneously.

The best place to begin an evaluation of the evidence provided by the different stocks of paper in Thornton's collection is with the texts that

[1] The example of National Library of Scotland MS Advocates 19.3.1, another fifteenth-century household anthology of mainly ME verse items, provides a possible precedent for this kind of informal book production activity. This anthology once consisted of a series of separate manuscript units eventually gathered together to form a single book. Prior to this time, these booklets seem to have enjoyed some kind of independent existence as portions of a local late medieval 'library *in parvo*'. See Phillipa Hardman (1978) and the account of different types of informal compiling activities in the forthcoming survey of fifteenth-century anthologies and miscellanies by Julia Boffey and John Thompson (referred to, 4, n. 15).

[2] Thornton's writing career, like that of the roughly contemporary metropolitan book producer John Shirley, probably extended over a considerable number of years. In this context, note the existing comments on the longevity and prolific output of Shirley which have already informed discussion of manuscripts like Bodleian Library MS Ashmole 59 (internal evidence suggests that the book was copied when Shirley was in his eighties). See Dr Doyle's published work on Shirley (1961, 1983), continued in an unpublished lecture given at the second York Conference on Fifteenth-Century Manuscript Studies (July 1983).

[3] See the description offered in the *Appendix*. It should be noted here that the hammer designs in watermark **viii** paper are really two different types of

64

Thornton probably copied either very early or else very late in his career. An obvious choice here is gatherings **a–b** (ff. 3–32) in the London manuscript. These contain the remaining fragment of *Cursor Mundi* in a manuscript unit that Thornton seems to have copied late in his career as an adjunct to an earlier sequence of material that originally began with *The Northern Passion*. As far as it is possible to tell from the surviving fragments, gatherings **a** and **b** were both made up entirely from watermark **i** paper. The only other surviving examples of this stock of paper are now found in gathering **K** in the Lincoln manuscript. This gathering was originally composed of eight bifolia but the final leaf is now missing, presumably cancelled by Thornton. The core of **K** is made up of three bifolia of watermark **i** paper, the next two bifolia are watermark **vi** paper, and the three outer bifolia contain watermark **xi**.

Fortunately, it is also possible to associate gathering **K** with a similarly early state in Thornton's compiling activities.[4] In the Lincoln manuscript Thornton commenced copying the romance of *Sir Perceval* in quire **I** (originally composed of eleven bifolia, only ten of which survive). However, by the time Thornton added *Sir Perceval* to the other 'Thornton romances' in the Lincoln manuscript, quire **I** had already been the subject of some rearrangement. At the first stage in its history, Thornton had used the opening leaves of his blank gathering to copy *The Awntyrs off Arthure*. This information is itself potentially useful but, for the moment, what is more interesting is that Thornton eventually completed *Sir Perceval* in **K**. *Sir Perceval* and gathering **K** were only added to the Lincoln manuscript as an afterthought, some time after gatherings **A–I** had been assembled in their present order to form nine 'romance quires'.[5]

The other types of watermarked paper in gathering **K** are also widely dispersed in Thornton's collection. In the Lincoln manuscript, examples of **vi** paper survive in **K** and also in gatherings **A** and **B**. The core of **A** is formed by two bifolia of **vi** paper and, although this opening gathering is particularly fragmentary, the outer leaves of **A** were probably originally composed of ten bifolia of **xi** paper. Gathering **B** now lacks its opening leaf but was originally made up from a core of three bifolia of **xi** paper, followed by nine bifolia of **vi** paper. Only half of gathering **C** survives and this consists of ten singletons, four of which contain watermark **xi**.[6] There are no other surviving examples of watermark **xi** paper in Thornton's two-volume collection, but it is certainly interesting that, in the Lincoln manuscript, watermark **vi** is shared by gatherings **A**, **B** and **K**. Gatherings **A** and **B** contain the bulk of Thornton's copy of the ME prose *Life of Alexander* and, together with **C**, they originally formed another seemingly self-contained manuscript unit. The Alexander biography in this unit was prepared for a very ambitious decorative scheme which was never completed but, eventually, it did supplant the Thornton copy of the ME alliterative *Morte Arthure* as the opening item in the Lincoln manuscript. This was probably at a late stage in the compilation of the Thornton 'romance' unit in the Lincoln manuscript but, intriguingly, the Alexander unit in gatherings **A–C** was already in its present position *before* Thornton copied *Sir Perceval* in gatherings **I–K**.

Watermark **vi** paper was also used to form the outer leaves of gatherings **e** and **f** in the London manuscript. Here Thornton used this stock of paper to copy the remaining lines of *The Sege of Melayne*, part of his Lydgate and 'song' sequence, *The Quatrefoil of Love* and his alliterating paraphrase of Vulgate Psalm 50. These are all items that were copied on the outer leaves of the two

paper. Watermark **viii** (I) now survives solely in the London manuscript, while watermark **viii** (II) survives solely in the Lincoln manuscript. Similarly, the crown designs of watermark **x** form two types of paper. Watermark **x** (I) survives solely in gathering **h**, and **x** (II) solely in **i** (both London manuscript).

[4] For details of the changing history of gatherings **A–K** in the Lincoln manuscript see Thompson in Derek Pearsall, ed. (1983).

[5] It was probably because of this later addition that Thornton returned to his note on f. 163v in the last leaf of gathering **I**. This originally read, 'here is ix quayers' but was eventually cancelled by a single ink stroke when a tenth quire (**K**) was added.

[6] For this revised collation of **C** see *thesis*, 23–4.

[7] Watermarks **i**, **vi** and **xi** need not, of course, represent three separate batches of paper since Thornton's paper stock must have passed through several intermediary stages between the time when it was first manufactured, imported, held by a paper supplier, purchased and then used by Thornton. One further complication is that the same medieval paper-mill sometimes produced a variety of different watermark designs for the one size of sheet. For these and other details concerning the early history of European paper production see Dard Hunter (1957), esp. 261–5; G. Thomas Tanselle (1971), esp. 37ff.; Jean Irigoin (1980).

[8] For the linguistic evidence see Angus McIntosh (1962); also discussion in *thesis*, 147, n. 47.

large and particularly fragmentary composite gatherings in the troublesome middle section of the manuscript. Again, Thornton's use of **vi** paper to copy this material can be associated with a period late in his career when he was also interested in filling up the limited remaining spaces in other partly-filled and sometimes rearranged gatherings. At this point, then, there are good grounds for assuming that Thornton's stocks of **i**, **vi** and **xi** paper were late supplements to his general paper supply, just as the items copied on this paper were also added at various late stages in his compiling activities.[7] Although it is not possible to determine fully the order in which Thornton copied the material in gatherings **A–C**, **a–b**, **e** and **f**, it is tempting to assume that the bulk of his stock of these three types of watermarked sheets had been used up before Thornton used the remnants to construct the gathering (**K**) needed to complete *Sir Perceval* in the Lincoln manuscript.

An entirely different, though equally useful, set of conclusions can be drawn from the watermark evidence in the quire in which Thornton eventually began copying *Sir Perceval*. Quire **I** originally contained Thornton's copy of *The Awntyrs* and is now made up exclusively of watermark **ii** paper. Elsewhere in the Lincoln manuscript this type of paper is found only in gatherings **D** and **E**, containing the bulk of Thornton's copy of the alliterative *Morte*. In the London manuscript, however, watermark **ii** paper is found in gathering **c** (ff. 33–53), containing *The Northern Passion*. Originally, Thornton appears to have copied the alliterative *Morte* into a separate 'Arthurian' unit which, like his *Awntyrs* gathering, was only later absorbed into the sequence of 'romance' quires in the Lincoln manuscript. Similarly, both the alliterative *Morte* and *The Northern Passion* were copied into manuscript units that, for a time, formed the opening sections of their respective collections. In each case, Thornton eventually updated his collection by adding new opening units to his two unfinished miscellanies. Therefore, it can be assumed that, despite their varied later histories, the three units containing *The Awntyrs*, the alliterative *Morte* and *The Northern Passion* were all copied at a fairly early stage in Thornton's career. Since these units include the only quires in his collection with watermark **ii** paper, it would seem that Thornton also used up this particular stock of paper at a similarly early point in his work.

It is difficult to be as precise about the rest of the stocks of paper Thornton used for the alliterative *Morte* and *The Northern Passion*. Gatherings **D–F**, containing the alliterative *Morte*, are mixed quires: the eight bifolia in **D** and the six outer bifolia in **E** consist of **ii** paper, but the three inner bifolia in **E** and all eight bifolia in **F** are composed of watermark **v** paper. As many as thirty-five other examples of this paper survive elsewhere in his manuscripts, making **v** the largest batch of any type of watermark design in Thornton's collection. Moreover, this paper is now far more widely dispersed than any other type of paper. In the Lincoln manuscript, gatherings **H**, **L** and **M** (containing eleven, ten and twelve bifolia respectively) are made up of **v** paper. The two inner bifolia of gathering **P** also contain the **v** watermark. Of course it might perhaps be expected that Thornton's copy of *The Privity of the Passion* in gathering **L** would have been copied using a similar batch of paper to the one used for the alliterative *Morte* since both seem to have been derived from a single Lincolnshire source.[8] But watermark **v** paper was obviously also part of the main stock of paper used to construct the gatherings that were eventually widely used in both the 'religious' and the 'romance' units in the Lincoln manuscript. This adds a further dimension to the discussion here since some of these gatherings may even have been assembled and stockpiled

in preparation for his compilation activities in the Lincoln manuscript some time before Thornton actually knew which items were eventually going to fill them.

Because of this latter possibility it is particularly interesting that, as far as can now be ascertained, only one example of a watermark **v** sheet has survived in the London manuscript. This originally formed the outer bifolium of gathering **d**. Like gatherings **E**, **F** and **L**, gathering **d** seems to have been assembled and partly filled at an early stage in Thornton's activities since it now contains the continuation of his copy of *The Northern Passion* and all of *The Siege of Jerusalem*. The single sheet of **v** paper here (which may have been left over when some of Thornton's other quires had been constructed) has also been added to an already mixed quire. Some of the other sheets in this quire provide a final series of links between the gatherings in each of Thornton's miscellanies.

The core of gathering **d** was originally formed by three bifolia of watermark **iv** paper. This type of paper survives nowhere else in the collection, but, in addition, **d** contains six bifolia of watermark **iii** paper. Elsewhere, the only other surviving examples of **iii** paper are in gatherings **G** and **P** in the Lincoln manuscript. In **G** they form the two inner bifolia of a gathering that also contains the only surviving example of a watermark **xii** bifolium in Thornton's entire collection. The outer leaves of **G** originally formed eight bifolia but only seven of these survive in their entirety and six of these contain one type of watermark **viii** paper (**viii** II).[9] The previous history of **G** can also be established with some accuracy. This gathering would appear to have been added to Thornton's collection so that he could complete the copy of *Octavian* he had commenced copying in the remaining leaves of **F**. This was after a time lapse of some kind during which **D–F** contained the alliterative *Morte*.

This discussion of the shared stocks of paper in Thornton's miscellanies brings us as close as we are likely to get to a definitive statement about the continuous nature of the physical links that can be made between his two manuscripts. These links confirm that Thornton's decision to create two miscellaneous collections – or perhaps more accurately his decision to complete one large collection and bind it together to form a book – need not necessarily have been a choice he had to make until very late in his writing career. It was a decision that may have been influenced by a series of lucky finds among his exemplars, or, indeed, it may even have been made after Thornton had already painstakingly assembled sufficient material to make such an ambitious project seem feasible.[10] Nevertheless, it must still be asked why the London manuscript seems a much less satisfactory and less complete collection. Naturally, part of the answer lies in the present fragmentary state of the book, due perhaps to the likelihood that it remained unbound for a considerably longer period than its sister volume. In its original state, the London manuscript was obviously far closer in number and size of pages to the Lincoln manuscript than its present appearance might suggest. If Thornton died before the task of copying and arranging the items in his second volume was complete, then this too would imply that part of the task of 'finishing' his second book was left to later, less able, hands. But, despite the relatively strong case that can be mustered in defence of the London manuscript in these ways, it may also be important to note that Thornton's second collection of items probably once began with one of the most obviously unfinished items in his entire collection.

[9] See n. 3 above. The bifolium ff. 108/ 117 is the only clear example of an unwatermarked sheet in Thornton's entire collection.

[10] There are a number of examples of both these possibilities in the two Thornton collections, but perhaps the most spectacular example of the direct influence of his exemplars on Thornton's own book production practices is his 'medical' unit in the Lincoln manuscript. The extremely large quire **Q** seems to have been tailored to fill *Liber de Diversis Medicinis* from a single stock of **xv** paper that does not appear elsewhere in Thornton's collection. See further Thompson (1982).

[11] For the defective Thornton text see Frances Foster, ed. (1913), 147 and the discussion in Foster (1916), 12–13, 71–72.

The Thornton text of *The Northern Passion* breaks off abruptly in the middle of the second column of f. 41r. It omits part of the interpolated story of how Seth was sent to Paradise and the interrupted text begins again on f. 42r.[11] The blank space on ff. 41r–42r would suggest that Thornton knew roughly how much room the missing lines from his own copy would have filled. Presumably his estimate here was based on his awareness of a textual *lacuna* at this point in his source. Certainly, the most obvious indication of this kind of gap would have been that the stub of at least one missing leaf appeared at the appropriate point in Thornton's exemplar. Moreover, despite the obvious care with which Thornton reserved an appropriate gap in his copy for the loss to be made good, and despite any efforts he may have made to fill the gap, at least part of the blank space still remains. At an early point in his career the incomplete nature of this item probably caused him little worry, especially since the unfinished manuscript unit containing *The Northern Passion* could easily have been set to one side until such time as the gap in his copy could be made good from a second, more complete, exemplar. But a suitable second copy of *The Northern Passion* never became available for his use and this may be why gatherings **c** and **d** were left over when the Lincoln manuscript was assembled. It was only at a later stage, when Thornton eventually added *Melayne* in the remaining space in **d** and in the opening leaves of **e**, that a second collection began to take shape. Watermark evidence suggests that this was probably around the same time as Thornton was adding his 'Alexander' unit, and then *Sir Perceval*, to the sequence of 'Thornton romances' in the Lincoln manuscript.

The Northern Passion is not the only item in his collection that may have been copied from an incomplete and therefore unsatisfactory exemplar. But it is revealing that the only other item where Thornton can be shown to have waited in vain for a second copy of a text is also found in one of the units that also ended up in the London manuscript. This is the copy of *Richard Coeur de Lion* in gatherings **g** and **h**. One of the reasons why this text is defective is the physical *lacuna* at the end of **g**. But Thornton's copy also ends abruptly on f. 160r where he left all of the second column blank; his copy recommences on f. 160v. The missing text corresponds to ll. 6381–6670 in Brunner's edition of the poem and Thornton could hardly have imagined that he could have squeezed this amount of text into the short space he left for the missing lines.[12] Nevertheless, despite this puzzle, the fragmentary nature of his exemplar is again the most likely explanation for the deficiency in Thornton's copy at this point. For a time, gatherings **g** and **h** containing *Richard* may also have been set to one side until eventually the remaining blank space at the end of **h** was filled by the Thornton 'romance' of *Ypokrephum*. Both these items would have fitted quite naturally alongside other 'romances' in the Lincoln manuscript, so, although they are copied on paper with the **ix** and **x** (I) watermark designs that are not shared by any paper in the Lincoln manuscript, their present isolated context, inserted near the end of the London manuscript, is obviously no clear indication of the production stage at which they were first copied.[13] It remains possible that the unfinished copy of *Richard* was available, but simply not selected, when Thornton finally began to assemble his 'romance' material for the Lincoln manuscript. At any rate, the 'romances' in **g** and **h** have had to find a place among the pile of quires from which the London manuscript was formed.

It seems likely too that Thornton's second miscellany became some kind of 'overflow' volume once the Lincoln manuscript had taken on a definite

[12] See Karl Brunner, ed. (1913), 5, 405–421.

[13] Cf. n. 3 above.

tripartite 'shape'. But perhaps other items in one or other Thornton miscellany could still equally easily have found themselves in a different volume. This category might include Thornton's copy of *The Three Kings of Cologne*, where the pages containing this item were rearranged and absorbed into **f** when Thornton added Lydgate's *Virtues of the Mass* to his collection. A similar fate seems to have befallen his gathering containing *The Awntyrs*. On this occasion Thornton needed extra paper on which to copy *Sir Eglamour*; his rearranged quire **I** satisfied this need and therefore ended up in the Lincoln manuscript. This type of radical rearrangement of paper may even have affected other gatherings and the items in them, but it is not always possible to detect such examples with any degree of certainty. On other occasions, of course, where it was no longer necessary to use all the remaining space in his quires for fillers, Thornton often seems to have removed individual leaves, probably as he required them elsewhere for other writing purposes.[14] On the credit side, the present opening items in each volume (the Alexander romance biography in the Lincoln manuscript and the *Cursor Mundi* account of religious history until Christ's death in the London manuscript) seem to have been variously 'tailored' for Thornton's specific purposes at fairly late stages in his compiling efforts, perhaps when the ambition to create two separate collections had already emerged as a definite possibility. Taking all these examples into account, therefore, it seems appropriate to characterise the final results of Robert Thornton's book-compiling activities as an intriguing mixture of obvious and sometimes happy accident, and occasional careful design.

[14] Thornton may not have been as prolific a correspondent as some members of the Paston family, but letter-writing, whether for day-to-day business matters or to maintain social contacts with family and friends, is one of the scribal pursuits for which Thornton – a fifteenth-century official and 'man of property' – may well have required a limited amount of paper. In this context, note too G. A. Lester's brief comments on the stocks of paper shared by part of Sir John Paston's 'Grete Boke' and by some of the Paston letters (Lester, 1984, 42, 15–17, 42–3).

APPENDIX

The watermarks in Thornton's collection

This description revises and expands the previous accounts offered in New Palaeographical Society (1913–14), pl. 45 and text; Karen Stern (1976), 27–8; Sarah Horrall (1979, 1980).

Watermark i   Bull (cf. *Briquet* 2804/5, 1438–46; *Beazeley* 128–9, 1444).

London Thornton manuscript	ff. 3, 8, 9, 11, 12, 13, 14, 16, 17, 21, 22, 23, 26, 31
Lincoln Thornton manuscript	ff. 170, 172, 174

Watermark ii   Bull's head (cf. *Briquet* 15203/6, 1437–45; nearest 15204, 1440).

London Thornton manuscript	ff. 34, 36, 38, 41, 42, 44, 47, 48, 50, 52
Lincoln Thornton manuscript	ff. 56, 57, 58, 59, 61, 66, 67, 68, 69, 72, 73, 81, 84, 85, 145, 148, 150, 151, 152, 154, 158, 160, 161, 163

Watermark iii   Cart (cf. *Briquet* 3528, 1429–61).

London Thornton manuscript	ff. 57, 59, 60, 69, 71, 72
Lincoln Thornton manuscript	ff. 113, 114, 254, 255, 257, 259, 261, 262, 268, 272, 274, 276, 279

Watermark iv   Crowned column (cf. *Briquet* 4398, 1421–69).

London Thornton manuscript	ff. 61, 62, 63

Watermark v   Fleur-de-lys and dolphin (cf. *Briquet* 5892/5, 1418–47; nearest 5895, 1431–47; *Beazeley* 122–3, 1438, 137–8, 1451).

London Thornton manuscript	f. 73
Lincoln Thornton manuscript	ff. 76, 77, 80, 87, 88, 91, 95, 96, 97, 99, 100, 123, 125, 126, 127, 130, 131, 132, 133, 137, 138, 142, 180, 184, 185, 187, 188, 191, 194, 195, 196, 198, 200, 202, 206, 207, 208, 211, 212, 216, 217, 218, 220, 263, 264

Watermark vi   Sole of shoe (cf. *Briquet* 13617/18, 1426–30).

London Thornton manuscript	ff. 74, 77, 78, 79, 95, 97, 99, 101, 102, 121, 124
Lincoln Thornton manuscript	ff. 7, 8, 20, 21, 27, 35, 36, 37, 38, 39, 42, 168, 176

Watermark vii   Serpent (cf. *Briquet* 13625/31, 1423–56; nearest 13625/9, 1423–44).

London Thornton manuscript	ff. 80, 82, 84, 86, 88, 90

Watermark viii   Hammer designs (I, cf. *Briquet* 11634, 1446–50; II, cf. *Briquet* 11631–2, 1410?–35).

London Thornton manuscript	(I only) ff. 104, 105, 106, 107, 108, 110, 116, 118, 119
Lincoln Thornton manuscript	(II only) ff. 106, 107, 109, 120, 121, 122, 238, 239, 240, 243, 244, 247, 248, 252

Watermark ix   Crossed keys (cf. *Briquet* 3867/9, 1420–58).

London Thornton manuscript	ff. 125, 127, 128, 130, 132, 136, 137, 138, 140, 142

Watermark x   Crown designs (I and II, cf. *Briquet* 4636/46, 1423–73).

London Thornton manuscript	(I) ff. 147, 149, 150, 151, 155, 156, 159, 160, 161, 165, 167, 168 (II) ff. 170, 171, 173, 174, 178, 179, 180

Watermark xi   Crossed axes.

Lincoln Thornton manuscript	ff. 1, 3, 6, 12, 13, 15, 31, 32, 33, 43, 45, 46, 49, 164, 177, 178

Watermark xii   Bull's head and cross (cf. *Briquet* 15103/10, 1434–69; nearest 15103, 1434–46; *Beazeley* 147–8, 174–5.

Lincoln Thornton manuscript	f. 115

Watermark xiii   Circle (cf. *Briquet* 2921, 1401; sometimes indistinct).

Lincoln Thornton manuscript	ff. 222, 223, 224, 225, 227, 228, 230, 232, 235, 253

Watermark xiv Catherine wheel (cf. *Briquet* 13261/68, 1402–44; nearest 13268, 1434).

Lincoln Thornton manuscript ff. 269, 270

Watermark xv Letter A and cross (cf. *Briquet* 7900/04, 1385–1442).

Lincoln Thornton manuscript ff. 286, 298, 299, 300, 301, 302, 303, 304, 305, 306, 307, 308, 310, 311, 312, 313, 314

SELECT BIBLIOGRAPHY

This section contains all works cited elsewhere in the book by author and date only. See also *List of Abbreviations*.

Alexander, J. J. G., 'William Abell "Lymnour" and 15th Century English Illumination', in *Kunsthistorische Forschungen Otto Pächt zu ehren*, ed. A. Rosenauer and G. Weber (Salzburg, 1972), 166–72

The Decorated Letter (London, 1978)

Aveling, Hugh, 'The Catholic Recusants of the West Riding of Yorkshire, 1558–1790', *Proceedings of the Leeds Philosophical and Literary Society, Lit. and Hist. section*, 10 (1963), 191–306

The Catholic Recusants of the North Riding of Yorkshire, 1558–1790 (London, 1966)

Bazire, Joyce, 'Mercy and Justice', *NM*, 83 (1982), 178–91

' "Mercy and Justice": The Additional MS 31042 Version', *Leeds Studies in English* NS, 16 (1985), 259–71

Benskin, M. and M. L. Samuels, ed., *So Meny People Longages and Tonges: Philological Essays on Scots and Mediaeval English Presented to Angus McIntosh* (Edinburgh, 1981)

Bergen, H., ed., *Lydgate's Fall of Princes*, 4 vols, EETS ES, 121, 122, 123, 124 (London, 1924–27, repr. 1967)

Blake, N. F., review of *MS Tanner 346*, introd., P. R. Robinson, in *English Studies*, 63 (1982), 71–3

Bliss, A. J., ed., *Sir Orfeo*, Oxford English Monographs (London, 1966)

Brewer, D. S. and A. E. B. Owen, introd., *The Thornton Manuscript, Lincoln Cathedral MS 91* (London, 1975, 2nd revised ed. 1977)

British Museum, *Catalogue of Additions to the Manuscripts in the British Museum in the Years 1876–1881* (London, 1882, repr. 1967)

Brown, B. D., ed., *The Southern Passion*, EETS OS, 169 (London, 1927, repr. 1971)

Brown, Carleton, '*The Cursor Mundi* and the "Southern Passion"', *Modern Language Notes*, 26 (1911), 15–18

—— ed., *Religious Lyrics of the XV Century* (Oxford, 1939)

Brunner, Karl, ed., *Der Mittelenglische Versroman über Richard Löwenherz*, Weiner Beiträge zur englischen Philologie, 42 (Vienna, 1913)

—— 'HS. Brit. Mus. Additional 31042', *Archiv*, 132 (1914), 316–27

—— 'Spätme. Lehrgedichte', *Archiv*, 161 (1932), 191–5, and *Archiv*, 164 (1933), 178–99

Buchthal, H., *Historia Troiana: Studies in the History of Medieval Secular Illustration*, Studies of the Warburg Institute, 32 (London, 1971)

Bühler, Curt F., *The Fifteenth Century Book: The Scribes, The Printers, The Decorators* (Philadelphia, 1960)

Casson, L. F., ed., *The Romance of Sir Degrevant*, EETS OS, 221 (London, 1949, repr. 1970)

Collins, F., ed., *Register of the Freemen of the City of York*, Surtees Society, 96 (London, 1897)

Cowper, J. Meadows, ed., *The Meditations on the Supper of Our Lord and the Hours of the Passion*, EETS OS, 60 (London, 1875, repr. 1973)

Davis, Norman, 'Another fragment of "Richard Coer De Lyon"', *N & Q*, 214 (1969), 447–52

de Wit, Pamela, 'The Visual Experience of Fifteenth-Century English Readers' (Unpublished D.Phil. thesis, Oxford, 1977)

Doyle, A. I., 'A Survey of the Origins and Circulation of Theological Writings in English in the 14th, 15th, and early 16th Centuries with Special Consideration of the Part of the Clergy therein', 2 vols. (Unpublished Ph.D. thesis, Cambridge, 1953)

—— 'More Light on John Shirley', *Medium Aevum*, 30 (1961), 93–101

—— 'The Shaping of the Vernon and Simeon Manuscripts', in *Chaucer and Middle English Studies in Honour of Rossell Hope Robbins*, ed. B. Rowland (London, 1974), 328–41

—— 'English Books In and Out of Court from Edward III to Henry VII', in *English Court Culture in the Later Middle Ages*, ed. V. J. Scattergood and J. W. Sherborne (London, 1983), 163–81

Edwards, A. S. G., '"The Whole Book": Medieval MSS in Facsimile', *Review*, 2 (1980), 19–29

—— 'Additions and Corrections To The Bibliography of John Lydgate', *N & Q*, 230 (1985), 450–2

Fisher, J. H., 'The Intended Illustrations in MS Corpus Christi 61 of Chaucer's *Troilus and Criseyde*', in *Medieval Studies in Honor of Lillian Herlands Hornstein*, ed. J. B. Bessinger Jr and R. Raymo (New York, 1976), 111–21

Foster, Frances, ed., *The Northern Passion*, 3 vols, EETS OS, 145, 147, 183 (Supplement with W. Heuser) (London, 1913–16, 1930, repr. 1971)

Furnivall, F. J., ed., *Hymns to the Virgin and Christ*, EETS OS, 24 (London, 1867, repr. 1973)

Gerardy, Theo, 'Die Beschreibung des in Manuskripten und Drucken vorkommenden Papiers', *Codicologica*, 5 (1980), 37–51

Gollancz, I., ed., *Wynnere and Wastoure*, Select Early English Poems III (Oxford, 1920, reissued Cambridge, 1974)

and M. M. Weale, ed., *The Quatrefoil of Love*, EETS OS, 195 (London, 1935, repr. 1971)

Görlach, Manfred, *The Textual Tradition of the South English Legendary*, Leeds Texts and Monographs NS, 6 (Leeds, 1974)

Gradon, Pamela, *Form and Style in Early English Literature* (London, 1971)

Greene, R. L., ed., *The Early English Carols* (Oxford, 1935, 2nd ed. 1977)

Guddat-Figge, Gisela, *Catalogue of Manuscripts containing Middle English Romances* (Munich, 1976)

Halliwell, James O., ed., *The Thornton Romances*, Camden Society 30 (London, 1844)

Hamel, Mary, 'Scribal Self-Corrections in the Thornton *Morte Arthure*', *SB*, 36 (1983), 119–37

Hanna, Ralph, III, ed., *The Awntyrs off Arthure at the Terne Wathelyn* (Manchester, 1974)

'The London Thornton Manuscript: A Corrected Collation', *SB*, 37 (1984), 122–30

Hardman, Phillipa, 'A Mediaeval "Library *In Parvo*"', *Medium Aevum*, 47 (1978), 262–73

Herrtage, S. J. H., ed., *The English Charlemagne Romances II: The Sege off Melayne and The Romance of Duke Rowland and Sir Otuell of Spayne*, EETS ES, 35 (London, 1880, repr. 1973)

Hitchcock, Elsie V., ed., *The Donet by Reginald Peacock*, EETS OS, 156 (London, 1921, repr. 1971)

Hodder, Karen 'Two Unpublished Middle English Carol Fragments', *Archiv*, 205 (1969), 378–83

Horrall, Sarah M., ed., *The Southern Version of the Cursor Mundi*, 3 vols, vol. 1 (Ottawa, 1978–, in progress)

'The London Thornton Manuscript: A New Collation', *Manuscripta*, 23 (1979), 99–103

'The Watermarks of the Thornton Manuscripts', *N & Q*, 225 (1980), 385–6

Horstmann, Carl, ed., *Sammlung Altenglischer Legenden* (Heilbronn, 1878)

ed., *Altenglische Legenden, Neue Folge* (Heilbronn, 1881)

'Nachträge zu den Legenden', *Archiv*, 74 (1885), 327–39

ed., *Yorkshire Writers: Richard Rolle of Hampole*, 2 vols (London, 1895–96)

and F. J. Furnivall, ed., *Minor Poems of the Vernon MS*, 2 vols, vol. 1 (Horstmann) EETS OS, 98 (London, 1892, repr. 1973), vol. II (Furnivall) EETS OS, 117 (London, 1901, repr. 1973)

Hunter, Dard, *Papermaking: The History and Technique of an Ancient Craft* (London, 1943, 2nd ed. 1957)

Irigoin, Jean, 'La datation par les filigranes du papier', *Codicologica*, 5 (1980), 9–36

Jackson, Charles, ed., *The Autobiography of Mrs Alice Thornton*, Surtees Society, 62 (London, 1875)

Jacobs, Nicholas, 'The Processes of Scribal Substitution and Redaction: A Study of the Cambridge Fragment of *Sir Degarre*', *Medium Aevum*, 53 (1984), 26–48

James, M. R., *A Descriptive Catalogue of the Manuscripts in the Library of Lambeth Palace: The Medieval Manuscripts* (Cambridge, 1930–32)

The Romance of Alexander, A Collotype Facsimile of MS Bodley 264 (Oxford, 1933)

Keiser, George R., 'A Note on the Descent of the Thornton Manuscript', *TCBS*, 6 (1976), 346–8

'Lincoln Cathedral Library MS 91: Life and Milieu of the Scribe', *SB* 32 (1979), 158–79

'Þe Holy Boke Gratia Dei', *Viator*, 12 (1981), 289–317

'More Light on the Life and Milieu of Robert Thornton', *SB*, 36 (1983), 111–19

'"To Knawe God Almyghtyn": Robert Thornton's Devotional Book', in *Spätmittelalterliche Geistliche Literatur in der Nationalsprache*, ed. James Hogg, Analecta Cartusiana, 106 (Salzburg, 1984), 2103–29.

Ker, Neil R., *Fragments of Medieval Manuscripts used as Pastedowns in Oxford Bindings* (Oxford, 1954)

Medieval Manuscripts in British Libraries, II (Oxford, 1977)

Kölbing, E. and Mabel Day, ed., *The Siege of Jerusalem*, EETS OS, 188 (London, 1932, repr. 1971)

Kreuzer, J. R., 'The Twelve Profits of Anger', *PMLA*, 53 (1938), 78–85

Krochalis, Jeanne and Edward Peters, ed., *The World of Piers Plowman* (Pennsylvania, 1975)

Kurvinen, Auvo, 'Mercy and Righteousness', *NM*, 73 (1972), 181–91

Latham, R. E., *Revised Medieval Latin Word-List* (London, 1965)

Lawton, David, ed., *Middle English Alliterative Poetry and Its Literary Background* (Cambridge, 1982)

Legge, M. D., *Anglo-Norman Literature and Its Background* (Oxford, 1963)

Lester, G. A., *Sir John Paston's 'Grete Boke': A Descriptive Catalogue, with an Introduction, of British Library MS Lansdowne 285* (Cambridge, 1984)

Louis, Cameron, ed., *The Commonplace Book of Robert Reynes of Acle, An Edition of Tanner MS 407* (New York and London, 1980)

MacCracken, H. N., ed., *John Lydgate The Minor Poems*, 2 vols, EETS ES, 107, OS, 192 (London, 1911, 1934, repr. 1961)

'Lydgatiana: III. *The Three Kings of Cologne*', *Archiv*, 129 (1912), 50–68

'Lydgatiana: V. Fourteen Short Religious Poems', *Archiv*, 131 (1913) 40–63

McIntosh, Angus, 'The Textual Transmission of the Alliterative *Morte Arthure*', in *English and Medieval Studies Presented to J. R. R. Tolkien*, ed. N. Davis and C. L. Wrenn (London, 1962), 231–40

'Scribal Profiles from Middle English Texts', *NM*, 76 (1975), 218–35

McSparran, Frances and P. R. Robinson, introd., *Cambridge University Library MS Ff.2.38* (London, 1979)

Madden, F., ed., *Syr Gawayne; A Collection of Ancient Romance-Poems by Scottish and English Authors*, Bannatyne Club (London, 1839, repr. 1970)

Magoun, F. P., ed., *The Gests of King Alexander of Macedon* (Cambridge, Mass., 1929)

Mehl, Dieter, *The Middle English Romances of the Thirteenth and Fourteenth Centuries* (London, 1968; first published in German, Heidelberg, 1967)

Mills, Maldwyn, ed., *Lybeaus Desconus*, EETS OS, 261 (London, 1969)

Six Middle English Romances, Everyman's Library (London, 1973)

Minnis, Alastair J., 'Late Medieval Discussions of *Compilatio* and the rôle of the *Compilator*', *Beiträge zur Geschichte der deutschen Sprache und Literatur*, 101 (1979), 385–421

Morris, Richard, ed., *The Cursor Mundi*, 7 vols, EETS OS, 57, 59, 62, 66, 68, 99, 101 (London, 1874–93, repr. 1961–66)

Needham, Paul, 'Johann Gutenberg and the Catholicon Press', *The Papers of the Bibliographical Society of America*, 76 (1982), 395–456

New Palaeographical Society, *Facsimiles of Ancient Manuscripts*, ser. II (London, 1913–14)

Offord, M. Y., ed., *The Parlement of the Thre Ages*, EETS OS, 246 (London, 1959, repr. 1967)

Ogden, M. S., ed., *The Liber de Diversis Medicinis*, EETS OS, 207 (London, 1938, revised repr. 1969)

Parkes, M. B., *English Cursive Book Hands 1200–1500* (Oxford, 1969)

'The Influence of the Concepts of *Ordinatio* and *Compilatio* on the Development of the Book', in *Medieval Learning and Literature: Essays Presented to R. W. Hunt*, ed. J. J. G. Alexander and M. T. Gibson (Oxford, 1976), 115–41

'The Impact of Punctuation: Punctuation or Pause and Effect', in *Medieval Eloquence, Studies in the Theory and Practice of Medieval Rhetoric*, ed. James J. Murphy (Berkeley and Los Angeles, 1978), 127–42

and Elizabeth Salter, introd., *Troilus and Criseyde: A Facsimile of Corpus Christi College Cambridge MS 61* (Cambridge, 1978)

Pearsall, Derek, *John Lydgate* (London, 1970)

Old English and Middle English Poetry, The Routledge History of English Poetry, 1 (London, 1977)

ed., *Manuscripts and Readers in Fifteenth-Century England* (Cambridge, 1983)

Pollard, Graham, 'The Company of Stationers before 1557', *The Library*, 4th ser., 18 (1937), 1–38

Renoir, A., 'A Note on the Third Redaction of John Lydgate's "Verses on the Kings of England" ', *Archiv*, 216 (1979), 347–8

Revard, Carter, 'Richard Hurd and MS Harley 2253', *N & Q*, 224 (1979), 199–202

'Three More Holographs in the Hand of the Scribe of MS Harley 2253', *N & Q*, 227 (1982), 62–3

Rickert, Margaret, 'Illumination', in *The Text of the Canterbury Tales*, 1, ed. J. M. Manley and Edith Rickert (Chicago, 1940), 561–605

Robbins, Rossell Hope, 'The Bradshaw Carols', *PMLA*, 81 (1966), 308–10

Robinson, Pamela R., 'A Study of Some Aspects of the Transmission of English Verse Texts in Late Medieval Manuscripts' (Unpublished B.Litt. thesis, Oxford, 1972)

'The "Booklet": A Self-Contained Unit in Composite Manuscripts', *Codicologica*, 3 (1980), 46–69

Ross, D. J. A., 'Methods of Book Production in a XIVth Century French Miscellany', *Scriptorium*, 6 (1952), 63–75

Alexander Historiatus, A Guide to Medieval Illustrated Alexander Literature, Warburg Institute Surveys, 1, ed. E. H. Gombrich *et al.* (London, 1963)

Illustrated Medieval Alexander-Books in Germany and the Netherlands: A Study in Comparative Iconography, Publications of the Modern Humanities Research Association, 3 (Cambridge, 1971)

'A Funny Name for a Horse – Bucephalus in Antiquity and the Middle Ages in Literature and Visual Art', in *Alexander the Great in the Middle Ages*, Mediaevalia Groningana, 1, ed. L. J. Engels *et al.* (Nijmegen, 1978), 302–3

Royal Commission on Historical Manuscripts, Ninth Report (London, 1884)

Sajavaara, K., 'The Relationship of the Vernon and Simeon Manuscripts', *NM*, 68 (1967), 428–39

Salter, Elizabeth, *Nicholas Love's 'Myrrour of the Blessed Lyf of Jesu Christ'*, Analecta Cartusiana, 10 (Salzburg, 1974)

'The Manuscripts of Nicholas Love's *Myrrour of the Blessed Lyf of Jesu Christ* and Related Texts', in *Middle English Prose: Essays on Bibliographical Problems*, ed. A. S. G. Edwards and Derek Pearsall (New York and London, 1981), 115–27

and Derek Pearsall, 'Pictorial Illustration of Late Medieval Poetic Texts: The Role of the Frontispiece or Prefatory Picture', in *Medieval Iconography and Narrative, Proceedings of the Fourth International Symposium organized by the Centre for the Study of Vernacular Literature in the Middle Ages*, ed. F. G. Andersen *et al.* (Odense, 1980), 100–23

Sargent, Michael, 'The McGill University Fragment of the "Southern Assumption"', *Medieval Studies*, 36 (1974), 186–98

Scott, Kathleen L., 'A Mid-Fifteenth Century English Illuminating Shop and Its Customers', *Journal of the Warburg and Courtauld Institutes*, 31 (1968), 170–96

Serjeantson, M., 'The Index of the Vernon Manuscript', *Modern Language Review*, 32 (1937), 222–61

Skeat, W. W., ed., *Alexander and Dindimus*, EETS ES, 31 (London, 1878, repr. 1973)

Smyser, H. M., 'Studies in the English Charlemagne Romances' (Unpublished Ph.D. thesis, Harvard, 1931)

Spector, Stephen, 'Symmetry in Watermark Sequences', *SB*, 31 (1978), 162–78

Stanley, E. G., Review of *The Thornton Manuscript*, introd., D. S. Brewer and A. E. B. Owen, and *The Findern Manuscript*, introd., R. Beadle and A. E. B. Owen, in *N & Q*, 223 (1978), 165–8

Stern, Karen, 'The London "Thornton" Miscellany', *Scriptorium*, 30 (1976), 26–37, 201–218

Stevenson, Allan, 'New Uses of Watermarks as Bibliographical Evidence', *SB*, 1 (1948–49), 149–82

'Watermarks are Twins', *SB*, 4 (1951–52), 57–91

'Chain Indentations in Paper as Evidence', *SB*, 6 (1954), 181–95

Observations on Paper as Evidence, University of Kansas Publications, Library Ser., 11 (Lawrence, Kansas, 1961)

'Paper as Bibliographical Evidence', *The Library*, 5th ser. (1962), 191–212

The Problem of the Missale Speciale (London, 1967)

Stones, M. Alison, 'Secular Manuscript Illumination in France', in *Medieval Manuscripts and Textual Criticism*, ed. Christopher Kleinhenz (Chapel Hill, NC, 1976), 83–102

Tanselle, G. Thomas, 'The Bibliographical Description of Paper', *SB*, 24 (1971), 27–67

Thompson, John J., 'Textual Lacunae and the Importance of Manuscript evidence: Robert Thornton's Copy of *The Liber de Diversis Medicinis*', *TCBS*, 8 (1982), 270–75

Turville-Petre, Thorlac, *The Alliterative Revival* (Cambridge, 1977)

Vaughan, M. F., 'Consecutive Alliteration, Strophic Patterns, and the Composition of the Alliterative *Morte Arthure*', *Modern Philology*, 77 (1979), 1–9

Watson, Andrew G., *The Manuscripts of Henry Savile of Banke* (London, 1969)

Westlake, J. S., ed., *The Prose Life of Alexander*, EETS OS, 143 (London, 1913, repr. 1971)

White, Helen C., 'Some Continuing Traditions in English Devotional Literature', *PMLA*, 57 (1942), 966–80

Woolf, Rosemary, *The English Religious Lyric in the Middle Ages* (Oxford, 1968)

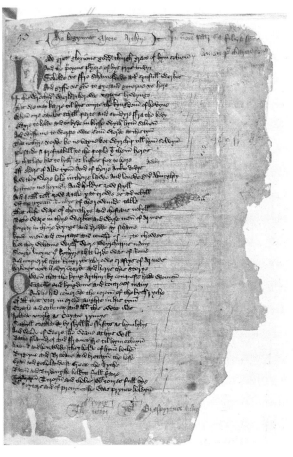

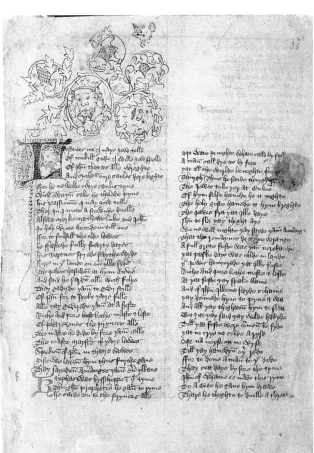

Frontispiece. Lincoln Manuscript, f. 53ʳ (above); London manuscript,
ff. 32ᵛ–33ʳ (below)

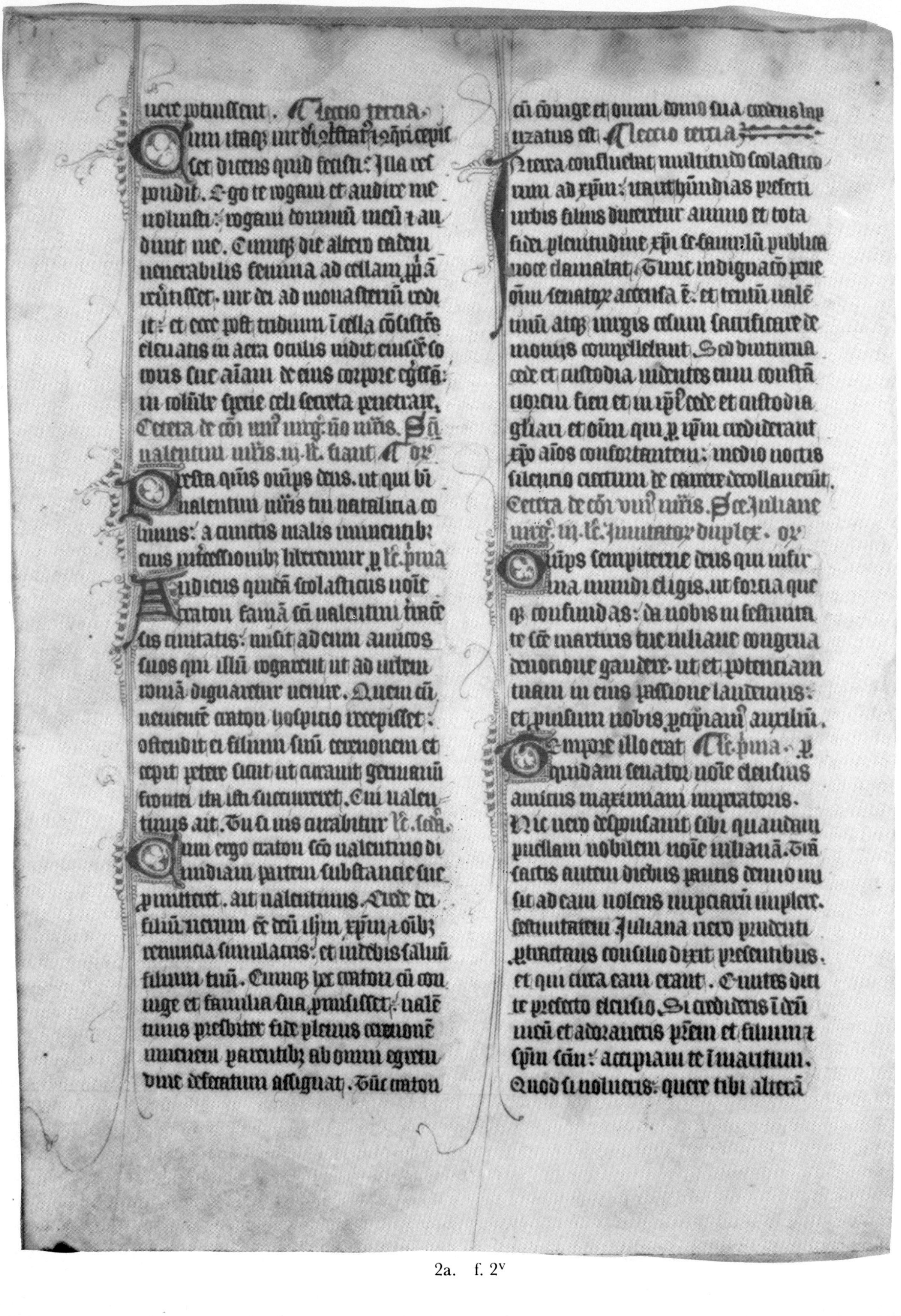
uenire potuissent. Leccio tercia.
Cum itaque uir dei conquereretur cepit
ei dicens quid fecisti: Illa res-
pondit. Ego te rogaui et audire me
noluisti: rogaui dominum meum et au-
diuit me. Cumque die altero eadem
uenerabilis femina ad cellam propriam
recessisset. uir dei ad monasterium redi-
it: et ecce post triduum in cella consistens
eleuatis in aera oculis uidit eiusdem so-
roris sue animam de eius corpore egressam:
in columbe specie celi secreta penetrare.
Cetera de communi unius uirginis non martiris. Sancti
ualentini martiris. iii. lecciones fiant. Oracio.
Presta quesumus omnipotens deus. ut qui beati
ualentini martiris tui natalicia co-
limus: a cunctis malis imminentibus
eius intercessionibus liberemur. Per. Leccio prima.
Audiens quidam scolasticus nomine
craton famam sancti ualentini interamne-
sis ciuitatis: misit ad eum amicos
suos qui illum rogarent ut ad urbem
romam dignaretur uenire. Quem cum
uenientem craton hospicio recepisset:
ostendit ei filium suum cheremonem et
cepit petere sicut ut curauit germanum
frontoni ita isti succurreret. Cui ualentinus ait. Tu si uis curabitur. Leccio secunda.
Cum ergo craton sancto ualentino di-
midiam partem substancie sue
promitteret. ait ualentinus. Crede dei
filium uerum esse deum ihesum christum et omnibus
renuncia simulacris: et uidebis saluum
filium tuum. Cumque hec craton cum coniuge et familia sua promisisset: ualentinus presbiter fide plenus cheremonem
iuuenem parentibus ab omni egritu-
dine desanatum assignat. Tunc craton
cum coniuge et omni domo sua credens bap-
tizatus est. Leccio tercia.
Interea confluebat multitudo scolastico-
rum ad christum: inter quos abundias prefecti
urbis filius diuertitur animo et tota
fidei plenitudine christi se famulum publica
uoce clamabat. Tunc indignacio pene
omnium senatorum accensa est: et tentum ualen-
tinum atque uirgis cesum sacrificare de-
monibus compellebant. Sed diutina
cede et custodia uidentes eum constan-
ciorem fieri et in ipsa cede et custodia
gloriari et omnes qui per ipsum crediderant
christo animos confortantem: medio noctis
silencio eductum de carcere decollauerunt.
Cetera de communi unius martiris. Sancte Iuliane
uirginis. iii. lecciones. Inuitatorium duplex. Oracio.
Omnipotens sempiterne deus qui infir-
ma mundi eligis. ut fortia que-
que confundas: da nobis in festiuita-
te sancte martiris tue iuliane congrua
deuocione gaudere. ut et potenciam
tuam in eius passione laudemus:
et prouisum nobis percipiamus auxilium.
Tempore illo erat. Leccio prima. Per.
quidam senator nomine eleusius
amicus maximiani imperatoris.
Hic uero desponsauit sibi quandam
puellam nobilem nomine iulianam. Trans-
actis autem diebus paucis desiderio in-
sit ad eam nolens nupciarum implere
solempnitatem. Iuliana uero prudenti
pertractans consilio dixit presentibus
et qui circa eam erant. Euntes dici-
te prefecto eleusio. Si credideris in deum
meum et adoraueris patrem et filium et
spiritum sanctum: accipiam te in maritum.
Quod si nolueris: quere tibi alteram

2a. f. 2v

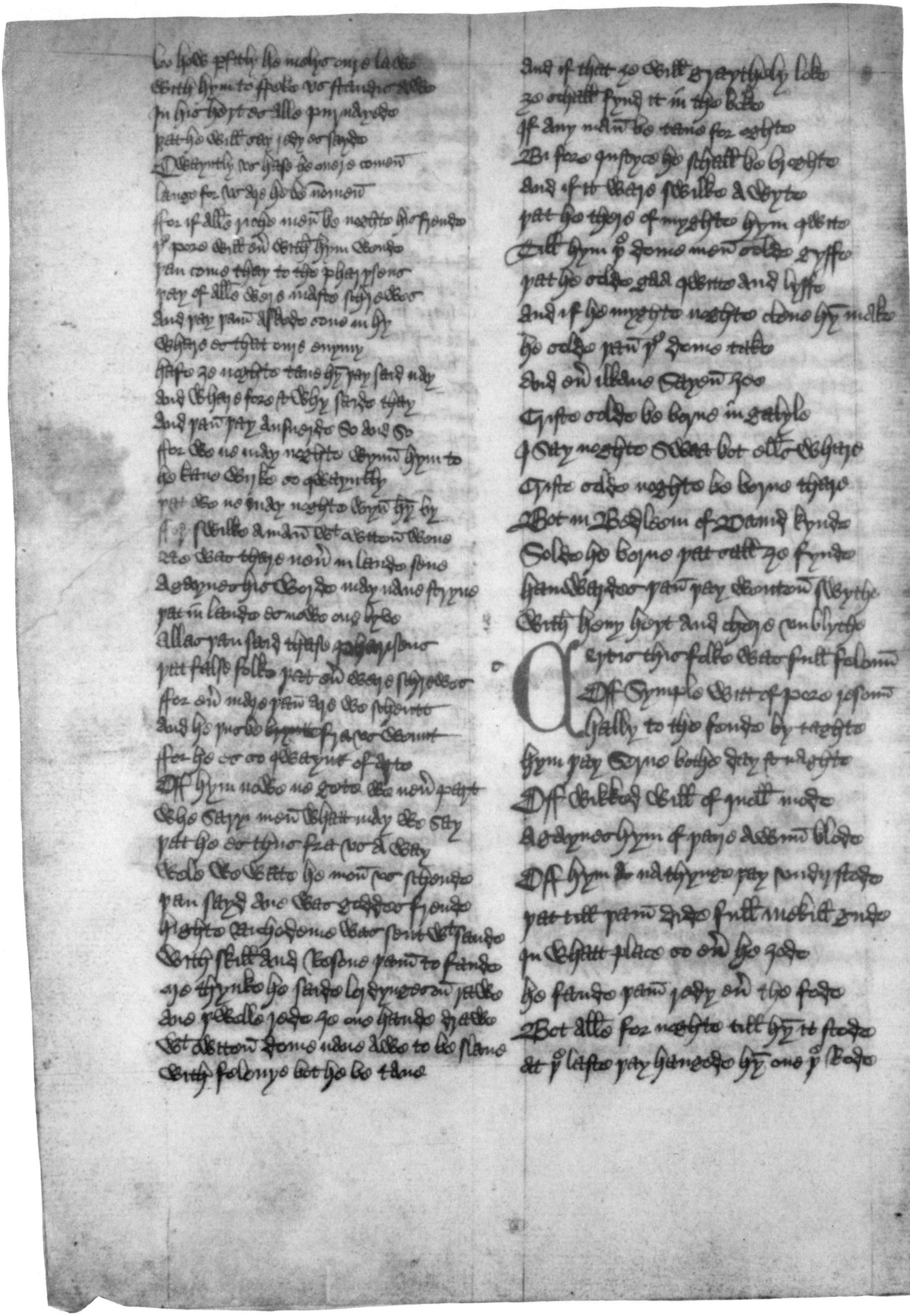

4a. f. 31^v

he hyghte adame that was for lorne
the tod child hyght abelle
that god almyghty lufed wele
theye faody odayned a wyse
that thay colde make otg afyre
the tende dele of alle a thynge
thay colde it to an hill hynge
a daye fell apon hande
ytt thay colde make yay offer ande
thay went on to ane heghe hill
alle theyr teynde yay hyghte to till
and alle yay fede therym to be brynt
thorow yay faody comandement
that was alle y alle ledes
that ehylom was by olde dedes
abelle teynde was alle onde
for he gaffe therym þat aylde mede
baynes gaffe the wet ensy
hym thoghte it was all fule folye
abelle tende hys onde full enow
they fore y onde went up on to g honow
and bayne it was of enylt will
the onde went dolen to bylde holl
bannede fthde bayne hoy co ensy
apy onde oys dolen a therym dose hyne
than ferde abelle bayne on till
wot fo ift ilt andno gud will
wot oust hys will a hys ded
did theye afty he oysse therym made
than styd baynes abelle on till
than luffed thys and me noghte dele
he tuke the ohebe bone of an asse
abelle dede he by oan to dasse
than hade adame oys de ynode
chow the to hyor the tothy slonghe
a odofull deorde yan stirt adame
alle thys oy olde rome theyode a domen
wot it dete dot hoy t oore
and oull non noghte hy moze
a hundeith tyme t fomty zere

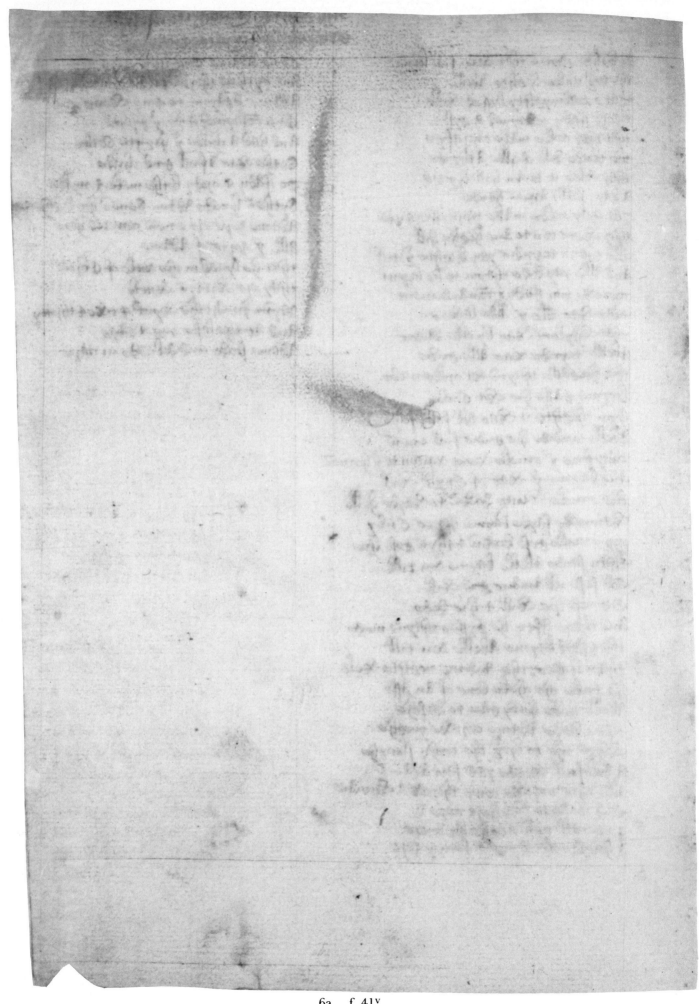

42

Lysteneo me / mayo ȝoꝛe telle
of mekill gude & ᵉville ȝoꝛe spelle
Of hym that coo alle dyȝhte
And ryhtor ony cꝛnꝺe ꝺay & nyȝhte

ffoꝛ he no cwlꝺe wꝺay cꝛnlio tyme
with ᵃll hyn cafe he tholꝺe hyme
hio paffionns ᵃ may ȝoᵈe tolle
Thoꝛ on ᵃ mote a fteꝺenꝺe ꝺwelle
Alſee: ᵃuaꝛ ᵇoꝛyᵃ tholle luke and gohn
In holy Gꝛto ᵈwoꝛꝺo m till ouꝛ
ffoꝛ to fulfill tho olꝺe lawe
he ffafteꝺo fully foꝛty ꝺaybo
hio ᵛaytueo hyꝺe flartha ꝺaybo
hyne m yᵉ lanꝺe on ciꝺyllee frꝺe
Tho ᵍalaeo hafaꝺon at hym enꝺro
And ſaiꝺ he ſeyꝺo alle with folye
Thay gaꝺy ꝺe ꝺaiu to gaꝺy fulle
Of hym foꝛ to fꝛoke yayo fulle
Allo yay gaꝺy ꝺo ꝺaiu at a fefte
Erthe did foꝛo ᵇeſt bothe maſto & lefte
of phaty oꝛonꝺo tho pꝛynceo allo
Tho maſto he ꝺiꝺo by foꝛo yaiu callo
Tho maſto aȝaynſt of yꝺyo laꝺeo
Spekew of hym m thayo ᵍaꝺeo
Lyſo ꝺo latew hym thyo fꝛytho gꝺno
Thay ſtyꝺow ꝺanꝺyꝛoo yaiu olꝺ yllano
mphao ꝺao byſthoppo i yᵉ tyme
Etymo tho pꝛophetio he ꝺaiu to pyne
⸱ʒ⸱ he cꝛꝺo cu to tho pꝛyncao allo

ȝꝛo ꝺefto ȝe noȝhto whato callo by full
a mau call ꝺyo cu by foꝛo
yat all tho ᵉꝺeylꝺo be noȝhto foꝛ
Thyngh Thuo he ſtꝛꝺo thynᵍ ᵉf
Tho galeo tuko yoy dt Enꝺio
Of hym ſelfo hittueꝺo he it noȝhto
Tho holy ᵍoſto haueꝺo it hym bꝛoȝhto
Tho galeo tha yat ᵍllo ꝺayo
hyn to flo yay thoȝht ꝺyo
Lo no eull noȝhto yꝺy ſtyꝺo yꝺiu ameꝺing
that tho ȝomꝺynao ꝺo ᵉoꝛno ꝺeꝛango
A full ȝꝛeto fefto ꝺaw yan noꝛoȝht ꝺo
yat paſke ꝺayo ꝺao callo m lanꝺo
yᵉ galeo honoꝛeꝺo yat ᵍllo fefto
Erthe and goꝛo bothe maſto & lefte
At yat fefto yay ſpako alleme
And of hym ᵍllone ſtyꝺe ochame
yay ꝺomeꝺo hym to pyne ᵃ ꝺea
And all yay thoȝhten hym to ſla
Eot ȝitt yay ſtꝛꝺ yay ꝺalꝺo haꝺyꝺo
Till yat fefto ꝺꝛayo comew to fuꝺo
yat no eyya no oolꝺo ᵃ yꝛfo
Lafe nᵈ noyſo on no ꝺeyfo
Till yay hanꝺyn cyᵉ ȝoꝺo
ffoꝛ to ꝺoue anꝺu to yᵉ ꝺoꝺo
Thay eull ꝺayo by foꝛo tho tynu
hyn of Whamo co mꝺꝺo thio pyme
Ro a ꝺatu he ᵍaue hym ᵍꝛaeo
Thayo he thoȝht⸱ to ꝺwelle ᵃ thyꝛe

ye his body & lay to hele
Pilate styrd of keyre nyghte so
yse ye knewe bode to doo
lay he was ye stollen fra
on all ewaye ys tomen or od
with eyote forse and wt eyot myght
yat he was stollen fra yow to nyght
ys ordll for yowe onest hane
als mekill als ye wellow thane
ffor this word so yay dyn sayne
ffor fryste yay wend to haf bow slayne
that jewes by yane od aythocken
ysy no sole it telle i solde no reden
y him was iesun therse his myghte
was y men come for hy to fyghte
yat many dymed men come full stille
and take his body as ydynes onys will

Nott Ihu cryst onys honour kynge
Off whayne so mad this sayynge
Send vs thy grace & pynynge
To hald it stabilly i onys momynge
As tyne y domyll onys what it be
show us ordll till honow flee
And late ws enys othno west dyghte
As tyne y donest for to fyghte
yat be redy to goys londe
yat on ordll last at dettyn onde
that so y thethe blyss of honour
Amen for his moder comoun
And also y haue hoy do this passioun
Ordll hane & thiss stonde goy to to pdone
Amen Amen x cryst tou
And longyng to god y for gyfe do

Explicit passio dni nri ihu xpi

Hic incipit destruccio ierusalem quam Titus & Vaspasianus
obsedit & distruxit ierusalem et vindicauit morte dni ihu xpi

The sege of Jerusalem
Of Tytus and Vaspasian

n tyberyno tyme that yere Emperyo
By Cesar hym seluyn was orssto in Rome
The while yat pilato was provosto endy y pynce yicho
And also justero of
and hey so ordy
kyng of galile alde de
thesho cesaro ordll o
Hitt thy osho pilati

To dele or chayene appynte for ponyse to ffele
thche gifte a feythyne had bene pleyoute an hynde othe
Bot q̄ ort a mychemento mitte in mynde of that othyo
that ort be hothynge to thytym oz q̄ herthow ffasse
Allo that thayo bodies by oz bayelyno of yaw matto
By a ladeyo pryffe oz q̄ paffe than thilty tho apheto otuldo
be matto in the myddo of the afto a mystoit to oyo
that alto that it that ffayo ceoldo be thaypio to haue
ffoz a gate of pyyto de to yayo ceelke
Thitty godeo matthyone theydow in yepo
So deayo yay bayelanto a bonghto de bele det of lande
and now of that thye come thayo fyeze of thytym aße
tho none yit lonede one thyno ayo ſtholeo a yt lande dwelle
that toyment tyelle oto and so ſtyno commando
gofteyno tho dontill eloy be a goynado ceto te ſtowe
and thayo of thyo matto and mo be matto ffayo buken
and ßulatto pnt ceto to tyofto to pynow foz ord
at ortteyw thayo dengolano and cile dodo tuke
and cehow otilo ceto donyd a done thily tuke vp thilyo tortio
Tputto dep thayo tyelonyo and tyomppooteo tho ſepo
donto fynoduto a deayo and hafe thytyo cotilo feythy do
and yyeno te ſteno thayo yede do onyo lazde Amen Amen Amen

Explicit la sege de Jerusalem

℞ Johnſon ſuteo q̄ ſcripſit ort benedictuo Amen

And to the Emꝑoures dette it tolde
That thei lo make ẜeȝ vppon þā wolde
Thei ẜote lo ȝar þā togety ẜt alle
It is bote yꝑ ẜeȝ of ẜayr tale
Than ẜent ptȳ to many an heþyn kꝓghte
Ptȳ baðe ȳat alle oðe come ȳat myghte
When ptȳ ẜeȝe foñllaðe seꝛoꝛly
Thty ꝑcōnoðe þ ẜołðteo ẜ ẜayr
Sexty knyghtis of þˢ łande
ẜlẜow ẜent hȳm ẜeȝe ꝑẜande
Thty þesẜðe on hȳ a dyaðeme
And make hȳm Emꝑō to hȳm ẜeȝe
Eȳno ꝑesent hȳm ẜth ȝolðe
And cronðe of ꝑayr ȳat ẜeẜ hołðe
The kȳnge of aȳmsoðȳm łande
ẜant þˢ ẜołðtȳo a ꝑeẜande
Sexty aȝeȝoȳs ẜayo of ẜteo
ẜt cheẜeẜte of hio kȳnge ẜome ẜeẜo
Sexty ẜtallecoms ẜayo of ẜhyðte
And ẜexti ẜteðo nolle and ẜeȝyðte
And vppon alle a ẜteðe a knyghte cẜttðe
ẜeth a fakecon aꝑꝓow hio hande
Sexty ẜꝑewehondeo on to þˢ ẜamen
And ẜexti ẜteacheo ȳꝓncðe a ẜamðe
Ho come hȳm ẜelfe ẜt thio ꝓẜande
And byoghte in hio aẜcoȳ hande
Jn cꝓstall a ẜnll ꝓche ẜtone
A ẜaẜꝓo þˢ beẜte ȳat myghte be one
The ẜołðtȳo ẜeo ẜull ẜayno of thio
And kyndoly ȝaẜ hio aẜwȳ byẜẜe
When ho hio ꝑaẜeȳo ẜoñllaðe haðe
A ꝑyẜẜo feẜte þˢ ẜołðtȳ maðe
Jn alle þˢ ẜamoẜðe kꝓghte a ẜþone
þˢ ẜołðtȳo haðe hȳ ẜelfe ȳ ẜono
By ȝaẜ aẜwȳ ho łłȳo aȳyghte
And ẜþiẜ myẜeðe hȳ on to a kꝓyẜt
So mokll lnẜo of ẜoðȝoꝑ
ẜeȝ amaȳoȝ ȳat cȝ̄anðly
þe aẜˢylo naðe ẜ ẜll ȳ tꝯno aðþȳne
ȳat ꝑaẜẜðe on aȝomẜȳyno a ꝑłoȳꝓo

(Cͦ ẜome ȳtt ȝo ẜeẜo ðone
And eȝaðẜwȳ hȳm ȳˢ ẜełðˍano ẜud
By þˢ hoȝhtoȳ ẜay it none
ȳat ẜołðano ẜeẜo to ẜeo
Cͦ ẜwt ẜnth ẜeẜtoȳ ẜeẜe
Theẜe kꝓghtio ȳat ẜeȝo bene
þˢ beẜte Ꝉ oȝtho myghto bene
þˢ ȝeȳꝓeẜte ona meðo
And ẜayeẜte þꝑon ẜelðe
Jn oñ alle ꝑñtay ẜeẜo
And a caꝑꝑe ẜnll of ȝoðo
þˢ beẜte in oȝtho myghte bo
Ꝉ ȳat ẜeẜo ẜeȝḡo thẜ̄e thꝯo
Cͦ ẜake alle Cȳẜteance
ẜt mokll ẜolomꝓteo
Ꝉ ẜexthȳ mañ in ẜeẜo
ꝑayo aẜ̄keȳo ȳaẜðȳẜte
... ɀ̄o heȳthoȳ łeðo
... ghte ẜeðo ẜꝯðo
... mo ẜeðo ho beo)

And when he come in to yat ꝑtede

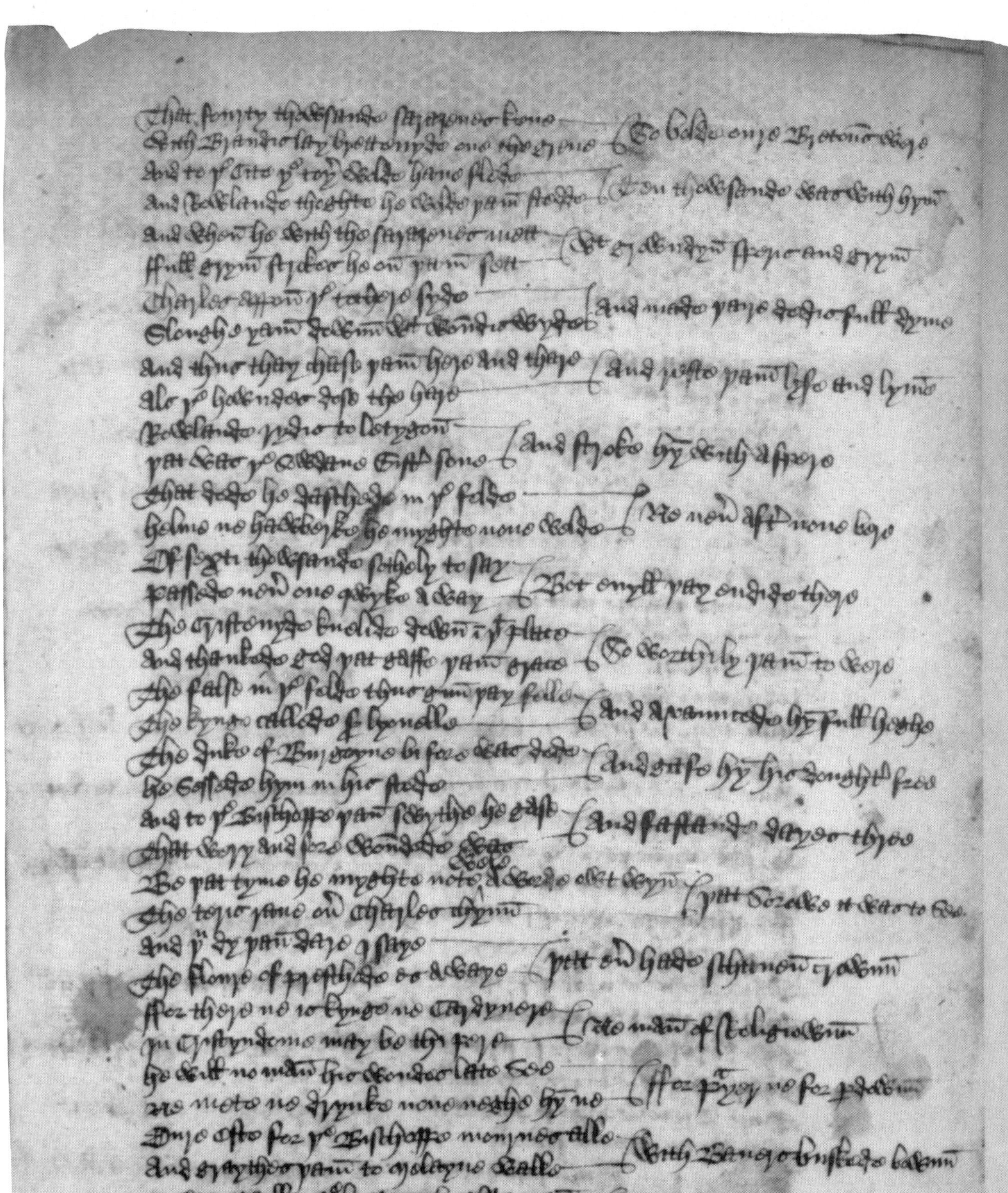

13a. f. 79v

With humble hert & prayer who gettyng
Lord & lady benygnyte and otheres celestialle
to hope & gette þe whiche I thynke deȝerne
And pray for gette to me in specialle
Seho be nott wroth I hy my lady calle
Bewte be þe spouse of gode full of grace
Redy & entendaunt to hir þynge I shalle

Deus flos Deus pulcherrime

O quene of blysse emperesse gardent
I my selfe which hath not bott þis
With albe thi helpe may none instrument
proforfforth dote to ende nocte be gyn
Where fore I þelfe to my tonge & wey þu
Thys instinctly þhyng of thi hyghe bewty
And whilo I lyfe to synge I will not blyn

Deus flos Deus pulcherrime

Tho bright ffldole ȝarnȝade in demus
Salemus fro þi ayente of galaad þependyng
So like most to thyn hore for gme bryghteous
ffllumenoth bryghteȝe ȝtu þ And shynyng
þ sterȝy henow þ tyme þ golde bryning
Bothe atȝtme ȝty thyne hore þ domyne souoȝynte
Of colo ȝhestho so listy ȝanoshȝynge

Deus flos Deus pulcherrime

Blyssed be thyn hore which fro thyn hore thore
Somyo also bryghte in tyssde to dese þ forpartyne
Grapartet wrtto & with his hbent so damo lore
Of þ ȝonely playfere gode do fone & thyn
So hosse thyn hore O lord selp witho domyn
So plestinte & brighte also I bele one thi kne
His synȝero suale dede bembe tt will & fyne

Deus flos Deus pulcherrime

Blyssed be þ fetyre ferahȝde snothe & platyne
Noȝe mynorlouȝly ȝapaynttode ȝonely & white
Thȝe mofthynct colorȝe sothȝ ȝofteȝme
þ eandȝono liloo freshoftee of goloto
þ langynȝe ȝloftene of þ aȝty eaȝyte
for to be solde þulosthes wt sibtolt
þ fetȝe hȝe fyne wtto thȝwo beȝ in deffote

Deus flos Deus pulcherrime

Blissed be þ braines concordande in fere
Noȝt to myche nor to lyte bot in mesure
Not ouer thikke ne nakid priȝs of here
Bot in mene set full temperatare
Silke thridys tlyinde gilted most honourlire
Stery radiant to prece may Absolon bere
In Blisse may passe þ beamynge of nature
O flos florum O flos pulcherrime

Blissed be þ nosse in profile lyne so euyn
In greynes euen thi vostre mesy yne
With onesty be euyn thi ey concordande in fere
With oute waste of ey bot in dry thynge
Humblyke adowne flowede i ostery yne
Pryo balsamyto fragrante in alle plante
Hey trenynge þ nose incense to goddes tonyne
O flos florum O flos pulcherrime

Blissede be thyn cehus of colour cristalline
In prede so thyste of penoschynge flostence
þ stery thonnys ledis frome pyne
Refrenyde yay bene in hoth of temperance
Alesyte vertuouslende in moyll vaylance
Zouȝt langynge yeu passe in vanoste
þ semeth liȝhte þ steyne sufferance
O flos florum O flos pulcherrime

Blissede be þ chekes frosheste of colour
Whyl likonede bene vn to þ lely whyte
þ whylke cssende hath þ rose to pryme
Cuthyn trein perayntede in vostere of dolyte
þ azounto ruby with the neyerpte
With yau in blisse myghte haue no payte
Bewte hath lyste to boke in orche a note
O flos florum O flos pulcherrime

Blisse be thyn cheo polityue fortuutte
þ fryste zette of onys saluacyone
In whome errye do þ prostret doly ette
Of cehyol pryo salutacyone
pry þti forme and thyne humylidcyone
Hand maydyn of goddo cehow þ styde ere
Bedder of the true in aynucyone
O flos florum O flos pulcherrime

Blissed be þ mouthe of cehomo siche birdes come
Thy fragrant lippes of honourlitye
Here hony swete yaw and ester þ hony combe

ye grace gode socour keste of thi body

Swetly to seye y frayede in none soygde

Whi ouff eke ye cryede dere on bestyrly

O flour flour O flour pulcherima

...of honour eke sche thi selfe subynde

...to thi body innocent and trewe

...suffre y falle yesse take and ....blynde

...to sustene and O ye cryste thyn

Whi leto ye tyken thi dedy payne yonde

...hay geste y temple vn to y

...stode hym sende a stylde on the yolle

O flour flour O flour pulcherima

O se angelle of oure ioy cryste

O monly oure kyngesfylde of alle honour

Whoso dede yen ye comforte to yo armonye

O honouly dede a O ye plenustre sonou

...stode helpe destrendt from yous full onou

To yo lady sone in aduey syte

Whi come ye nostyte a sonde wt ledde frenou

O flour flour O flour pulcherima

y owe no moze bot blyssede be al daye

Of cryste y solempne Joyssoryoun

yo .... y bedte onou for ay

And stablide it thy che hecte affonoyone

Wrty angelle of sonoy cryste stnyte

yo stede dedouno on to my mansyone

O flour flour O flour pulcherima

To ferthe and see y dethete do of yeou

...sonoy oure lady serfyofte of yeesse alle

yo cryede deye for to see Salamou

...dedouno honoude and wrty yelle

lat be lat be O soldeny yele nlle

...lady oo flour of fermoste

...down obey to hy ...yse ye shall

O flour flour O flour pulcherima

Of wrty gederyng Salamou yothe wryte

Wrty fonyostere comonbynow folebynen

And wtnusette eke of stonde a in fonyte

wt alle y dethety o of yeou dede and soueu

Wyche dente to see y bodte y conostynew

O my stede lady moste indonyte

O libede a blyste yen sosede nostyte to synye

O flour flour O flour pulcherima

O cryzte lady cyoyo afferede and leyte

O saloyon thi hoste thi payne nyede to thi chylde

yo hostro ....do y cherys fouz lyfe
to styede bro stayn for oure deyke oulde
And alowy ort y flo y non dete folde
wt dete onde y ezamed well to see
thyn hoste bedte a to synze wt yoyt ....
O flour flour O flour pulcherima

Explicit · Amen Amen

Otuell stroke his stede fflorryne
With the spoyre of golde full fyne   A bolyffe he to hym come
May he the stryde be slayne hastyne   Bot here the moste betone
then shall neghte to y townd to dyne
Otuell these the tene y enyd   to chyvallorye hathe hys sort
yat he ne hath loste no he hone   the eyyponde he alle p thent
knyghtis spoghte in all a stonne
token vp this tome and tome   ffull brightly one y ye saye
how yey had chroste one styll on keyst
home yey chonte yt to payge
And chey lloo lovede god of the empyre   of all cedrede he wolofent
And so Otuell yat worthy do
And than yey hade a memory   yat comely dere to see
With alle y noble chevalry
yey nede hys lorde of lombarldy
to have it alle in hire blysh   y comye stays a free
And thorghe goddhoste do a heye
Couslande folake and thymede   A ens yf horyn med dette doe
And thoo yste y knyghte vo here
bryngo vs to thy blessed bere   Amen p charyte

Maylles   Hoye endde y romance
            Of Duke Rollande of Otuell of Spayne

            Explicit Otuell

                Passio Christi Tercius

Hic yncypt quedam tractatus Passionis Domini nostri ihesu christi in Anglico

O... to Iesu thyne Chylde and thy loss
   ffrom payadye place of moste plesture
   Thi to Iesu I hange vppon the crosse
   Crouned with y thorne blonnded with the synnes
   Handes & feete to me jest my endutes
   With sharpe nayles my body nede yeur donne
   When and then fell hyn pendance
   Loke one my blonde... and my passion
   Thynke and yemembr thee apon my blody face

In bathelem in that fox fete⸺ that was borne of mare fre:
for he ys prout

Explicit celu[m] laudatur

mare mag[ister] ad [christum] fo[re] / in nemus deus ayt[] ye nasyd on tre /
deus sont / q[uod] qui qwa may not go / y[e] thyssyd qydeyr tappyd in two
y[e] thyssyd oft

man to reforme theyr gyle and thi losse
ffrome paradyse place of moste gladnes
the to jesus I hange apone thro crosse
Crownyd with the thorne womdede wt tho lance
hande and fete to enclese my grenesse
with scharpe naylde my blode made ryne downe
whan ou thou folte any grytnsance
loke one my womdes thynke one my passyonn

Thynke and remembre apon my blode ffare
the jede the sponge asyxde mengyde with galle
still feld jabixo I man for thi tyssixo
with hatoffull spyttynge y one my wysto dide falle
kyng of jewes in scorne ye dide me calle
Blyndfelde woblyde by fals reprshonn
O man for thi comforte amonge th tnoubled all
loke one my womdes thynke one my passyonn

Thynke one tho wttys that went in suche blen
deu celily whon I deste apo tho cryste
Remembre in floeryo apone tho ptlycrine

A riche tresorne kynges of his councell
rr & zere with streiffe & ryote tyrannille
ho bare his regne hade he no ryste
att ponschin lythe he beryed . his chest

Henricus Secundus

Henry ý secunde sone of ý emperice
Better regnede nexte a full manly knyghte
Also boke olde pleynly dothe expresse
this seyd henry by fredam of wyll & myghte
Sleete seynt Thomas for holy chirche ryghte
zere xxxv he regnede it comethe mynde
At Fount Euerarde he lythe beryed worþ frynde

Ricus Primus

Richerde his sone nexte bi successton
Kynge of þat name stronge hardy & notable
Better regnede kynge callede cuyr de lyon
with treason hede ý regnede at his table
Slayne at Galyarde by deth full lementable
ý stature he regned fully of ys zere
his herte beryed in Roone at the heghe Awtere

Johes Rex

Nexte kyng Richarde regnede his broþ Johñ
ytt after sone Entrede in to fraunce
leste Almayne & Normandy on none
this londe enterdyttede by his mysgouernñce
and att it be putt in remembraunce
xviij zere kyng of this reaume
he lythe at Croxdé dede of poyson

Henricus Tercius

Henry the thyrde his sone of ys zere Age
Etto at Gloucestre regnede a long zere
longe dyyes he hade at his Warde
Holy félittede he hym in almonse dede
r by zere here regned in dede
Beryed at Westmynstre be regede of kyttyng
Dayes of seynt Edwarde a very wyfe a kynge

Edwardus Primus

Tho firste Edwarde let ý stodioñ langs
Etto after regnede ý Etto over ý a knyghte
Wan scotlande inwardy ý Scottis stronge
And alle Weldo in despite of all þ yer my ghte

Be neythir hastty nor sodenly vengeable
To þore folkes doo no violence
Jnjurye of langage of seyyng worshipable
And sodeyn motion not engely at thi table
Jn hauyng gentill & prudent in substance
Chaste of tong of wordes not dissoynable
To sytt the beste set & sytte thi plesaunce
Haue in dyspite tho merthes þat bene donble

Suffre at thyn table no detraccyone
Haue dyspite of folkes þat bene nyoble
Of false sclaundering and adulttryow
With yn thyn howse suffre no dokyssion
Broke in thyn housholde shall cawse grete in grosse
Off alle þolo sayse dyspite and foyson
With thy nought done to luste in joste & rose
Be clenly clope after thyn astate
Passe neythir bolender bezo thi pennye blyne
Sayth thyse folkes be nought at dabate
Hyspite set thi botty be obesye for to styne
Losyne thy seluike no quasott to contryme
With thi sugott to sty no trbozo grete stthyme
Where fes I confett amysoke allo thi lyfe
To lyfe in proso and grete tho a gud name
Hyse at tho moms and to loryde bezo at onem
A sodyne mysteir and blake dyozo of peßylence
Be tymly at grosse y shtill tho botty chone
Hyste at tho pylynge to do to god sonescute
Cresott y grore with cartiere daliience
And allo noey haue conpißyonne
And ted othill songe syted & influence
tho to enegesse and thi poßeßyonn
Suffre no enfottie in thi howse at nyghte
Be bayse of tozosonpozo a of grete grosse
Of nodyyng hoßse and of candill lyghte
Of slaκho one moynyngo & slouegynge ydilnesse
Broke of alle enco to chese peztegesse
Bayse allo dronkenhede lyejo & lechogye
Off alle vn thryfty grete tho manstze
yit co to then dyso playoye and hatfoly doyes
After note be arno make nought to longe tlago
Bolo feote and womale psoyne ay fromo thi colde
Be nothte to grenffse if thoghte take no keye

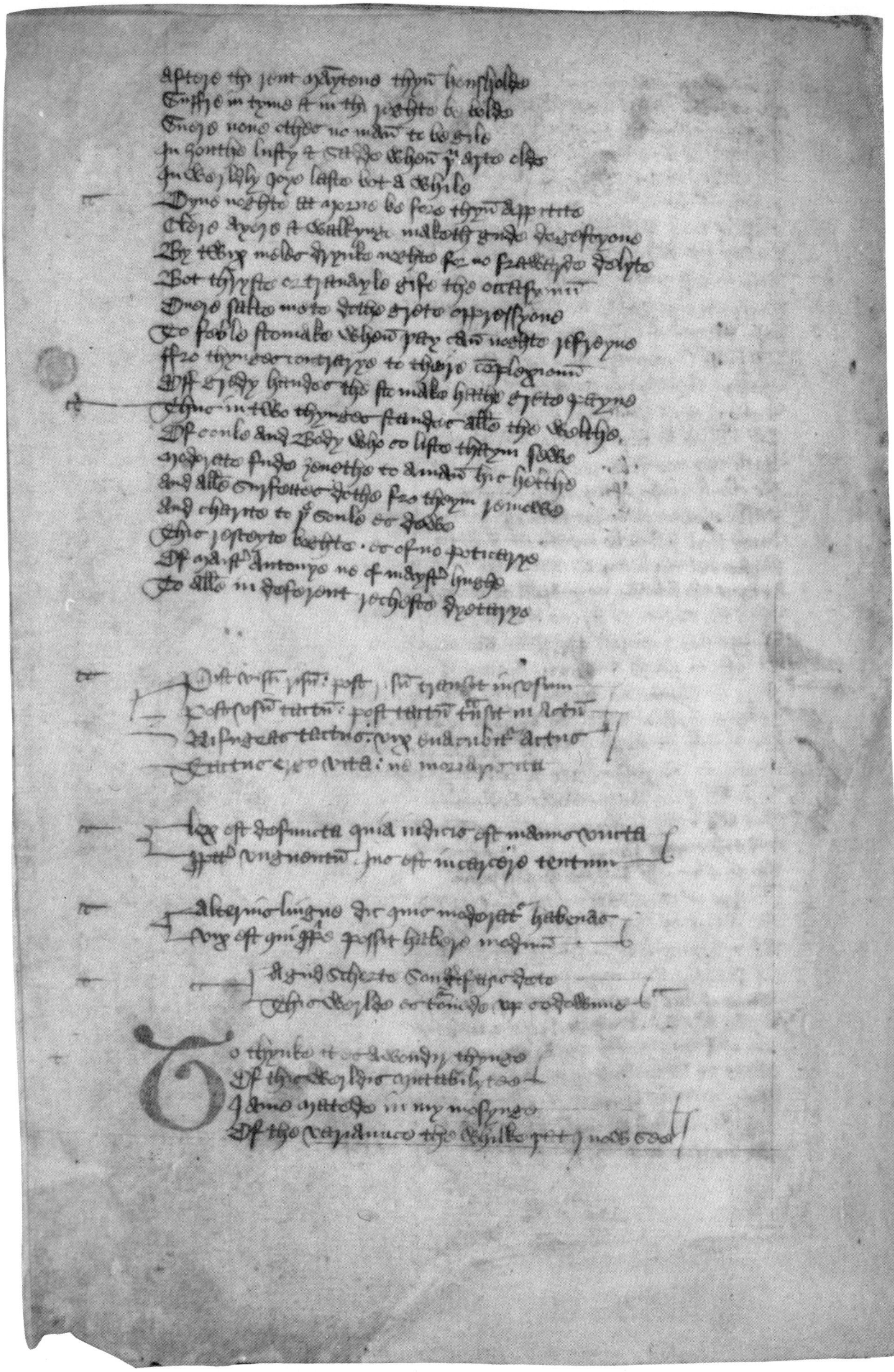

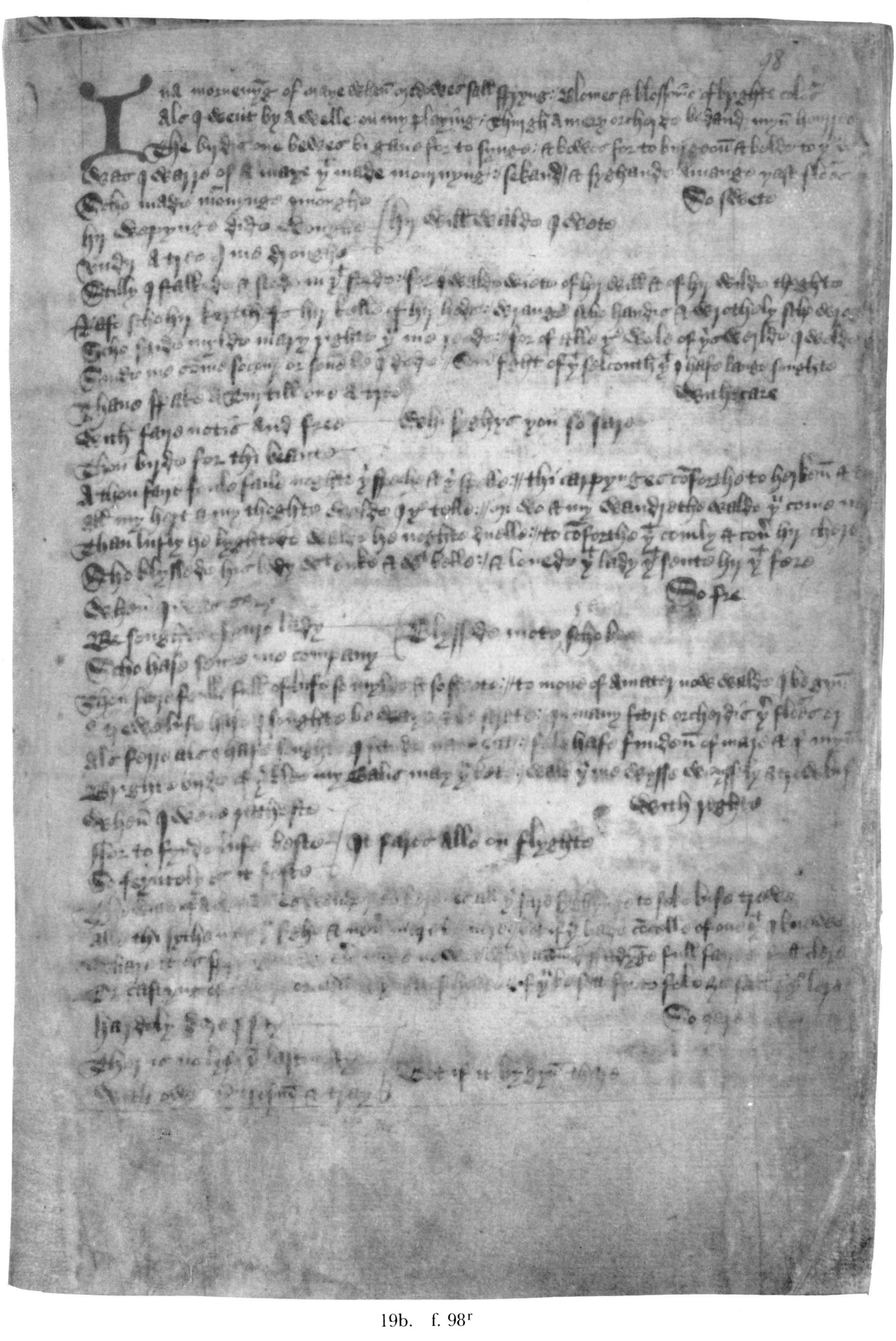

19b. f. 98r

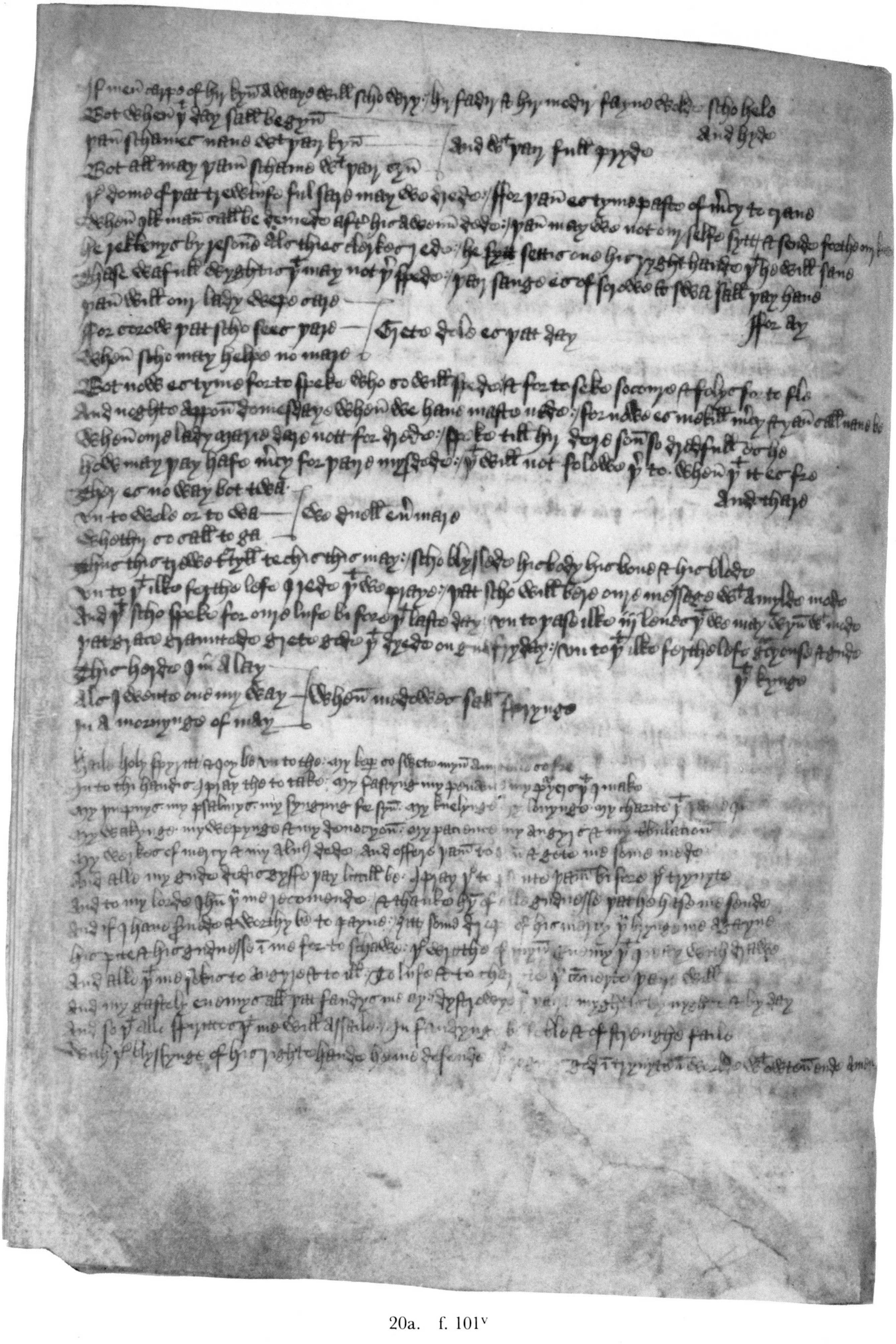

20a. f. 101v

Miserere mei deus secundum magnam misericordiam tuam

MLord you haue mercy of me after thi mercy mekill of myghne

Lord you haue mercy on me and geue my thoghte & penance playne

Lord you haue mercy on me that suffred for my syn deth slayne

Lord you haue mercy on me that chaunge es giue you gete agayne

Agayne you gete me to þi ese and gones no ud in gude þey be

So þat I thirkly take þi grace god you haue mercy on me

Et secundum multitudinem miseracionum tuarum dele iniquitate meam

And thurgh thi mercy mekill to mell whase myghte no man here myster may

And also you arte of my sheslys I dsall my sekkkle soper you clenshe aday

Gan you suffrede þi selfe to sell vo fer to stare þe sothe to say

you halde thi hand keyke ouere of helle ds helpe to gouon while hele today

thy coy blysse þinou satt blyn to pam þt þsatt balde and bee

thi iuge you to þat welthe may keyn þan you haue mercy on me

Amplius lama me ab iniquitate mea & a peccatto meo munda me

Washe me lorde if þi sett degy oiser es þat wykio ilk deallly vesyghte

Gou you git named suppost me e dealle of mercy and mekill of myghte

And clense me lede þat gbo dege of synno þt gbo saldo in þi sysghte

And sewe me hert while I am here þte by chip alc glhane gisghte

shoure hane gvet hert & will souerayne to syne the

that I my fersekkyd myghte sulfull þan þi haue mercy on me

Quia iniquitate meam ego cognosco & peccatum meum contra est semper

full deale I knalle my selfe certayne þt wykll do deyker þ I hafe degsyghte

And hell sye symes my synto hafe slayne I sere to slauyng hafe I senghte

my synde ays ud me doyne bot thy su I thynke in thoghte

Yasy mercy es mekse of myjyne you my syn þat mds de moghte

yesyste none en mede man do þt nyee þi þ ue qt mde of mercy fse

And syyw I thaysthy thalle a mere þan þi haue mercy on me

Tibi soli peccaui & malu cora te seci vt iustificeris þ monibz & vicerou induly is

On to þlorde bathe lorde & still ofte haue I synd & sothe it do

Be fore þ Iesu haue I done ill es dome I may my dede grantte chase

Bo þ þorgeo lede at thi will you may dealte alle my eyeklkynesse

Be foe þ þ I tyme sulfell to make endynge of mide & lesse

Lesse & mde I mde to mene þt mde hede dege nede to be

After pyyo de poles deyyg be den þan þi haue mercy on me

EEcce enim in iniquitatib

The kynde of mde to ill gy you oe endeyten & eayer tene

ful well þuste cospeyone a yng inde milke þyde deur sene

yn mdy cosy dee me my f mde hafe me syd de sothe es sene

On to cyste I ctys & syp It on fozthys me & make me clene

store you make me to haue mede in heuen before thi face oo ffye

Crthou mercy co may þ than my mysse to : þen you htue mercy on me

Que ayne lorde oothe it co : Als othe soo thi lake oo on here seye
you knowe hisee noghte a noghte deseue : you forther faythe to folke in feye
keper of þ noghte bathe maye a lesse : þt þ certe co noghte to þge
And to come men þ go progsso : on to me you hast made þam cloo
cloo of þ maker me fee to ben : the commandemento in ilke contyo
And so yow I am megkede amonge the men : þen þ hase mercy on me

Styentull me lorde berth þ stynde : And make me clene my kynde to kulde
bot þsse sall be departte thi cearde : yat we sall be to loue thi litte
lorde þ sall deaithe me bot thi hande : þan sall I be whit þen þ sall be
yat co noghte ello I vnderstande : bot my mysse þ you may beyth þ alle
beyth þ alle þ deseo þ dose me dose : And put þam bodene bot thi ponte
And yat I forellen do þam forlede : þen you haue mercy on me

to my herynge myn eye let qu : lorde seye o solase ouill you sende
berth þy a blysse þat now sall blywe : And laste in helthe to weten ende
to loue god sall yow baner by gyn : þ on þe molde for mebe the bende
And my this make bathe mage it myn : vn to mylde þ stille may mende
mende you may one myo let mayne : And stille one o stynde by stande it oo
Sen ezendure ezeke oo we end a deyne : þen þ haue mercy on me

lorde you terme þ face fra my own in haste : when my mysse þo makes vs to thkyne
And lete þ thige fra me be caste : oo yat you se noghte on my sty
Bot eyante me of þ halyg oo oo : þj aco come grauer to by gymne
And oo my styrke oo styke oo þ deaste : And weysse me sone deailye to thkyne
kyn me lorde fra dea a deay : in entelde it oothe to deonne berth the
efene oo medyne mende me may : Bot god þ haue mercy on me

Sed put my bete co alithy beste : And yon to blyo fra bailes me beghte
A clene herte in my oeste you beste : of oeythe nebbe þ aye deoo noghte
A noghte soy itt let in me to yste : lorde in my body you late be thi oeste
oee yat þ oeyke by este a deeste : no bayke bot yat þ welde dea o deeghte
deeghte þ has this beylde oo oeyte : oo deate þ of thi oeeke aye dee
And this to thoste in ilke a tyste : þen þ has mercy on me

Alat me noghte lorde fra thi face : ult if þ falle ... ...

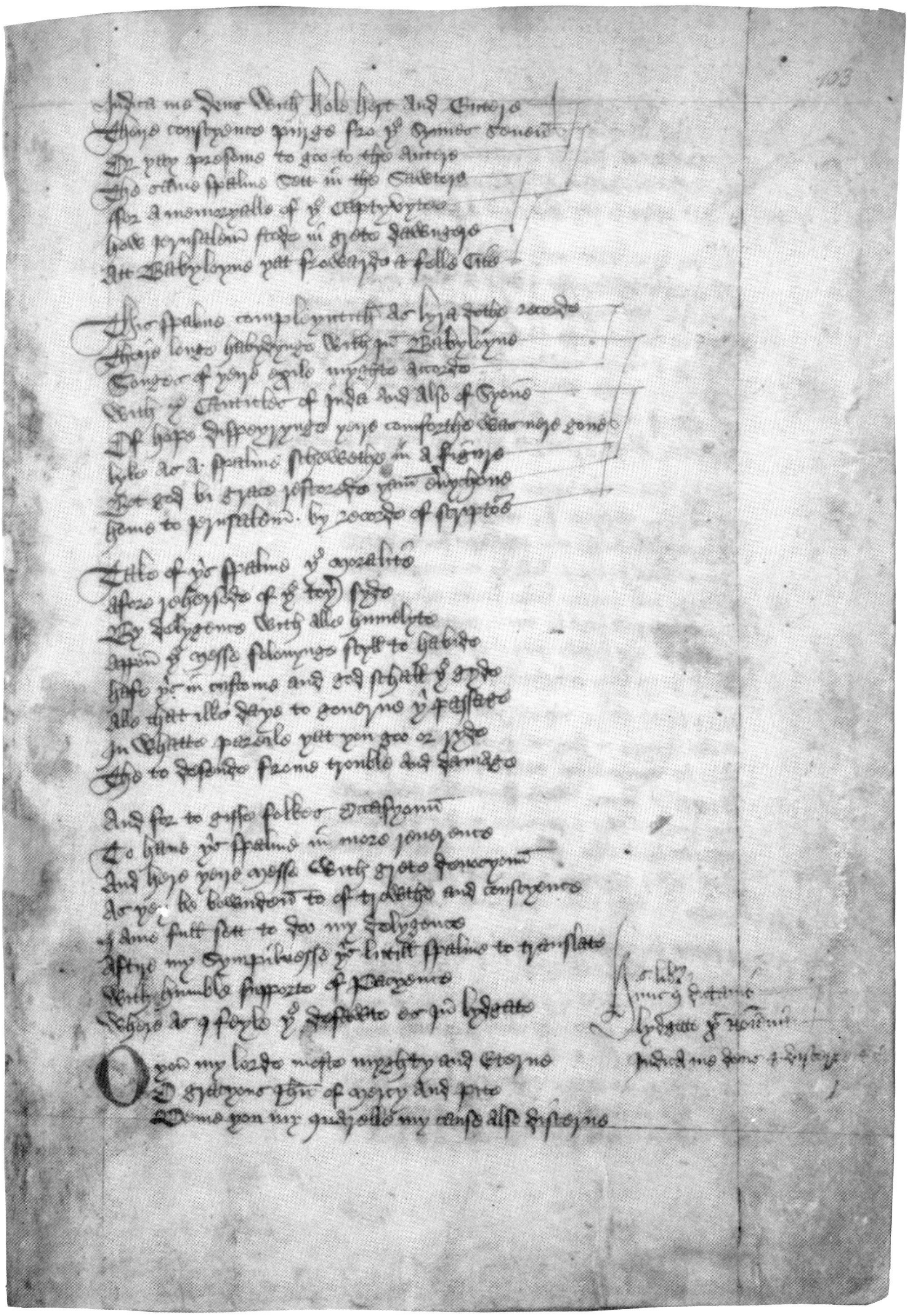

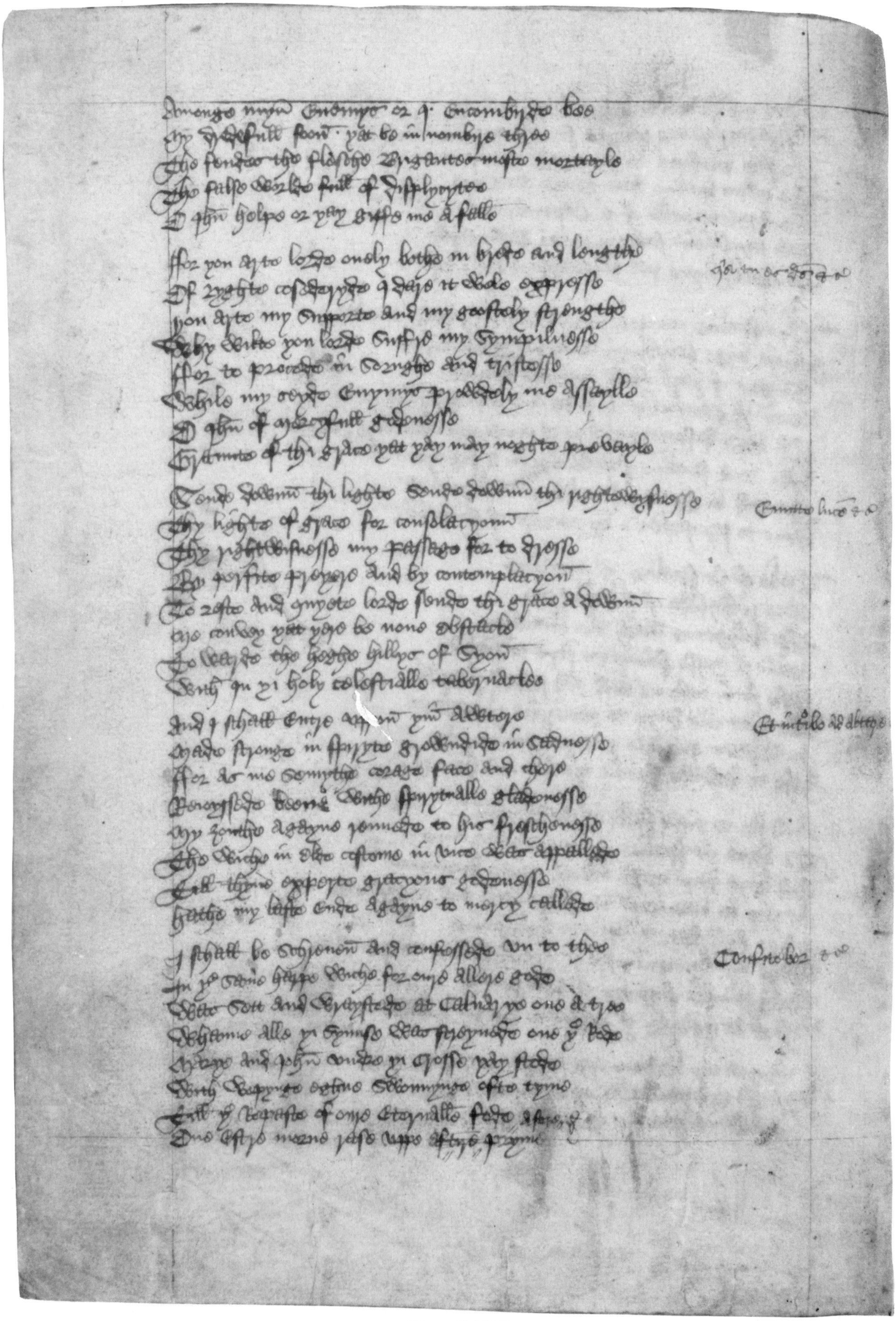

22a. f. 103ᵛ

O þou my saule whi arys þou heuy bee — *Quare tristis es &c*
Sythen criste hathe boughte þe with his passyoun
What cause haste þou for to troubled bee
Thi lorde was slayne for thi redempcyoun
Truste in god and bee welle righte certayne — *Spera in deo &c*
Voyde of dispeyre or ambiguytees
For þou to hym I schalle be schryuen agayne
My gostely gone agayne alle aduersytees
Þe helthe of my chere is my felicytees
Which he my sauyour is allas whome schulde I drede
Agayne worldely perylles and infernalle powstees
He spared noghte his blode for me to blede

Moralisacio Sacerdotis vestimentorum apparatus in missa &c

Vpon his hede an amyte firste he leythe
Which is a sygne a token and a figure
Outwardly a schewynge grounded in faythe
The longe albe by cours of scripture
Rightwysnesse perpetually to endure
Þe longe gyrdille clennesse and chastytee
Bowende of þe arme þe ffanon dothe assure
Alle sobyrnesse knyttes with humylitee
The stole alsoo strechynge ferre in lengthe
Is of doctours þe angelike doctryne
Agaynes of heretikes to stande in his strengthe
Fro cristes lawes now to declyne
The chesiple abouthe with charyte to schyne
Brighte as phebus in his myddaye spere
Holdes one his cours in the righte lyne
To frende and foo strechyng with his bemys clere
A worthi preste made stronge with armure
Afore the awter as cristes champyoun
Schalle stonde vp righte and make a discomfitures
Alle oure thre enemys conquere and here dominioun
Þe flesche · þe worlde · Sathanas þe felle dragoune
Firste to bygynne or he ferther passe
With contricte herte and his confessyoune

22b. f. 104r

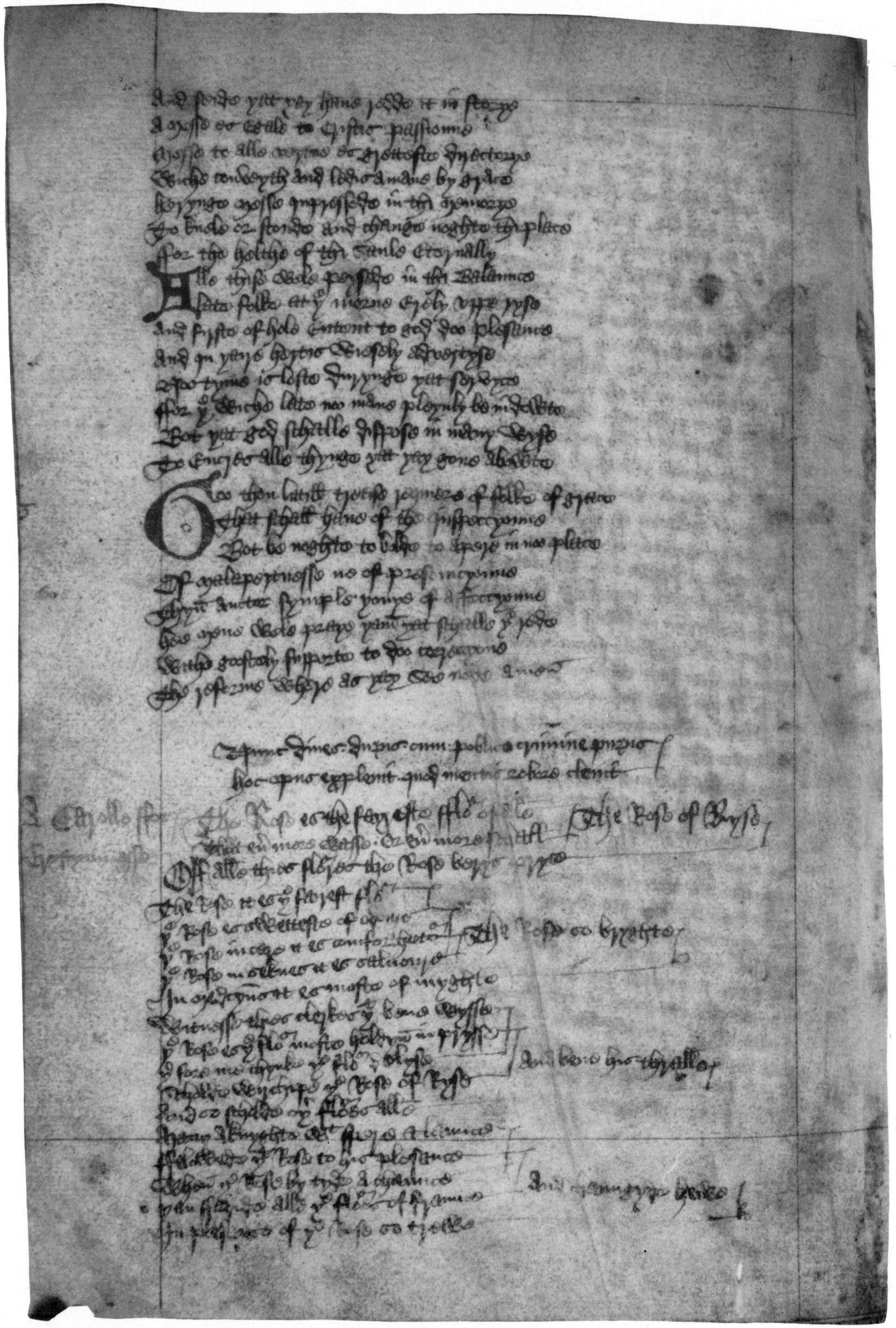

23a. f. 110v

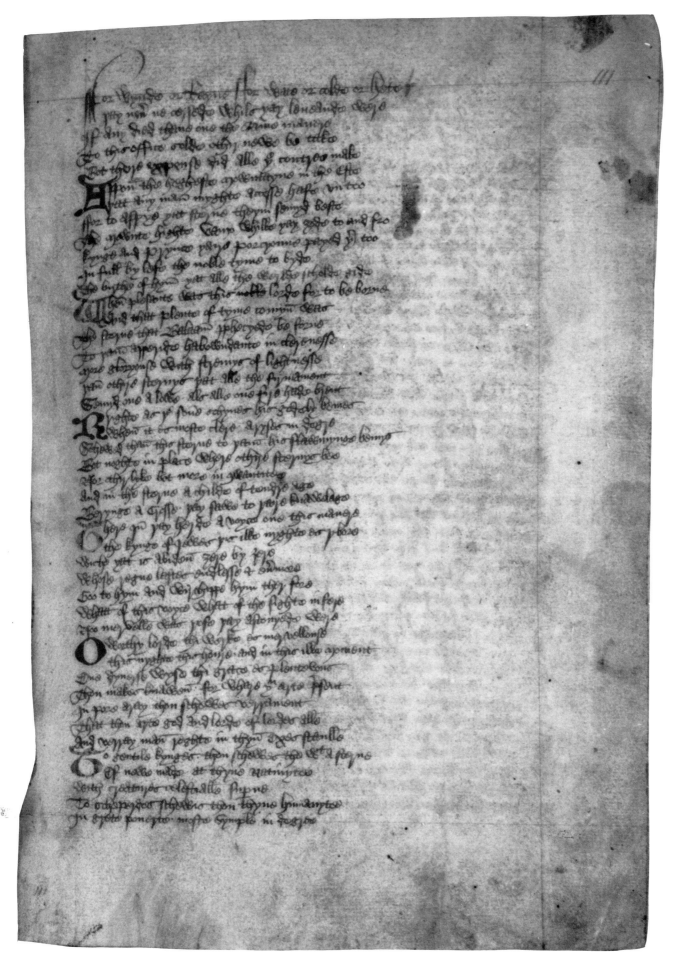

24a.   f. 119ᵛ

Hic incipit tractatus cuiusdam Sapientis

Here by gynnyth a litill tretis of Wysdome

Waste maketh a kyngdome in nede
And nede maketh a man to trauayle
ye more trauayle ye more nede
for whi if it be done by euyll conseyle
The man yat trauaylleth ofte in fere
moche thynge may loyyne yat will auayle
Amonge gud men this lyfe is lere
The shall no man helpe the assayle
The man yat lyffeth in Waste to spende
And hauntes wikked company
ffrom this contrey if soo he shall his nede defende
thasse the kyng his tyme and cely
It shull the kyng a tonge y accorde
And her y whoso stonde faste they by
Wikkednesse comes on us sonde
No man ken telle y enoyseon why
he yat loues Witt and wisdome by Witt
And andmade preyone men in store
unknowthly he kens no skyll
ffor nedeles myche wolde hase more
Wit in and out Wayes now Witt
a thynges y Wayes may andaw so lere
In man counthe both sonere yere suffre ill
than Witt a gode ofte to the nede by fere
Whatt kyngdome or oo Wayes yet on oo
the comone distroye y glonghe wokkayne
then Wikkenny y soroille woo
And soyyes ofte or lirlesse men be slityne
fraghe Wastede Wit Wayes and Woo
yat maketh a kyngdome yare dedyne
And When yat aysthete liddio tyme hoo
then now Wolke knewe yatyo oft full slityne
Who now man in this kyngdome oo Wyse
Alonett to shyppe Witty they don of yesene

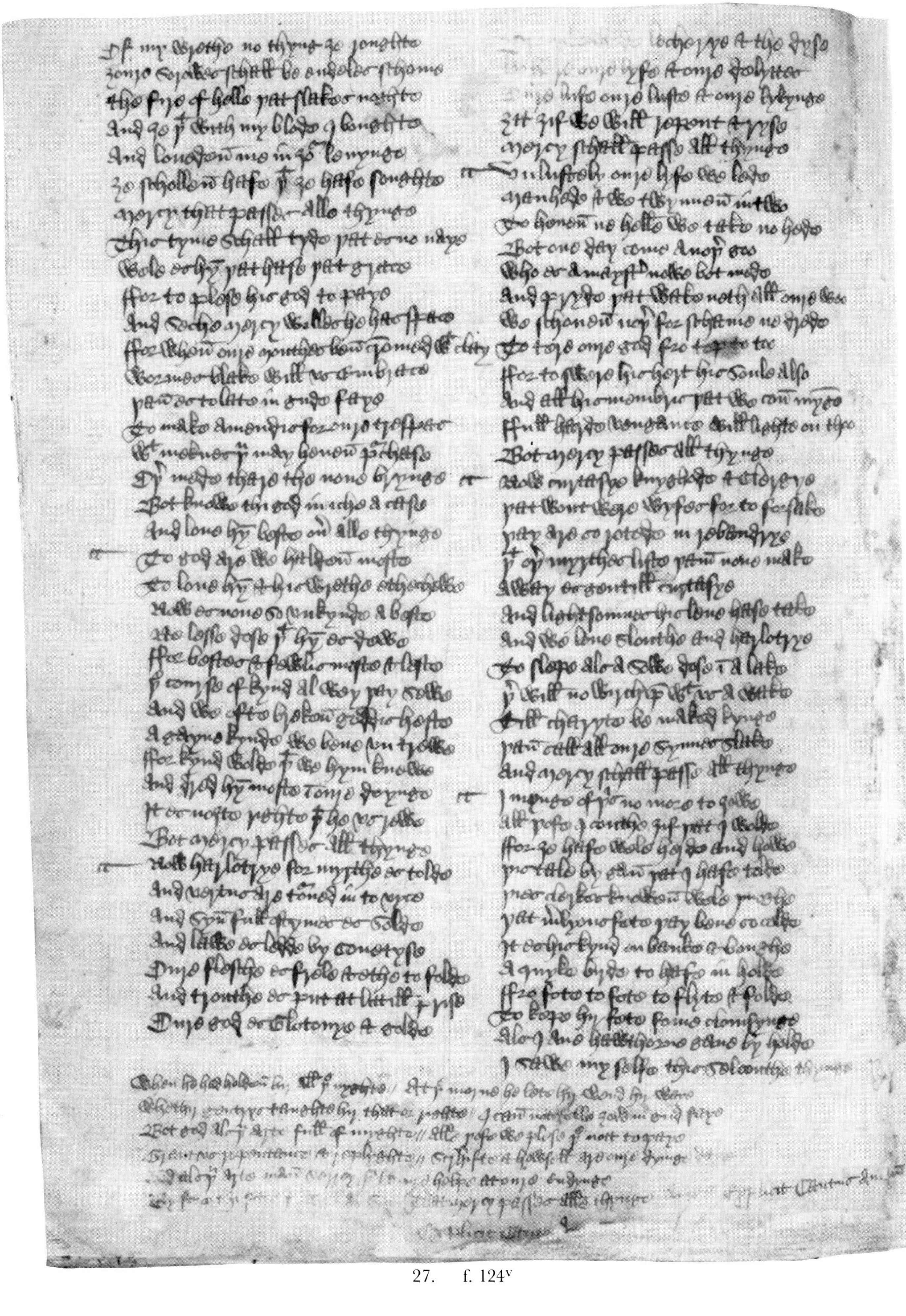

27. f. 124v

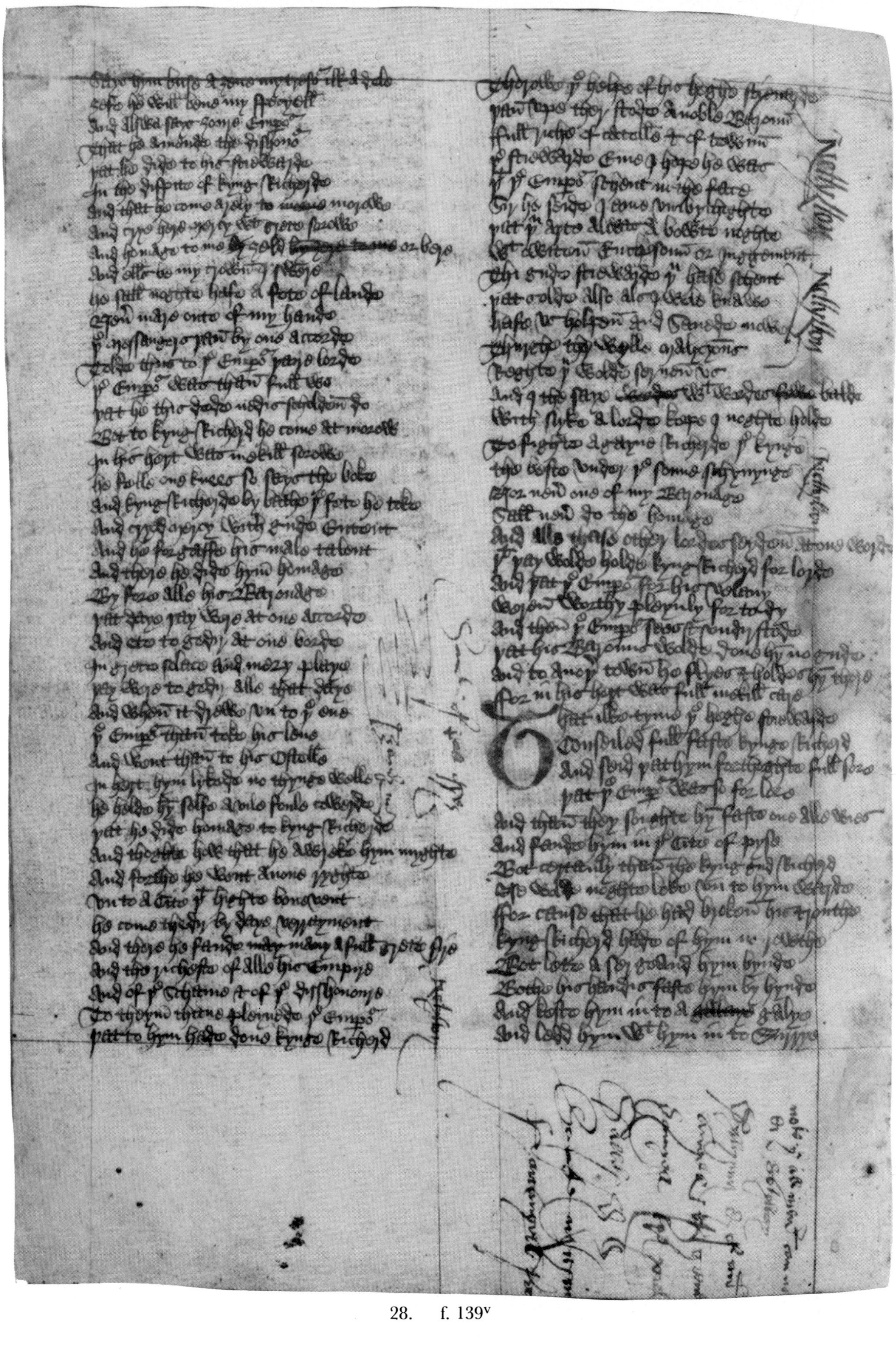

28. f. 139^{v}

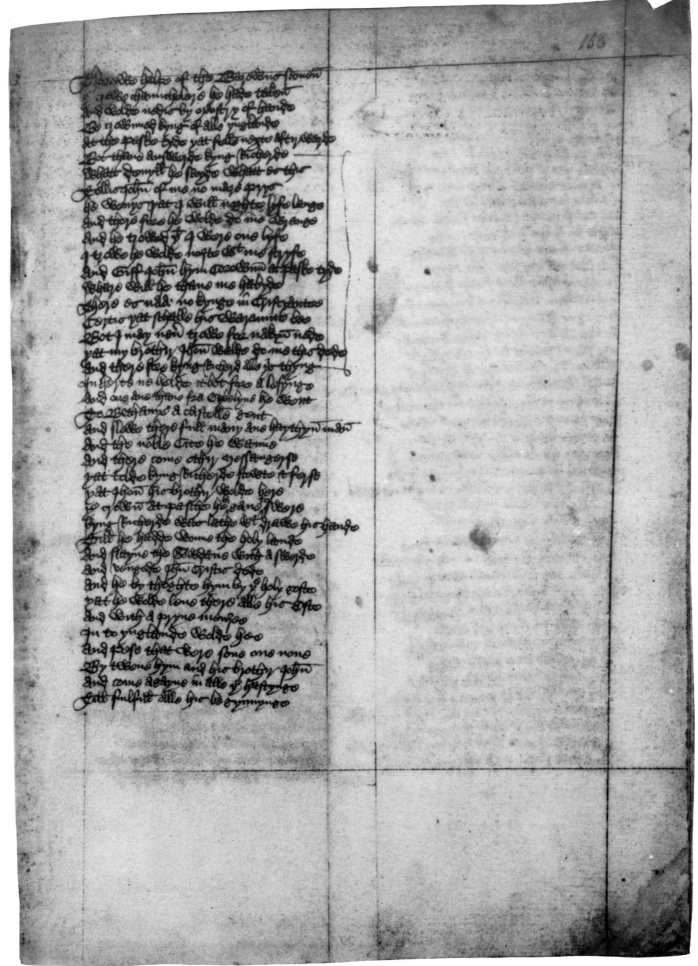

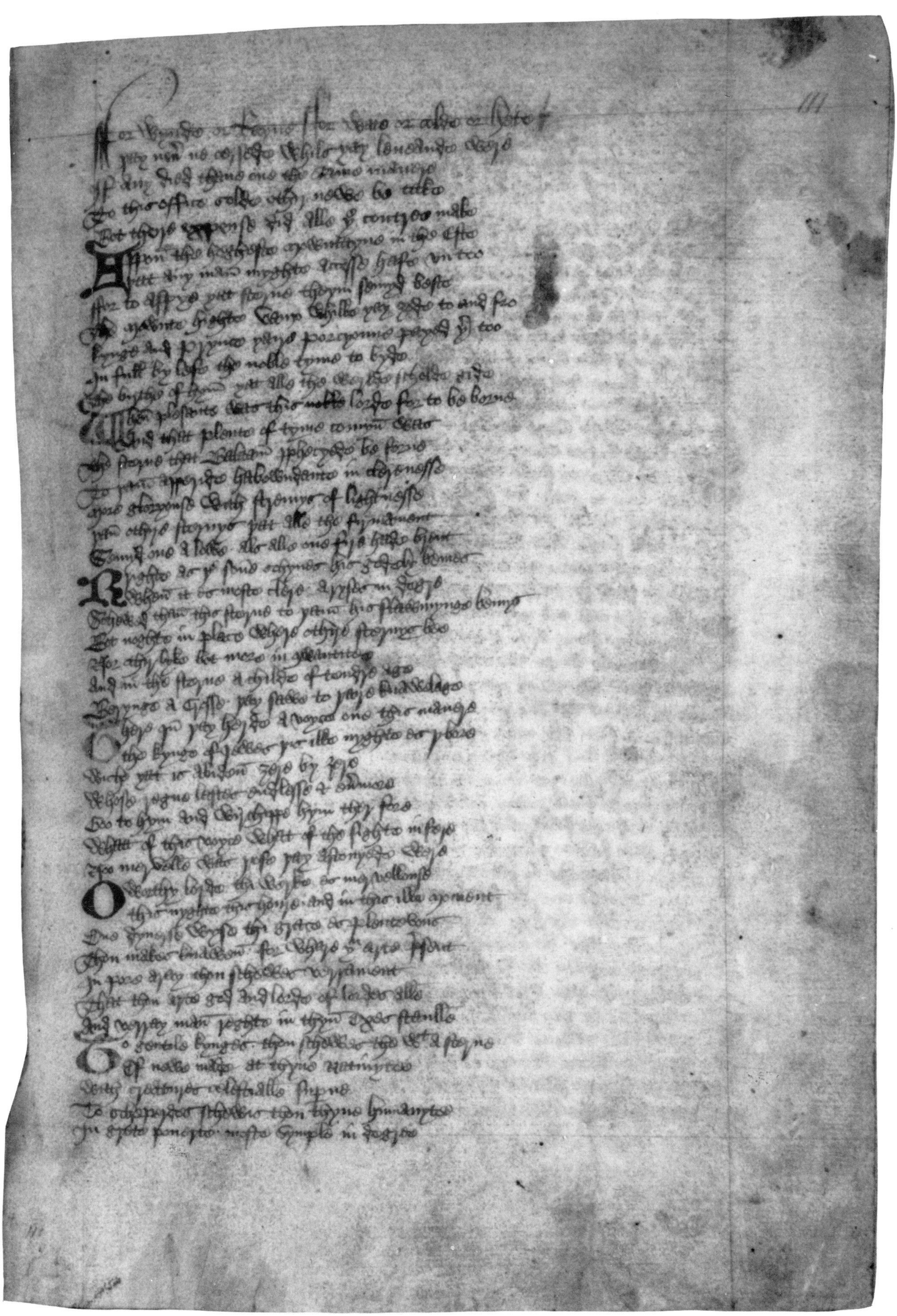

31b. f. 169r

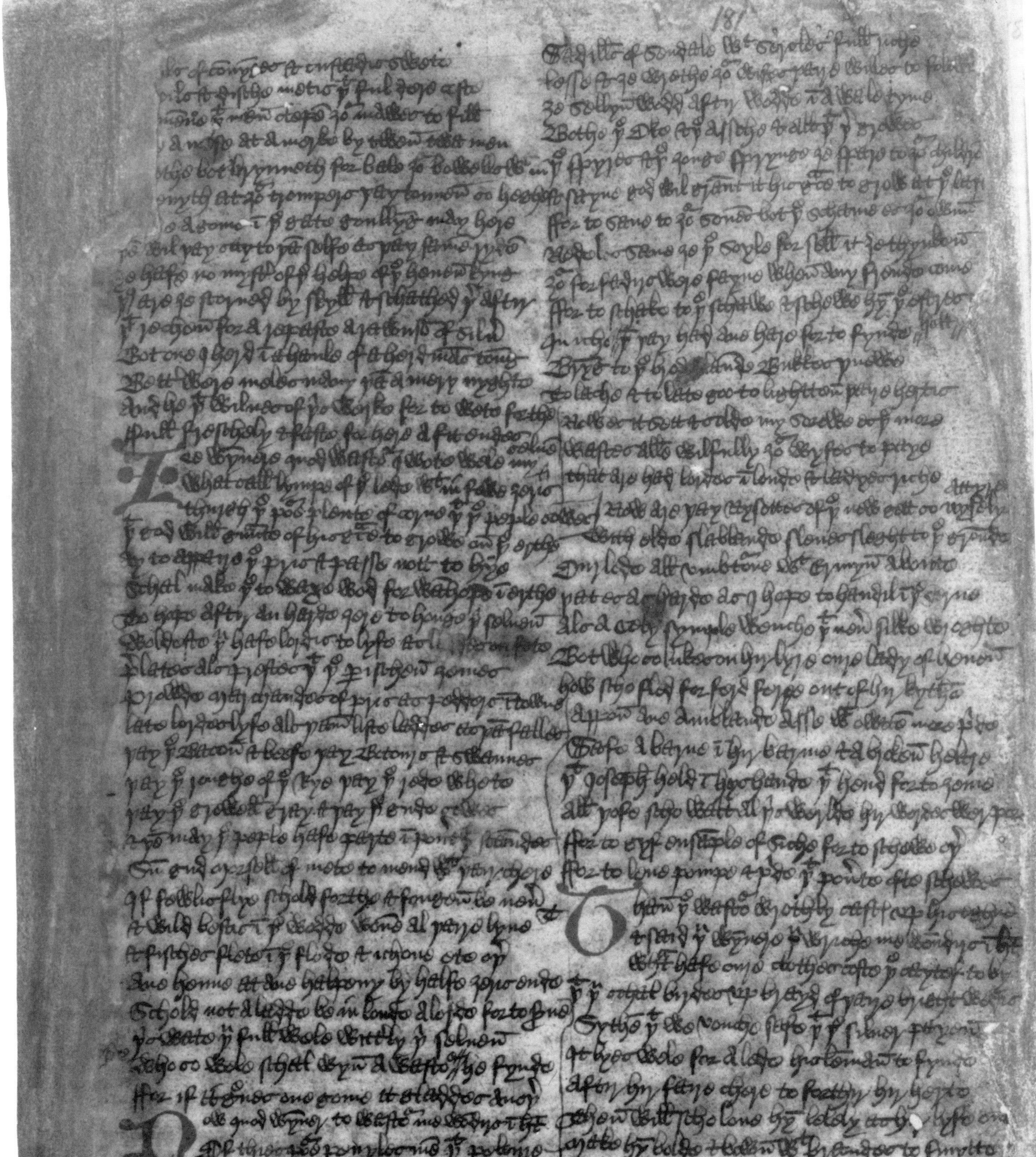

32b. f. 181ʳ

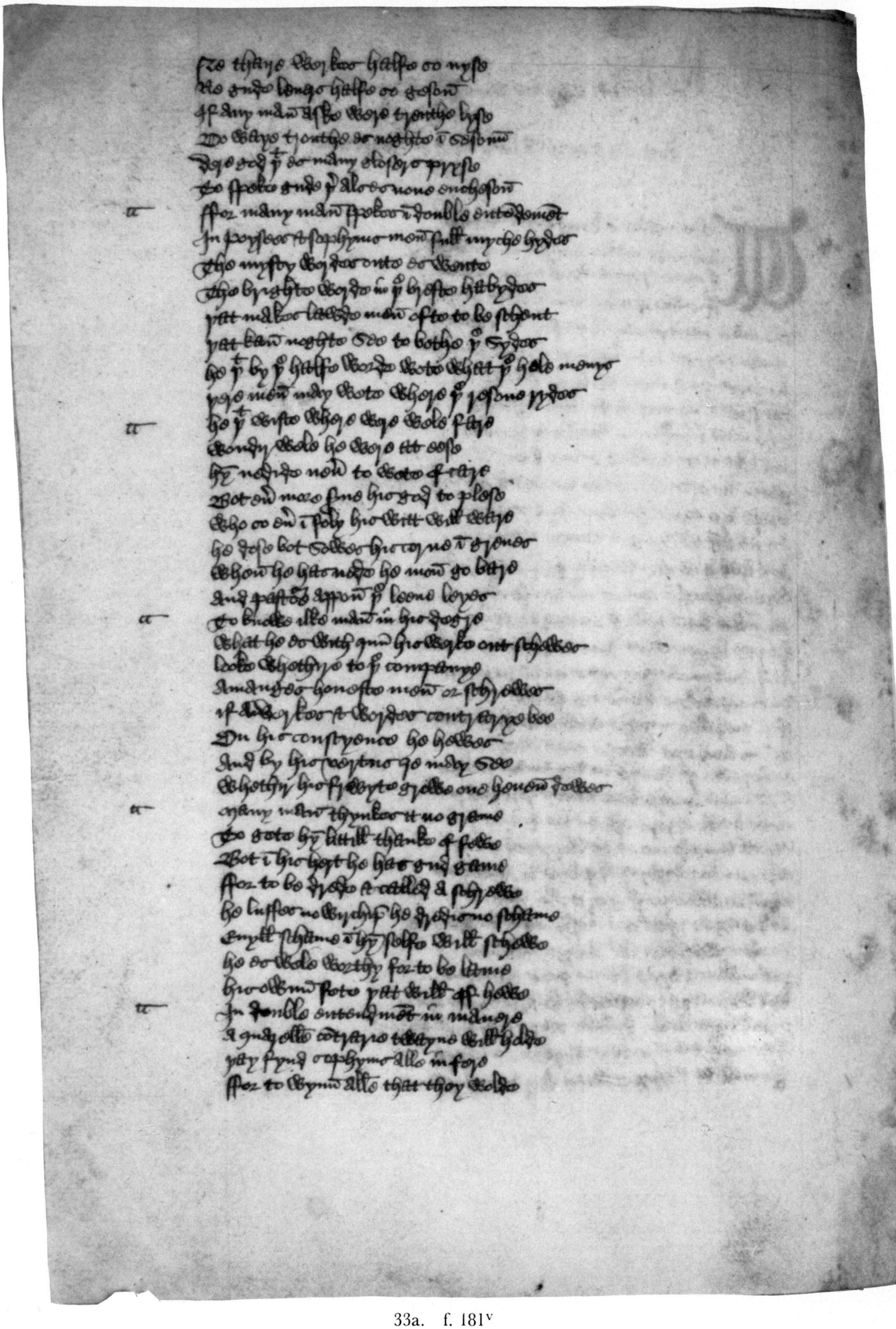

33a. f. 181v

And sua to make vr ransuning for vs him self he said
a þu blissed mai of all of þe quen mai i say
Of þi sorn mari milde þu hade in hert þat day
þat dai it was þi prsunue mai naue þai wid sai nay
Quen þu þi suete sun sua sau be ledd wid tene and tray
of comen it es þe nu þe snow þat þorn þine herte strang
þat symeon wid when had hight þe forwid lang
Bot of ioy ane hundreth fald he dubh̄d þe þi sang
Anen he ras fra dede to lyf widhis goddehed sua strang
ath þe birth and þe passion of iho þat vs boght
If he ne had resun fra þe dede had bene vs all fornoght
Nu mai we se all opun þe fight till end es broght
þe world suurrid þe feind es feld þat man wid sorn soght
u þe þau leuedi hang all vr trouth and fai
All men was in dute and were lor þu leue hah mai
Till þi suete sun up ras þi trouth was stabil ai
Nu men agh vr lauerd leue þu lered vs þar þe wai
in ari neke þu moder es ful of reuth and pete
myrthful maiden mild of all fulfild of all bimte
Na man mai tell þe tend part þe blissednes of þe
vr trouth vr hope all lar þu þau vr wild leuedi mi te
And þus vs wid þi suete sun þat hang for vs on tre
Thim i haue þe passiun in said eftir in might
Bu he egain vr wither deuie vr bataile toke to fight
þogh his it war þe panies all vs it was þe plight
He giue vs grace haue part of blis þat he tilhis has light
a nd þat we mai widuten end be wid him inhis sight
þar ioy and blis es lastand ay þat es in heuenes light
And specialy for me ȝe pray þat þis boke gart dight
John of lindbergh i ȝu sai þat es in naue ful right
If it be tint or dune away treuli in trouth i plight
Qua bringes it me wid uten delay i sal him ȝeild þe might
And qua it helis and haldis fra me treuli i ȝu tell
Curced in kirc þau sal þai be wid candil boke and bell

Ihc of mari born
for sinful man þat was forlorn
I forsok in fadir blis
And come in til erde i wis

I let me take and hard bind
For lime i had to manes kind
I tholid pouert pine and schame
All for sinful manes ane

35. Göttingen University Library MS theol. 107ʳ, f. 114ᵛ

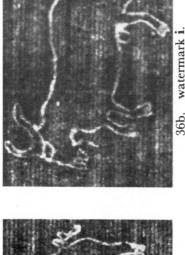

36a. watermark **i.**
London manuscript, f. 13

36b. watermark **i.**
London manuscript, f. 21

37a. watermark **i.**
Lincoln manuscript, f. 170

37b. watermark **i.**
Lincoln manuscript, f. 174

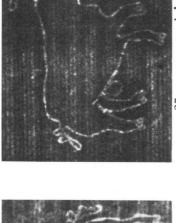

38a. watermark **ii.**
London manuscript, f. 36

38b. watermark **ii.**
London manuscript, f. 50

39a. watermark **ii.**
Lincoln manuscript, f. 61

39b. watermark **ii.**
Lincoln manuscript, f. 58

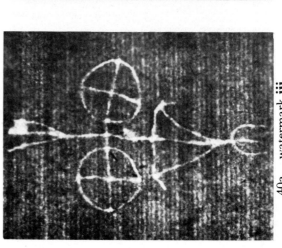

40a. watermark **iii.**
London manuscript, f. 57

40b. watermark **iii.**
London manuscript, f. 71

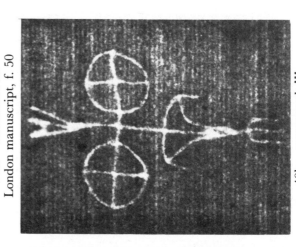

41a. watermark **iii.**
Lincoln manuscript, f. 257

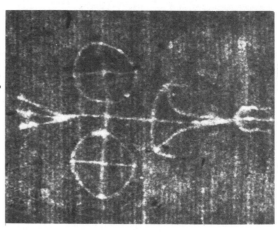

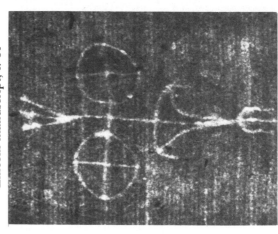

41b. watermark **iii.**
Lincoln manuscript, f. 254

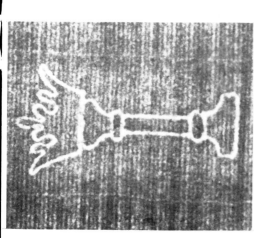

46a. watermark **vi.**
Lincoln manuscript, f. 37

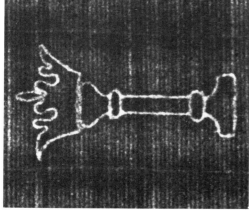

46b. watermark **vi.**
Lincoln manuscript, f. 38

47a. watermark **vii.**
London manuscript, f. 88

47b. watermark **vii.**
London manuscript, f. 90

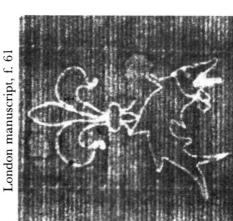

44a. watermark **v.**
Lincoln manuscript, f. 76

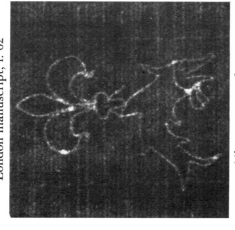

44b. watermark **v.**
Lincoln manuscript, f. 137

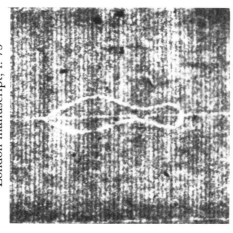

45a. watermark **vi.**
London manuscript, f. 99

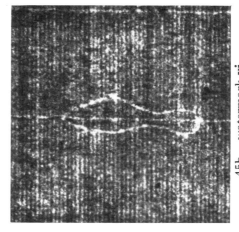

45b. watermark **vi.**
London manuscript, f. 102

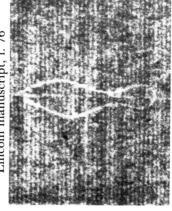

42a. watermark **iv.**
London manuscript, f. 61

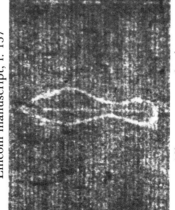

42b. watermark **iv.**
London manuscript, f. 62

43. watermark **v.**
London manuscript, f. 73

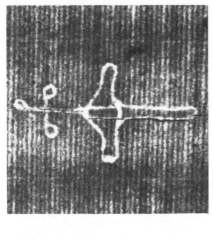

48a. watermark **viii** (I).
London manuscript, f. 106

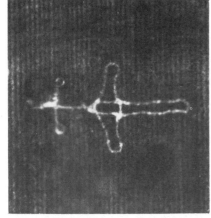

49a. watermark **viii** (II).
Lincoln manuscript, f. 107

49b. watermark **viii** (II).
Lincoln manuscript, f. 106

52b. watermark **x** (II).
London manuscript, f. 171

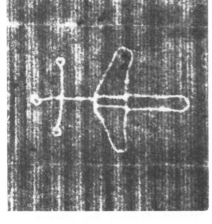

48b. watermark **viii** (I).
London manuscript, f. 119

50b. watermark **ix**.
London manuscript, f. 136

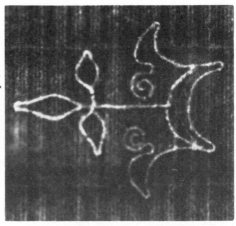

52a. watermark **x** (II).
London manuscript, f. 170

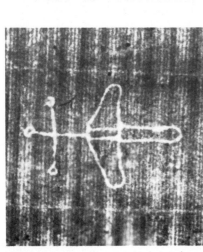

50a. watermark **ix**.
London manuscript, f. 125

51b. watermark **x** (I).
London manuscript, f. 165

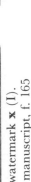

51a. watermark **x** (I).
London manuscript, f. 147